SUPPORTING
Children's Health
and Wellbeing

D1338777

Sara Miller McCune founded SAGE Publishing in 1965 to support the dissemination of usable knowledge and educate a global community. SAGE publishes more than 1000 journals and over 800 new books each year, spanning a wide range of subject areas. Our growing selection of library products includes archives, data, case studies and video. SAGE remains majority owned by our founder and after her lifetime will become owned by a charitable trust that secures the company's continued independence.

Los Angeles | London | New Delhi | Singapore | Washington DC | Melbourne

Jackie Musgrave

SUPPORTING
Children's Health
and Wellbeing

⑤SAGE

Los Angeles | London | New Delhi
Singapore | Washington DC | Melbourne

Los Angeles | London | New Delhi
Singapore | Washington DC | Melbourne

SAGE Publications Ltd
1 Oliver's Yard
55 City Road
London EC1Y 1SP

SAGE Publications Inc.
2455 Teller Road
Thousand Oaks, California 91320

SAGE Publications India Pvt Ltd
B 1/I 1 Mohan Cooperative Industrial Area
Mathura Road
New Delhi 110 044

SAGE Publications Asia-Pacific Pte Ltd
3 Church Street
#10-04 Samsung Hub
Singapore 049483

Editor: Jude Bowen
Associate editor: George Knowles
Production editor: Nicola Marshall
Project manager: Jeanette Graham
Copyeditor: Sharon Cawood
Proofreader: Rosemary Campbell
Indexer: Anne Solamito
Marketing manager: Dilhara Attygalle
Cover design: Wendy Scott
Typeset by: C&M Digitals (P) Ltd, Chennai, India
Printed and bound by CPI Group (UK) Ltd,
Croydon, CR0 4YY

Library of Congress Control Number: 2017933081

British Library Cataloguing in Publication data

A catalogue record for this book is available from
the British Library

ISBN 978-1-4739-3031-5
ISBN 978-1-4739-3032-2 (pbk)

At SAGE we take sustainability seriously. Most of our products are printed in the UK using FSC papers and boards.
When we print overseas we ensure sustainable papers are used as measured by the PREPS grading system.
We undertake an annual audit to monitor our sustainability.

This book is dedicated with love and joy to the
memory of my daughter, Nicky.

*When you are joyous, look deep into your heart and you shall find it is only
that which has given you sorrow that is giving you joy. When you are
sorrowful, look again in your heart, and you shall see that in truth you
are weeping for that which has been your delight.* (Gibran, 1923)

CONTENTS

ABOUT THE AUTHOR

Jackie Musgrave is senior lecturer and the leader for the BA (Hons) in Early Childhood (Professional Practice) degree in the Centre for Children and Families at the University of Worcester. Her research interest in children's health and well-being emerged from her experiences as a Registered Sick Children's Nurse in a children's hospital and from working as a practice nurse in inner-city Birmingham. Jackie moved into education in 1996 and she started teaching child health to level 3 students in a college of further education.

Jackie went on to teach a child health module to foundation degree students. Working with experienced early years practitioners, she realised how the knowledge, skills and qualities of the practitioners had helped them to develop inclusive approaches for children with on-going health conditions. The practitioners' experiences inspired Jackie's doctoral research. However, whilst carrying out her research, she became aware of how early years practitioners supported children's health and wellbeing in other areas that extended beyond long-term conditions.

This book is the product of post-doctoral research which informs practitioners of a range of contemporary health conditions. The content of the book highlights how practitioners can maximise young children's participation in their early education by developing their knowledge and, in turn, addressing the implications for practice that arise as a consequence of health conditions.

ACKNOWLEDGEMENTS

I am grateful to a great number of people who have made this book possible. I have worked with many colleagues who have generously shared their knowledge and offered me the opportunity to become an 'academic' and write books. I consider myself fortunate to have worked with colleagues at Oxford-Brookes University developing the Early Years Foundation Degree, where I was first offered the opportunity to become involved in higher education – in particular, thank you to Nick Swarbrick. Thank you to my former colleagues at Solihull College, most notably Helen Perkins, who demonstrated outstanding leadership in developing higher education in further education. I would also like to thank Rachael Levy at the University of Sheffield, who could not have been a more patient and supportive doctorate supervisor.

Since moving to the University of Worcester in 2012, I have had the privilege of working with published authors in the Centre for Children and Families. In particular, I would like to thank Michael Reed for sharing his authorship with me and giving me my first opportunity to write a chapter in his and Rosie Walker's book, *A Critical Companion*.

The wisdom and leadership in supporting children's health and wellbeing demonstrated by the Early Years Foundation Degree and undergraduate students with whom I have worked over the last 14 years have been the inspiration behind this book.

Without the participants in my research, I would not have been able to write this book. I am grateful to the contributions made by the practitioners, parents and, most of all, 'DJ' who taught me so much over the year I observed him. He will always have a special place in my heart.

I am grateful to all at Sage Publications, in particular Jude Bowen, Amy Jarrold and George Knowles for their support and encouragement.

Thank you so much to my friends and family for their support and interest in the book, especially my husband, Paul, for his proofreading and love, and my daughters, Jenny and Laura for their support and love.

1

CHILDREN'S HEALTH IS EVERY PROFESSIONAL'S RESPONSIBILITY

CHAPTER AIMS AND OBJECTIVES

- To explore definitions of health and wellbeing
- To identify the responsibility of professionals in relation to supporting children's health and wellbeing

Introduction

The title of this chapter reflects the ideology that all adults have a responsibility for supporting the health of our youngest citizens. This responsibility links to the UK Government's approach to safeguarding children. The Working Together to Safeguard Children (HM Government 2015) guidance states that part of safeguarding is 'preventing impairment to health' (p. 5). This statement suggests that we all have a responsibility to maintain good health as well as to prevent children from acquiring health-threatening conditions.

In order to consider the responsibility of professionals in relation to supporting children's health, the chapter adapts Bronfenbrenner's ecological systems theory (1979, 1994) to illustrate how each of the systems surrounding the child bears a responsibility to support children's health. By supporting children's health and doing your utmost to promote good health and avoid ill health, your actions will, in turn, help to promote children's wellbeing. As well as supporting children's health, part of your responsibility is to avoid injuries that can leave a legacy of disability or even death. However, before we can explore how your responsibility for supporting children's health can be carried out, it is important that you have an understanding of the definitions of health and wellbeing. It is also important that you have an understanding of the factors that can contribute to and cause children to have *ill* health, in order to be able to carry out your role in preventing and maintaining good health. An aim of the chapter is also that you will develop your own definition of health (and the causes of ill health) that is useful to apply to the children and families in your setting.

Defining health

Health is a nebulous concept and defining what we mean by health can be challenging. Part of the difficulty associated with our understanding of health is possibly that there is no universally accepted definition of what health is. However, a book about health would not be complete if it did not include the World Health Organization (1986) definition of health, which is as follows:

> The extent to which an individual or group is able, on the one hand, to realize aspirations and satisfy needs; and, on the other hand, *to change or cope with the environment*. Health is, therefore, seen as a resource for everyday life, not the objective of living; *it is a positive concept emphasizing social and personal resources*, as well as physical capacities. [Italics added]

This definition is an ambitious attempt to offer an explanation that fits all. The words *to change or cope with the environment* are important because part of your role is to enable the environment for all children. However, your ability to understand how to change the environment for children with a health condition may make the difference to their being included in their early learning. Asthma is an example of a health condition that will require you to adapt the environment by removing or reducing 'triggers' that may provoke asthma symptoms (this will be discussed further in Chapter 9).

Helena Green, a student practitioner, offers an explanation of what health means to her:

> Supporting children's health means to me, that their basic needs are met. Additionally, they are supported by family and professionals to develop mentally and physically at a rate that is suitable to the individual and their context.

Helena's explanation of how she sees her role in supporting children's health takes an holistic view of the child, and the child's health is an intrinsic part of the child. Helena sees the context of children's lives and the support of family and professionals as being essential to supporting children's health. Her definition resonates with Bronfenbrenner's ecological systems approach and also lends itself to a social model of health.

The medical and social model of health

These terms are often used to describe approaches to health and ill health. As the complexities and determinants that influence health are better understood, it is important that health conditions are not looked at in isolation, that is, the social model is used to improve health. However, for early years practitioners, there is a need to adopt a medical model as well.

The social model of health takes an holistic view of the impact of health, or ill health, on individuals, meaning that the social, emotional and environmental factors are taken into account. In relation to children, it is vital that their care and education needs are also taken into consideration. As early years practitioners, it is likely that this will be a natural tendency to address the whole child and their family when looking at the impact of health on children's inclusion.

The medical model of health can be described as taking a biological or physical approach to health, which focuses on a specific health condition. Diagnosis of a condition, such as diabetes, means that there is an evidence-based approach to treatment. Knowing the signs and symptoms and understanding the treatment and management of health conditions means that you will be better equipped to minimise the impact of the condition and maximise children's participation.

Defining wellbeing

Wellbeing can be examined from philosophical, economic, psychological, sociological and health perspectives. The range of contexts that can influence wellbeing means that the concept of wellbeing is also nebulous and, again, there are many definitions. The *Oxford English Dictionary* defines wellbeing as 'the state of being comfortable, healthy or happy'. Statham and Chase (2010) define wellbeing as 'generally understood as the quality of peoples' lives ... it is understood ... in relation to objective measures, such as ... health status' (p. 2).

Children's health and wellbeing: a personal view

Your understanding of health and wellbeing will be shaped by your experiences and your professional role. For example, many years ago when I worked as a sick children's nurse in a hospital, I nursed children who were unwell and the aim of my work was to make a contribution to restoring children back to health. At that time, I considered that children's health could be interrupted by an event that made them 'sick', they came into hospital for an intervention that restored them back to health and, in turn, their wellbeing would be improved.

My view of children's health and wellbeing changed after I became a lecturer in a college where I taught child health modules to early years students. I realised that my experience as a nurse caring for sick children had given me a snapshot of one perspective. When I started to teach experienced practitioners who were students on an Early Years Foundation Degree, I learnt from students about how they worked to promote and maintain children's health. I realised that the students had developed a rich fund of knowledge. Much of this book draws on the rich fund of knowledge and the unique wealth of experience that have been developed by practitioners.

An aim of this book is to examine the inter-relationship of health and children's wellbeing. So far, it is apparent that definitions of health and wellbeing are difficult to apply in a way that is helpful to young children. I am reminded of Janet Moyles' (2010) thoughts on defining play – she used the analogy of bubbles to explain how just when we think we are clear about a definition, changes occur which affect our understanding and thinking. In a similar way, I think that the same analogy can be applied to defining health and wellbeing. When we consider children's health and wellbeing, it can be even more complex to define.

The link between health and wellbeing

The part of the WHO definition that states that health is a *positive concept empha-sising social and personal resources*, suggests that there is a link between health and emotional wellbeing (WHO 1986). This part of the definition can be interpreted as meaning that our emotional wellbeing is reliant on our social interaction with oth-ers. In addition, it suggests that emotional wellbeing is linked to our relationship with ourselves. Therefore, this highlights the importance of developing self-reliance and resilience in young children, so that they develop good wellbeing and improve their mental health (this area is addressed further in Chapter 6).

There is a strong case for you to be equipped to fulfil your role in supporting children's health and wellbeing because there are influences that are potentially beneficial not just to the individual, but to all of society. Figure 1.1 summarises the rationale for addressing children's health and how this can reduce the need for access to health services.

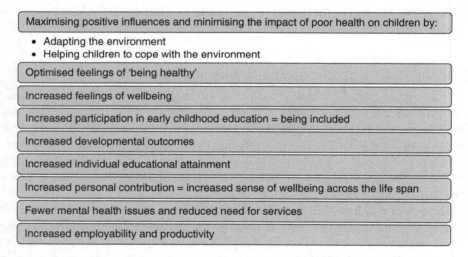

Figure 1.1 Rationale for supporting children's health and wellbeing in the early years

Determinants of health

A determinant of health is defined as a factor that influences health. The World Health Organization (2015a, p. 1) states that

> many factors affect the health of individuals and communities. Whether peo-ple are healthy or not, is determined by their circumstances and environment. To a large extent, factors such as where we live, the state of the environment,

genetics, our income and education level, and our relationships with friends and family all have considerable impacts on health.

The following sections explore the determinants of health (influences on health) within various systems.

Bronfenbrenner's ecological systems and children's health in early years settings

Bronfenbrenner's ecological systems theory (1979) is useful for consideration of the influences of different contexts on children's health. In McDowall Clark's (2013) adaptation of Bronfenbrenner's systems in relation to children in the early years, she points out that children have two microsystems – that of their home and that of their early years setting. Figure 1.2 defines the layers in relation to early years settings.

Chronosystem

The chronosystem is the historical events that have shaped the changes in relation to children's health. Such changes include societal and medical advances. Knowing

Chronosystem
The long-term context of historical changes which impact on social factors at all levels.

Macrosystem
The broader context of social structures, political ideology, economic forces and wider value and belief system.

Exosystem
The localised context or community within which micro- and meso-systems exist.

Mesosystems
The interaction and communication between the child's various microsystems.

Microsystem – family
The child's immediate context where all their first experiences are mediated. The microsystem is impacted on by all the surrounding levels, e.g. local and national.

Microsystem – the setting
Nowadays, most children spend a large proportion of their time within different settings which form a major site of socialisation.

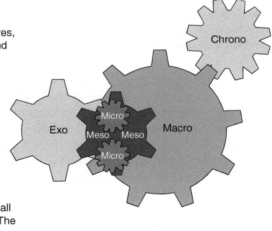

Figure 1.2 Bronfenbrenner's ecological systems and children's health in early years settings as adapted by McDowall Clark (2013)

the historical context of children's health helps us to understand the contemporary issues relating to children's health, as discussed in Chapter 2.

Macrosystem: national influences and global perspectives

The macrosystem in relation to children's health can be regarded as encompassing national influences such as legislation and policy. However, it is also important that the macrosystem embraces global influences on children's health. This is especially important at a time when many children are migrating from their country of origin, bringing with them their culture, religion and ethnic diversity, all of which can be an influence on all aspects of health. The level of deprivation and poverty experienced by children and their families remains a negative influence on health. Conversely, the higher the socio-economic status of children and their families, the better their health outcomes are likely to be. Therefore, as Figure 1.1 shows, there is a benefit for governments in promoting positive health and wellbeing in children.

National influences

An aim of children's health policy is to reduce inequalities in health so that all children reach their full developmental potential in childhood and across the lifespan. Marmot (2010) pointed out that the health inequalities are caused as a consequence of children living in poverty in the UK. His report informed changes to legislation aimed at reducing the disadvantages caused by poverty to children's health. Legislation and policy are discussed in Chapter 3 where the aims of global and current government policy are examined. This encourages you to critique government policy and reflect on whose voices are heard within legislation. The chapter discusses your role in developing policies in your settings that are meaningful for children, their health condition and their families.

Global perspective on children's health

Within the macrosystem, it is important to highlight some of the global health issues that can influence children's health and that, in turn, may have implications for practice. The country that a child is born in has an important influence on their health. Therefore, it is important for us to examine children's health from a global perspective so that we can appreciate that there are stark differences in the standard of children's health in some areas of the world. As previously stated, we need to understand how the child's environment influences their health status. Children living in poor countries of the world have a higher chance of dying before their 5th birthday than children in developed countries. Some of the reasons why this is so, are similar to those for the UK in the 1800s. Children who live in countries that do not have the infrastructure to provide safe drinking water and to support sanitation are more likely to come into contact with infectious diseases. In a world where immigration and migration result in many children moving between countries and cultures, we need to appreciate, as professionals, the context within which children's understanding of their world is shaped by their environment. Therefore, throughout this book consideration will be given to the influences on health that have implications for your practice.

Exosystem: working with other professionals and the local community

The influence of the local community is a powerful determinant of health. If your setting is in an area of deprivation, it is likely that there will be a higher number of people living in poverty and, consequently, more children are likely to have health problems and poor social and emotional development. Areas that are home to people from diverse communities bring with them their associated health beliefs and behaviours, all of which can bring challenges and, in turn, present implications for practice. To some extent, the kind of setting that you are working in will influence the services that are available for you to access. Consequently, you may have extensive or limited contact with the professionals involved with children's health. For example, a privately owned setting may have limited contact with a child's health visitor. On the other hand, the staff of a Children's Centre may work closely together to support children's health. Therefore, it is important that you understand the socio-economic factors and the ethnic diversity of your neighbourhood, in order to be able to anticipate the likely health needs. In turn, this information can help you to plan how to address the health needs that are likely to be issues for the children and their families. Furthermore, this information can help you to understand the services and professionals that are available to meet such needs. (The need for collaborative and integrated working is discussed in Chapter 4.)

Mesosystem: working with parents

The role of parents is located in the mesosystem and your role in working with parents (or carers) is critical to making links between the two microsystems of children. Crucial to this role will be communication between parents and you about the health issues affecting the children. This may be around the management of an individual child's health condition, or it may be about a health promotion initiative, such as healthy eating, in your setting.

Some of the information that is communicated by parents to you may be as a consequence of advice from healthcare professionals. This may add another layer of complexity to your relationship with parents, especially if the parents hold religious or cultural beliefs that conflict with your beliefs. (How you can support parents is discussed further in Chapter 5.)

Microsystem: the role of the practitioner in promoting and maintaining children's health

As McDowall Clark (2013) has pointed out, more children now are in a second microsystem in out-of-home day-care settings for many hours each day. The hours a child spends in your setting may be equal to those spent at home. However, the need to support children's health and wellbeing remains in place and becomes your responsibility to fulfil during the time the child is with you. Your role in supporting children's health is challenging. It is likely that you will have children in your setting who are regarded as having multiple disadvantages which may exacerbate their health issues. Therefore, the content of this book encourages you to consider your role in the broadest sense. The content will challenge you to consider the knowledge you already hold and help you to identify the knowledge that you may need to acquire in order to equip yourself to carry out your role.

Theory into practice: bringing it all together

At this point, it may be useful to start thinking about how Bronfenbrenner's ecological systems theory can help you to consider the influences on the health and wellbeing of the children in your setting.

CASE STUDY 1.1

Stargazers Children's Centre, Moonbeam day-care setting and Sunfield Primary School all share a site in an inner-city area of a large city. The area of the city in which the settings are situated is bordered by three very different neighbourhoods. Very close to the site, there is an affluent suburb that is situated en route to the city centre. Over a main road from the site, there is a council estate that has benefitted from investment and regeneration programmes in recent years. Next to the site of the settings are several streets that have small, dilapidated terraced houses.

The different types of housing are home to a diverse range of children and families:

1 Think of the different sorts of families that you are likely to encounter in all three settings. What are the 'determinants' of (factors that can impact) children's health?

2 Thinking of the different sorts of children and families that attend your setting, what are the relevant determinants of health that need to be considered?

3 List examples of some of the health and wellbeing issues that may affect the children in the setting, and make suggestions for how these might be tackled.

Conclusion

This chapter outlined your responsibility in supporting children's health. In order to carry this out, it is important that you recognise the specific conditions affecting the children in your setting, as well as understanding the ways that those conditions can impact on children's development and early education. Part of your responsibility in supporting children's health is to fully grasp the determinants that affect the children (and their families) in your setting.

Further reading

Blair, M. and Barlow, J. (2012) Chapter 6: Life Stage – Early Years in the Chief Medical Officer's Annual Report: Our children deserve better. Available at: www.gov.uk/government/uploads/system/uploads/attachment_data/file/252656/33571_2901304_CMO_Chapter_6.pdf (accessed 23 July 2016).

Hall, D. and Elliman, D. (2006) *Health for All Children* (4th edn). Oxford: Oxford University Press.

2

HISTORICAL PERSPECTIVES AND CONTEMPORARY ISSUES RELATED TO CHILD HEALTH

CHAPTER AIMS AND OBJECTIVES

- To examine the influence of the chronosystem, that is, the long-term context of historical events which have impacted on children's health and wellbeing

- To convey an understanding of why we are where we are in relation to children's health by examining the legacy of historical events

- To identify contemporary factors and influences affecting children's health and causes of poor health

As you read the chapter, you are encouraged to think about the following:

- Your role in relation to promoting and maintaining the health of the children in your professional care

- How an understanding of the history of child health can help you to educate children, colleagues and parents about the importance of promoting and maintaining good health

- The health needs of children who have not had, or do not have, access to healthcare.

Introduction

The French philosopher, Michel Foucault (MacNaughton 2005) claimed that in order to understand the present we must examine the events of the past. This assertion is especially true in relation to children's health. Some of the conditions that were life-threatening as recently as the 1950s have now become regarded as 'extinct'. For example, poliomyelitis was a common cause of death and disability. During the 1950s, there were 8,000 cases of paralytic poliomyelitis reported. The discovery of a vaccination for this infectious disease and the introduction of immunisation programmes for all children mean that the disease is unlikely to infect children in contemporary times in countries where immunisation is available. The last-known natural polio infection in the UK was reported in 1984 (Public Health England 2013). When a health condition is no longer a danger, the impact of the disease starts to fade from memory. We forget the devastation it can cause and even forget the epidemiology (how a disease is caused and spreads) of the condition. Forgetting about a threat to health that is perceived as no longer existing is understandable, however there is also a danger. This is because we can become complacent about certain health conditions and we can forget that the condition has not disappeared, but is, rather, being contained. In the example of poliomyelitis, it is being contained by prevention of the disease through immunisation programmes. Therefore, it is important that we have an understanding of why some threats to health appear to be no longer problematic. Equally, it is important to understand why there are now conditions that affect children's health that were unheard of until recent times, for example we are now facing an epidemic of childhood obesity (Hall and Elliman 2006).

Global perspective

It is also very important to bear in mind that not every child who attends your setting was necessarily born and brought up in this country. As discussed in Chapter 1, many children who have migrated from other countries may not have had the benefit of a health service that was freely available to all. Consequently, they may not have benefitted from health interventions such as immunisation programmes.

Societal influences on children's health

The factors that affect children's health and wellbeing are linked to how their role in society is constructed and the expectations that society has of children (see McDowall Clark 2013). Therefore, gaining an understanding of the changing role of children in society will help to understand what has affected their health and why some changes have come about. However, societal changes must also be viewed alongside medical advances. Such advances include changes in approaches to health as well as important discoveries such as antibiotics.

Historical overview of child health

Pre-Industrial Revolution

Before the Industrial Revolution, most children lived in rural areas. Little is reported about children's health at this time, possibly because there was little treatment available for illnesses. It was common for babies to die at birth from complications resulting from labour or as a result of undiagnosed congenital abnormalities. If babies survived the hazardous birth process, rates of infant mortality were high and there was still a high risk that they would not reach their first birthday. After the start of the Industrial Revolution, infant mortality increased because of urbanisation and the accompanying unsanitary conditions. Consequently, many young children died because of infectious diseases. The high level of infant mortality started to improve once organised, evidence-based ante- and post-natal care and qualified midwives and health visitors became a legal requirement in 1918.

Industrial Revolution

This was a time of social and economic upheaval and the changes in society had a profound effect on children and their health. A large workforce was required to meet the demands of new industry. Food was expensive and mothers and fathers, as well as children, were required to work in factories to earn money for food. A lack of childcare meant that babies often accompanied their mothers to work in the hazardous working environment of the early factories. Babies were frequently sedated with laudanum (a compound derived from opium) to quell their crying, as well as rendering them incapable of crawling into the machinery and being maimed or killed.

Children started to work in factories at the age of 4. Their small stature meant that they were valuable assets in the cotton mills because they could squeeze underneath the machinery to remove fibres that could create blockages which could cause a breakdown and delay in production of the material. In his notes on the Industrial Revolution, Pike (1966) recounts harrowing descriptions of such children being scalped because their hair became trapped in the machinery. The hard work undertaken by children when their physical development was incomplete, and in the inhospitable environment of the factory or coalmine, combined with poor nutrition, meant that people often died before they reached the age of 25.

This period of history was a bleak time for children. It is worth considering at this point that in contemporary times we can be dismissive of and cynical about health and safety. However, it was because of such events as described in this section that it was realised that regulation and legislation were necessary to make children's lives safer and, in turn, healthier.

Post-Industrial Revolution: The Victorian Age

At the start of Queen Victoria's reign in 1837, the effects on children of being part of the workforce were being highlighted in parliament and consequently many changes were made to improve children's health during the Victorian Age. Victorian philanthropists influenced changes to improve children's lives. It was during this period that public records started to be kept and this meant that it was possible to find out the causes of death and ill health in children. Such records revealed that a high proportion of children died before their first birthday (Horn 1974). Children who lived in rural areas had a higher rate of survival than those living in urban areas. The figure for rural areas was that 1 in 10 children (i.e. 10%) died in the first year of life, compared with a mortality rate of 50% for children living in cities (Horn 1974).

A common cause of death was babies dying as a consequence of accidental smothering because of bed sharing with their parents. This cause of death was called 'overlaying' and arose as a consequence of crowded housing and the lack of a safe place for babies to sleep.

Sedation of babies with opium continued well into Victorian times. Women frequently had large families and had a great deal of essential work to do, therefore babies were often given a compound known as Godfrey's cordial which contained opium. Consequently, another frequently recorded cause of death was opium overdose.

Infant mortality rates were high and as many as 150 babies out of 1,000 live births died (Corsini and Viazzo 1993), often from infectious diseases, however the deaths associated with infection reduced as sewers were built and lavatories became widely available. Common infectious diseases at this time included diphtheria, measles, whooping cough, scarlet fever, typhoid and cholera. The viruses and bacteria that cause these infectious diseases thrived in the crowded and poorly ventilated schools. The symptoms of such conditions had a profound effect on children's education, general holistic wellbeing and everyday lives. Children were often absent from school because of an epidemic of a condition such as measles. There were frequent school closures because of epidemics, which also affected the teachers. Again, a contemporary example of the devastation that can be caused by an infectious disease is the ebola outbreak that swept West Africa around November 2014. In a similar way, children missed out on their education as a consequence of the fear of contracting the virus.

When children became unwell, there were few treatments available. Those that were around included cod liver oil, quinine, Epsom salts and alcoholic drinks. Natural and inexpensive treatments included herbal remedies – for example, remedies for whooping cough included fried mouse and mistletoe berries. According to Horn (1974), witchcraft and superstitious practices abounded. As more pharmaceutical treatments and preventions have been discovered, the use of and belief in such practices has receded. However, in some countries of the world witchcraft remains a firmly held system of beliefs.

Infestations with fleas and head lice were endemic. Children were sewn into their underwear in the autumn until spring. This created a breeding ground for body lice; the attendant itching caused skin infections, sleep disturbance and resulted in a lack of concentration and cognitive impairment during the day.

The increased importation of affordable sugar in the 1860s meant that children were given sugar in their diet. However, an absence of toothbrushes and toothpaste and a lack of clean water meant that the unpalatable teeth-cleaning practice of dipping a wet rag in salt and scrubbing children's teeth was an unpleasant experience. Consequently, children started to develop tooth decay. However, tooth decay (dental caries) remains a contemporary problem and is still a threat to children's health (see Chapter 7).

During the Victorian era, medical pioneering work included the opening of children's hospitals. These were usually situated in poor areas of cities, because then, as now, it was recognised that poor children were more likely to have poor levels of health when compared to children of affluent families. Other advances included the development of anaesthetics and a greater understanding of how infection acquired as a consequence of surgery could be reduced by the use of antiseptics. This meant that surgeons could perform operations that were hitherto impossible. However, the smaller stature of children and the unpredictability of children's responses to being ill and to medication meant that surgery on children remained fraught with difficulties, a situation that did not change until the 1950s.

1900–1945

Margaret McMillan, a pioneer of nursery education wrote in 1919 (McMillan 2012):

The fate of vast numbers of little children given over to all the dangers of the streets, and in homes where no real nurture is possible, was brought very forcibly before us this autumn, when after a holiday we found that one third of all our nursery were diseased, and obliged to spend a week at the clinic before they could come back to our school.

The McMillan sisters worked to improve the health of the children who lived in poverty and attended their nursery by providing 'nurture' as well as education. They were advocates for outdoor play, healthy food and they promoted good standards of hygiene and encouraged self-care in small children. The legacy of their work can be seen in the principles of contemporary Early Childhood Education and Care (ECEC).

1945–1989

The period of time following the end of the Second World War in 1945 was a time of austerity, however it was also a time of medical advances that dramatically improved the health of children. For several years beyond the end of the war, there were food shortages which meant that children's diet had restricted fat and carbohydrate content. On a social level, this was a time when communities were located in close geographical areas and the availability of and need for transport was not great, so children walked. Outdoor play was the norm (if you get the opportunity to speak to somebody who was a child in this period, ask him or her where, what and how they played at this time). The combination of a diet that did not contain excessive amounts of fat and carbohydrates and access to the outdoors and plenty of opportunities for physical exercise resulted in what we would now consider to be a healthy lifestyle for children.

One of the major medical milestones was the introduction of antibiotics during the 1940s, which meant that infections that are regarded as commonplace nowadays, but are life-threatening without antibiotic treatment, could be treated. Another medical milestone during this period was the introduction of immunisation programmes to prevent some infectious diseases. At this time, the branch of medicine dedicated to children's health was gaining its own identity and evolving. Paediatric medical advances included developments in surgical procedures and safer anaesthesia. This development had a significant impact on children who were born with heart defects that were previously inoperable. Many more children were able to have life-saving heart operations that meant they survived and were able to have a good quality of life.

Pregnancy and childbirth continued to be a dangerous time until the middle of the 20th century, however the care of pregnant women became a medical specialism and improved ante-natal care meant that the crucial time around birth was safer and more babies survived this critical period. In turn, the care of newborn babies who had congenital conditions, or survived a difficult birth, became a specialism and the opening of units for babies who required neonatal care was started around 1950.

The National Health Service (NHS) was introduced in the UK in 1949 and this heralded the start of free healthcare at the point of need in the UK. Before the NHS, parents had to carefully consider the affordability of paying for a medical consultation for a sick child. This inevitably meant that sometimes parents left medical consultation too late, or not at all, because they could not afford the fees. As well as the cost of consulting a doctor, it is likely that parents considered whether there was any point because there was little that could be offered to cure a child who was sick besides castor oil and bed rest. This was before antibiotics were available to cure infections. The sophisticated scans to aid diagnosis that we now take for granted were not available and surgery for children was not a common procedure. The NHS removed the concern of not being able to afford medical care for people in the UK and free medical care is still available today. However, it is worth bearing in mind that lack of access to health services and lack of ability to pay for them is a situation that continues to exist around the globe for many people.

The post-war period saw a move away from simply curing the symptoms of disease and illness to the prevention of disease becoming a focus. The concept of screening for medical conditions was introduced. The aim of screening at this time was to detect the signs and symptoms of a medical condition in order to diagnose it in the early stages before the symptoms became problematic. An example of screening was the introduction of the heel prick test (Guthrie Test) for all babies. This was introduced to identify babies with phenylketonuria (PKU), a rare genetic condition; early identification meant that treatment could be offered, for example dietary restriction, and the child could avoid the long-term brain damage caused by PKU.

As a consequence of the changes in society and in medicine, during this period children's survival rates improved, and with this improved mortality rate there was a shift in the need to focus on improving the quality of children's lives and health, not just on preventing the death of children.

1989 onwards

As the 20th century progressed, so too did the medical advances that contributed to improving children's health. The pioneers of children's health of the past would probably be surprised that curing and preventing illness were not enough to ensure that children had good health. For example, it became clear that simply providing a free national health service did not ensure that all children could access the benefits that the service offered, nor did it mean that all children could reach their optimal level of health. It became evident that promoting and maintaining children's health is complex, and as a consequence of the complexities there are obvious inequalities in children's experience of health. In addition, it became apparent that there are many influences on children's health which this period of great advancement in medicine had not yet addressed.

The United Nations Convention on the Rights of the Child (UNCRC) in 1989 was a turning point for children's position in the world. For the first time, most countries of the world signed up to a declaration that recognised children as citizens who had rights. Article 24 of the Rights confers:

> the right of the child to the enjoyment of the highest attainable standard of health and to facilities for the treatment of illness and rehabilitation of health. States Parties shall strive to ensure that no child is deprived of his or her right of access to such healthcare services. (UN 1989)

The reality of ensuring that children receive their right to health is not straightforward because of the many influences in the child's environment that affect their health. One of the biggest factors in how healthy a child can be is where they are born in the world.

In the United Kingdom, the Every Child Matters (ECM) agenda in England and Wales (DfES 2003) followed the aims of the UNCRC right to health. One of the outcomes of the agenda was the aim that children should benefit from 'being healthy, enjoying good physical and mental health and living a healthy lifestyle' (p. 6). The ECM agenda set the scene for the current child health legislation in the UK, which is discussed in Chapter 3.

As well as policy which offered early interventions designed to promote good health in children, medical advances continue to mean that conditions that were previously untreatable are now treatable. For example, 80–90% (Office for National Statistics 2016) of children diagnosed with cancer now survive in countries where treatment is available. This is compared with a survival rate of 20% in previous years.

Ante-natal care and post-natal care of babies has also improved and this has resulted in higher survival rates. The consequence of this medical advance is that there are greater numbers of children living with complex medical needs (this is discussed further in Chapter 10).

Contemporary issues in child health

The chapter so far has attempted to summarise how the 20th century was a time of change for children's lives and the previous sections have illustrated how some of the societal changes and medical advances have improved children's survival rates. The challenge for professionals working with children has moved away from working to ensure children survive, to improving their health and wellbeing and quality of life.

Contemporary approaches to strategies designed to improve and address children's health issues include policy aimed at preventing or combatting the effects of a range of conditions. This is being approached by offering universal services to all children (from conception) using early interventions (this will be discussed in Chapters 3 and 4). However, here is a list of the contemporary high priorities for children's health:

- reducing levels of childhood obesity and improving nutrition (see Chapters 7 and 12)
- improving levels of dental care and addressing dental caries (decay) (see Chapters 7 and 12)
- preventing infectious diseases (by increasing immunisation uptake) (see Chapter 8).

However, there are many conditions that are not addressed in government policy but that continue to affect children's lives in the short or long term and are a source of *ill* health for children. In order to understand the contemporary issues relating to children's health, Table 2.1 summarises some classifications or descriptions of the types of health conditions that are commonly seen in children.

Classification of health conditions

It may be more helpful to consider children's health in relation to the cause of the condition and the effect it is likely to have on children and their families. In

Table 2.1 Classification of conditions in contemporary medicine

Classification	Example	Implications for child and family	Implications for practice
Acute: meaning sudden	Infectious diseases such as gastroenteritis	Children, especially babies, can become dehydrated and dangerously unwell; children miss out on their early education; parents have to keep child away from the setting and are unable to work	The spread of infection can affect other children and staff and require them to be away from the setting; strategies and policies that prevent and minimise the spread of infection are vitally important
Chronic: long-term; each chronic condition has a range of signs and symptoms which require management via medication, diet or the environment; some conditions which are chronic may have an acute exacerbation, for example asthma	Asthma, coeliac disease, cystic fibrosis, diabetes, epilepsy, sickle cell anaemia Mental health issues	In order to minimise the symptoms of a chronic condition, children may have to avoid 'triggers'; additional time required for medication or other interventions such as physio or bandaging; on-going management may require children to attend hospital visits	Knowledge and understanding of the management of conditions; policies for medication; integrated working with health professionals
Complex medical needs: are when children have a great number of medical needs and interventions to support bodily function or to maintain life	**Life-limiting** conditions are those for which there is no reasonable hope of cure and from which children or young people will die **Congenital** conditions are present at birth, such as cerebral palsy and foetal alcohol syndrome **Life-threatening** conditions are those for which curative treatment may be feasible but can fail, such as cancer	Some conditions cause progressive deterioration, rendering the child increasingly dependent on parents and carers; the child may have developmental delay; may require on-going treatment and interventions; families may need to provide on-going personal care and medical treatment	Management of condition is likely to include the need for clinical skills to support the child's bodily function, for example suction; may require training of staff to continue medical care in settings; may impact on ratios as children may require extra attention
Injuries	Accidental and non-accidental	Child may need to have child protection procedures initiated; parents may need parenting support	Knowledge of safeguarding; education of parents and children, e.g. road safety

particular, it is important to think how the condition is likely to impact on young children's ECEC and what the implications are for practice.

Reflection on your experience

The examples given in Table 2.1 are deliberately brief and the effects on children and their families and the implications for practice will be developed further in later chapters. However, the headings in the table may be useful for you in considering some of the conditions that children have.

Table 2.2   Examples from practice of the most common health conditions

Classification	Condition
Acute conditions	First aid situations, such as asthma attacks, anaphylaxis episode, falls
Allergic conditions (chronic)	Allergic rhinitis
	Allergy
	Anaphylaxis
	Hayfever
Chronic conditions	Coeliac disease
	Cystic fibrosis
	Diabetes mellitus
	Eczema
	Epilepsy (including febrile convulsion)
	Galactosaemia
Infectious diseases	Chicken pox
	Conjunctivitis
	Coryza (common cold)
	Diarrhoea and vomiting
	Ear infections
	Foot and mouth
	Mumps
	Slapped cheek
	Whooping cough
Infestations	Head lice
	Ringworm
	Threadworms

RESEARCH FOCUS

My continuing doctorate research explores the question: how do practitioners support children's health and wellbeing? (Musgrave 2014). Student practitioners' and working practitioners' responses to the question 'what are the most common health conditions affecting the children you have worked with in your setting?' are summarised in Table 2.2.

(Continued)

(Continued)

The findings from this research have many implications for practice (these conditions will be discussed in the relevant chapter). At this point, answer the following questions in relation to Table 2.2:

1   How similar would your list be? Are there any other conditions that you would add to the list?

2   Which conditions have you not encountered?

3   What is your knowledge level of all of these conditions?

4   What strategies, policies and interventions are you aware of for tackling these conditions?

5   Identify your role and priorities in relation to the contemporary health issues in your setting.

6   What do you think are the implications for practice and policy within your setting? For example, what measures can you put in place to minimise the impact of these conditions on (a) the individual children in your setting, and (b) all children in your setting?

7   What challenges can you anticipate in your role supporting children's health?

Theory into practice

Having reflected on the health conditions that you have encountered in your own practice, you may have come to the conclusion that children frequently do not have just one health condition. You may also have had the thought that children who are regarded as being disadvantaged are more likely to have multiple health concerns. Consider Case study 2.1.

CASE STUDY 2.1

Ayania is 3 and her brother Canab is 6. They arrived in the UK six months ago with their mother, Ceebla, from Somalia. The children are picking up English, but Ceebla does not speak any English and she is very shy. The family is currently living with distant relatives in a privately rented house, which is over-crowded and in poor condition. The children's father remains in Somalia. The family's uncertain immigration status means that it has been difficult for them to be given benefits. The family is relying on what the relatives can spare to give them, however Ceebla is known to frequently visit the food bank for extra food. Ayania has been in your pre-school room in a privately owned day-care setting for the last 3 months. When she first started, she would smile readily and practise her English with enthusiasm. Over the last month, you have become concerned about her. The concerns are that she appears to be losing weight; she is lacking concentration; and she doesn't seem to want to eat much of the food provided by the nursery, but will eat the fresh fruit. You have noticed that she has been coughing and scratching her head a great deal.

This morning, when you asked her how she is, she became tearful and could not communicate with you. It is now lunchtime and you have noticed that Ayania appears very hot and lethargic.

REFLECTION

- What are the possible causes of Ayania's being unwell?
- What are your concerns? Think about her previous healthcare; and the other children.
- What actions can you and the manager take?
- Which other professionals can help you to help Ayania?

As you may have considered in response to the questions, Ayania was not born in this country, therefore it is unlikely that she will have received the immunisations that are a universal service aimed at preventing infectious diseases. Her food intake has decreased recently and this has resulted in weight loss. The considerations here are that she simply cannot tolerate the different food she is being offered, or has she picked up worms and this has affected her appetite? Ayania has a high temperature – what are the possible causes of this? If she has a contagious illness, is there a risk to the other children in your room? How are you going to communicate with Ceebla? Is the family likely to be registered with a local medical practice? If so, what will the staff there know about her health and previous medical history?

Clearly, Ayania and her family are experiencing multiple disadvantages and these are impacting on her health and wellbeing. However, it is important to bear in mind that children who do not live in poverty can also have health issues that are potentially going to have a negative effect on their developmental progress and long-term health. Consider Bethany's situation in Case study 2.2.

CASE STUDY 2.2

Bethany is 2 and she is an only child. Mum and dad live near to your setting and they work nearby in the financial area of the city. Bethany's mum drops her off in the morning and, when they arrive, Bethany is in her buggy and is often asleep. Mum says that this is because she has been up in the night because her eczema has flared up and she is very itchy. Bethany gets wheezy when she tries to run about; her parents say that they don't want her running around because they are concerned that she may be developing asthma, like her dad. You have noticed that Bethany is starting to look larger than other 2-year-old children and that she is already wearing clothes that are labelled as being the

(Continued)

(Continued)

right size for 4-year-olds. Bethany's weight gain is puzzling you because, at mealtimes, Bethany picks at her food. When you mention this to her mum, she suggests that it may be because Bethany prefers to eat sweet food at home and refuses to eat normal family meals. She enjoys breakfast cereals and will eat food products which have a picture of Peppa Pig on the packaging. Mum also mentions that she has been trying to cut out some foods like dairy because she is concerned that this is provoking her eczema.

REFLECTION

- What are the possible reasons for Bethany's eating habits?
- What are the possible consequences of Bethany's lack of physical activity both in childhood and adulthood?
- How can you work with Bethany's parents to promote physical activity and healthy eating for her while she is in the setting?
- What are the challenges for you in working with Bethany's parents?
- Which health professionals can you work with?
- What legislation and strategies are you aware of that can help you to support Bethany's health?

You may have concluded that Bethany's health problems can be considered as being caused, in the first instance, by the symptoms of her eczema and by her parents' concerns about the possibility of developing asthma. The impact of both eczema and asthma can be underestimated and it is natural that parents want to reduce the possibility of provoking the symptoms. Many people believe that dietary manipulation, for example, as in Bethany's case, by cutting out dairy produce, helps to reduce the symptoms of eczema. Unfortunately, this approach can result in children becoming 'fussy eaters' which has long-term consequences. Similarly, inhibiting Bethany's physical activity also has long-term consequences because she may be more prone to obesity. Bethany's case is one where there are a number of overlapping issues, all of which influence each other. Working with the parents in a way that is supportive will be essential. In this situation, working with the health visitor to conduct a 2-year review may be a good opportunity to involve the parents in a sensitive way.

There are no straightforward answers in such cases. The families' situations are meant to provoke your thinking. It is hoped that as you read the other chapters in this book you will gain knowledge and develop your thinking about some of the contemporary health issues that can affect children in your setting.

Table 2.3 is a timeline which summarises notable events that have made a contribution to children's health. The events selected are by no means all that have made a positive contribution to preventing death and illness in children, but they have been chosen to give a sense of how recently some events have occurred.

Table 2.3 Timeline of events influencing children's health and wellbeing (adapted from Blair et al. 2010)

Date	Event	Impact on children
1800s The Industrial Revolution	Industrialisation of cities A move away from rural living Children become part of the workforce	Crowded and unsanitary living conditions Children from the age of 4 employed in cotton mills, factories, coal mines and as chimney sweeps
1837–1901 Victorian Reforms	Philanthropists highlight the negative impact of child labour on children's health	Acts of Parliament are passed to reduce the hours of work for children
1840s	General anaesthetics start to be used	Surgeons could perform operations that were hitherto inoperable
1841	Antiseptics used for preventing infections in wounds, and greater awareness of the need to use gloves during clinical procedures	A reduction in the incidence of life-threatening infections
1850s and '60s	Smallpox immunisation starts to be developed and first attempt at vaccination programme	Led to worldwide eradication of smallpox
1850s	Children's hospitals opened in Birmingham and London	Recognition that the health needs of children are different to those of adults
1862	The pioneers of neonatology research develop interventions to avoid the high death of newborns Infant incubators developed	The care of premature and ill newborn babies becomes a speciality
1870	First health visitors appointed in Manchester	Poor mothers were visited to teach them how to care for their children's health
1880s	The Education Act introduced free state education for children under the age of 10 District nurses introduced with a focus on supporting mothers and babies	Children's health became a focus of government attention Aimed to improve standard of hygiene and reduce infant deaths from gastroenteritis

(Continued)

Table 2.3 (Continued)

Date	Event	Impact on children
1901–1950 First half of 20th century	End of the Boer War	
1901	Interdepartmental Committee on Physical Deterioration set up	Investigated the health of school children which led to school health services being set up
1918	Maternity and Child Welfare Act	Committees set up to address the health needs of pregnant women and children under 5
1919	Margaret McMillan published *The Nursery School*	Highlighted the role of nursery education in improving children's health
1921	Register for Sick Children's Nurses created in England	Recognition that children require specialist nursing skills
1939–1945	The Second World War	Rationing meant that many foods were unavailable
1940s	Antibiotics are created and become available for use	Infectious diseases caused by bacteria were treatable
1940s	The 'first special care baby units opened in Bristol and Birmingham	Developing practices that contributed to reducing the number of babies dying because of premature birth and illnesses present at birth
1946	United Nations Children's Fund (Unicef) set up	Aims to provide emergency healthcare to children in developing countries
1948	Introduction of the NHS (in the UK)	Free treatment available to all
1948	World Health Organization created	Aims to improve international healthcare for all
1950–1989	Vaccinations/immunisations for some infectious diseases became available	Reduction in the numbers of children disabled and dying from polio, whooping cough, measles, mumps, rubella
1950 onwards		
1950s	Surgeons start to develop techniques to correct congenital heart defects	Children with heart defects that were previously inoperable survive and go on to be unaffected by the heart defect they were born with
1959	The Platt Report made recommendations about the welfare of children in hospital	The recommendations led to improvements for children in hospital
1960s	A shift from curing diseases to prevention of ill health	Approaches to health education and health promotion were developed
	Introduction of screening of babies for conditions that require early treatment	The heel prick test (Guthrie Test) was introduced to identify babies with phenylketonuria
1970s	Technological advances in medical equipment	Diagnosis and treatment of conditions more reliable

Date	Event	Impact on children
1989	UNCRC: Article 24	Every child has the right to the best possible health. Governments must provide good quality healthcare, clean water, nutritious food and a clean environment so that children can stay healthy. Richer countries must help poorer countries achieve this
2003	Every Child Matters in England and Wales – the Green Paper identified five outcomes that are most important for children	The five outcomes are mutually reinforcing. For example, children and young people learn and thrive when they are healthy, safe and engaged; and the evidence shows clearly that educational achievement is the most effective route out of poverty
2004	The National Service Framework for Children, Young People and Maternity Services was published – an integral part of the ECM outcomes	A 10-year programme designed to improve the health and wellbeing of children and young people
2007	Child Health Promotion Programme introduced (changed name to the Healthy Child Programme the following year)	A universal public health programme for children
2008	Scotland: Getting it right for every child	Included an aim to improve children's health
	The Healthy Child Programme (HCP)	A universal public health programme for children. Introduced a review for 2-year-olds
2011	'Supporting Families in the Early Years' was published – a joint publication by the DfE and DoH	Designed to promote the implementation of the HCP, increase the number of health visitors and develop closer partnerships between health and early years services
2013	Wave Trust in collaboration with the DfE published 'Conception to Age 2: The age of opportunity'	This was an addendum to the government's vision for the Foundation Years: Supporting Families in the Foundation Years. Aimed at tackling the roots of disadvantage
2014	Children and Families Act – supporting pupils with medical conditions	Statutory guidance to achieve better outcomes for children aged 5 and over with long-term health conditions in state-maintained schools
	The (revised) Early Years Foundation Stage	Introduced the progress check at age 2. To include the Healthy Child Programme health and development review
	Overview of the Early Years High Impact Areas, a joint publication by the Department of Health, NHS England, Public Health England and others	Aimed to support the transfer of commissioning and to help health visitors to implement the HCP
2015	From 1 October, transfer of 0–5 years commissioning to local authorities	The responsibility for commissioning public health services for children aged 0–5 years transferred from NHS England to local authorities

Conclusion

This chapter has helped you to examine the chronosystem in relation to children's health. The first part of the chapter has summarised the main developments in children's health that have taken place over the last 200 years. One of the main messages is for you to be conscious that many conditions have not disappeared; they are simply being contained as a consequence of the societal changes and medical advances that have occurred in relatively recent years. The chapter content has hopefully made you realise that you have an active role to play in preventing some of the conditions that can impact on children's health, whether the prevention of infection is in the microsystem of your setting, or whether it is being aware of the immunisation schedules that are part of the macrosystem and playing your part in promoting the uptake of immunisations in your setting.

Another message of the chapter is to consider that despite having a free national health service, there are many health issues that continue to be problematic for children. Conversely, the presence of the NHS means that many more children are surviving but their healthcare needs the management and support of practitioners.

Further reading

Blair, M., Stewart-Brown, S., Waterston, T. and Crowther, R. (2010) *Child Public Health* (2nd edn). Oxford: Oxford University Press

Cunningham, H. (2006) *The Invention of Childhood*. London: BBC Books.

Hall, D. and Elliman, D. (2006) *Health for All Children* (4th edn). Oxford: Oxford University Press.

3
CURRENT GOVERNMENT POLICY AND LEGISLATION

CHAPTER AIMS AND OBJECTIVES

- To summarise legislation and policy in relation to children's health and wellbeing since Every Child Matters (2003)

- To critically evaluate legislation in relation to children and families in your setting

- To consider the implications of legislation and government guidance for policy and practice in ECEC settings

Introduction: Why is understanding policy important?

There are several reasons why it is vital as a professional practitioner that you have an understanding of child health policy. However, learning about policy can be viewed as less interesting than other areas of learning. No matter what your personal view is on policy, it is an area that you need to engage with, not least for the following reasons:

- government policy influences priorities for funding
- government policy will influence your policies in practice
- policy is based on research evidence and reflects what is regarded as the best approach to take in supporting children's health.

Evaluating child health policy

In common with many countries in the world, successive UK governments have invested heavily in child health policy with the aim of improving outcomes for children in childhood and adulthood. The services that are available have been developed with the best of intentions, however it is important to evaluate the aims and sometimes the effectiveness of some aspects of child health policy. It is important to apply criticality to policy and not accept the aims at face value. As you read the chapter, bear in mind the following questions:

- What is the value of the policy/legislation in relation to all children?
- What are the challenges and benefits in the macro- and microsystem?
- Are the needs of 'hard to hear' voices reflected in policy?

Your roles and responsibilities

Early years practitioners are central to many of the aims of the government child health policy. Therefore, the success and value of child health policy in part relies on the skills, knowledge and understanding of the workforce. As you read the chapter, you are urged to consider your role and responsibilities in relation to meeting the aims of child health policy. In addition, you are asked to keep in mind the children and families who attend your setting and to consider their individual perspectives and needs. Most importantly, you are asked to consider how you can lead on developing good practice in children's health.

Explanation of terms used in this chapter

The word 'policy' can be used in several contexts. Policy is described in the *Oxford English Dictionary* as a 'course or principle of action adopted or proposed by an organisation, government or business'. Fitzgerald and Kay (2016, p. 3) define policy as

> An attempt by those working inside an organisation to think in a coherent way about what it is trying to achieve (either in general or in relation to a specific issue) and what it needs to do to achieve it.

In the context of this chapter, the word policy is used in two ways. First of all, it is used to examine the approach – that is, the policies that have been published by government to improve children's health and wellbeing. Some of the policies are statutory, that is, legislation has been passed in parliament and it is required by law that the policy is followed and not to do so is to break the law. The guidance and principles of the Early Years Foundation Stage is an example of statutory policy. The second use of the term policy is in relation to the courses of action that you take in your settings to work with children and their families to support children's health and wellbeing.

Policy and legislation for children's health and wellbeing

Global child health

It is important that we consider children's health policy in a global and not just a national context. The United Nations Convention on the Rights of the Child (UN 1989) states in Article 24 that all children have a right to health. This right is reflected in the UN Sustainable Development Goals, which ensure healthy lives and promotes well-being for all at all ages as goal number 3 (UNDP 2015). The focus on improving health and wellbeing for children in developing countries includes improving maternal health, a similar aim to the Healthy Child Programme (see below). Another main aim of the goal is to tackle the threat that malaria poses to children in affected areas of the world (Chapter 8 explores malaria in more detail).

National child health

The organisation and provision of child health policy in the UK is complex. Policies can be inter-related and overlapping, meaning that there may be several policies from different stakeholders with similar aims. Table 3.1 is an overview of some of the specific pieces of legislation, policy and reviews that are relevant to children's health and wellbeing. The table is chronological and is designed to give you a sense of the way that child health policy has developed. It is designed to enhance your understanding of the legislation and/or policy. It includes the main aims and some of the considerations to bear in mind relating to the aims. The policy and legislation included in this chapter are not exhaustive. For example, where there is policy and/ or legislation relevant to a specific health condition, as in Chapter 7 where children's dental health is discussed, specific policy relating to this area of health is included in that chapter rather than in this one.

In addition to legislation and policy that are specifically aimed at children's health and wellbeing, it is important to consider other legislation that contributes to keeping children healthy and preventing children from becoming unwell. For example, the Reporting of Injuries, Diseases and Dangerous Occurrences Regulations (RIDDOR) (Department for Work and Pensions 2013) is legislation that is general to all of the population and not just children.

Considering the perspectives of all stakeholders

In order to critique the value of policies, it is useful to consider the perspectives of all stakeholders involved in planning and implementing government child health policy. The stakeholders involved in the UK could include:

- the child/children
- parents, carers and families
- early years practitioners
- other professionals: health visitors, general practitioners, midwives
- local communities – Children's Centres/private, voluntary and independent day-care providers; local authorities
- drug companies
- the NHS
- government – including opposition government.

There are advantages and disadvantages for each of the above stakeholders related to the implementation of some aspects of child health policy. As you will see below, childhood immunisations are a significant preventive measure in the Healthy Child Programme (HCP) (DoH 2009). Using the example of childhood immunisations and considering the list of stakeholders above, you may realise that there can be a tension between the different aims of each stakeholder. For example, a child in the UK has the right to receive a schedule of free immunisations as part of the HCP. However, some parents do not believe in the safety or efficacy of childhood immunisations in preventing infectious diseases. Therefore, they may refuse to have their child immunised because of their beliefs, which may

Table 3.1 Summary of legislation and policy relevant to children's health and wellbeing

Name and date of policy	Aim	Advantages of policy/ legislation	Comment
Every Child Matters (2003)	To maximise opportunities and minimise risks for all children and support them to 'be healthy'	Promoted interagency approach	Ambitious agenda
		Built on the Children Act and the UNCRC. A legacy that helps us to understand the importance of working with others – e.g. school nurse, HV	difficulties in developing good models of IAW
			Disregarded/reduced importance during the coalition government
Children Act 2004	Related to welfare and safeguarding	Required LAs to publish an overarching plan setting out their strategy for improving the ECM outcomes	A positive move which helped to give a voice to children, in particular to children with disabilities
National Service framework for children, young people and maternity services (2004)	10-year plan for health, education and social services to work together to reduce inequality	Set national standards of care to improve services for children	Regarded the mother as most influential in their children's health
		Acknowledged the importance of the ante-natal period	
		Promoted an understanding that 'Healthy mothers produce healthy babies who become healthy children and adults; much preventable adult ill health and disease has its roots during gestation, infancy and childhood' (p 4).	
Early Years Foundation Stage (2007)	The Childcare Act (2006) made a statutory requirement for local authorities to specify the learning and development that early years providers must secure in providing early years provision	Helped to highlight the importance of the 0-5 year stage of learning and development	Shaped the concepts of the need for positive relationships and enabling environment that are essential for the learning and development of children, as well as recognising that each child is unique
The Healthy Child Programme 0-5 years (2009)	A universal approach using early intervention for all children from conception to 5 to improve health and wellbeing	Based on progressive universalism, meaning the HCP can help to identify children who are at risk of poor outcomes and make referrals to other service to provide early support	Requires willingness and participation of families, therefore some vulnerable children will not benefit from the services
	Introduced the 2-year old review		Requires collaborative working with voluntary and community services

Name and date of policy	Aim	Advantages of policy/ legislation	Comment
The Healthy Child Programme 5-19 years (2009)	Good practice guidance which sets out the recommended framework of universal services for children and young people to promote optimal health and wellbeing	An evidence-based approach aimed at delivering efficient and high quality services that make a measurable contribution to the prevention of ill health and the reduction of inequalities	Requires willingness and participation of families, therefore some vulnerable children will not benefit from the services Requires collaborative working with voluntary and community services
Working Together to Safeguard Children (2006, 2010 and 2015)	The governments' responses to cases relating to the need for everybody to take responsibility for safeguarding children	Demonstrates across party commitment to the concept of a multi-agency approach to working together to keep children safe	The complexities associated with safeguarding children is reflected in the number of revisions of this document that have been published
Fairer Society, Healthy Lives (Marmot 2010)	Public health review highlighted the health equalities that are caused as a consequence of children living in poverty in the UK	This report informed changes to legislation aimed at reducing the disadvantages caused by poverty to children's health	The review continues to influence successive government policies, in particular the concept of 'school readiness' as a way of promoting equality
Supporting families in the Foundation Years (2011) Department for Education and Department of Health	The coalition government's vision for those who commission, lead and deliver services for mothers and fathers during pregnancy and for children until the age of 5	Aimed to create an effective support system for parents and practitioners	A focus on improving health for children which drew on research which highlighted how high quality early education can contribute to improving children's health
Family Nurse Partnership Department of Health	The FNP is a preventive programme for young first time mothers. It offers intensive and structured home visiting, delivered by specially trained nurses (Family	FNP has three aims: to improve pregnancy outcomes, child health and development and parents' economic self-sufficiency	Evidence based research from the US shows improvements in ante-natal health Cost savings in the US are substantial, ranging from $17,000 to $34,000 per child by the time they reach 15, with a $3-5 return for every $1 invested

(Continued)

Table 3.1 (Continued)

Name and date of policy	Aim	Advantages of policy/ legislation	Comment
	Nurses), from early pregnancy until the child is two		The outcomes that are being measured include smoking during pregnancy, breastfeeding, admissions to hospital for injuries and ingestions, further pregnancies, and child development at age two
Health Visitor Implementation Plan 2011-15	Aims to increase the number of health visitors by approx. 50%	HVs to play a key role in coordinating the delivery of the HCP. Introduces the 6 high impact areas where HVs can impact on children and families' health and wellbeing	Some families' needs are increasingly complex. Recovering from the deficit is leaving a gap in services
EYFS (2012, 2014)	Statutory guidance which sets the standards for learning, development and care Children learn best when they are 'healthy'	2 year check introduced – links with the HCP supports an integrated approach acknowledges the uniqueness of each child offers general guidance about promoting positive health and preventing the spread of infections within settings medicine	Training for 2-year old check not easily available Some 2-year olds may not access ECEC Not very specific in terms of health
Life Stage: Early Years (2012)	The annual report of the Chief Medical Officer included a chapter on the early years	The chapter highlighted how practitioners in the early years play a key role in promoting, educating and supporting children's health	An aim of the recommendations is to reduce the incidence of disease. the recommendations promotes the concept of ' proportionate universalism' (p 1)
Ensuring a good education for children who cannot attend school because of health needs (Department of Education 2013)	Statutory guidance for local authorities to follow when carrying out their duty to arrange suitable full-time education for children who cannot attend mainstream school because of their health	If a child is away from school for 15 days or more, this may be continuous or intermittent, liaison with health professionals is necessary to arrange good quality alternative education	A challenging statutory duty in times of austerity Differing interpretations of when a child is deemed unfit/unable to attend fulltime mainstream school may lead to tensions about what is a justifiable reason. LAs are not allowed to have lists of specific health conditions

Name and date of policy	Aim	Advantages of policy/ legislation	Comment
SENDA (2014)	Outlines the legal requirements of local authorities, health services and education settings in meeting the needs of children with SENs	Health care plans must be reviewed every 12 months	Extends the age range 0–25 years which may be challenging
Children and Families Act (2014) Supporting pupils in schools with medical conditions	Statutory guidance which requires schools to have policies in place which support children with medical conditions	Aims to include children in all aspects of the curriculum Strengthen the links between education, health and care settings All children with a medical condition to have an Education and Health Care (EHC) plan	Logistical issues relating to staff training Only applicable to maintained schools, excludes maintained nursery schools Only applicable to school age children The guidance relies on schools having access to the School Nursing Service, regional variations in availability of the support may impact on the level of support schools can access
Conception to age 2 – the age of opportunity. Wave Trust in collaboration with the Department for Education (2013)	Addendum to the government's vision for the Foundation Years: Supporting Families in the Foundation Years	A multi-disciplinary approach which makes specific recommendations about the importance of high quality ECEC in promoting infant mental health	Report highlights issues relating to 0–2-year-olds
Promoting the health and wellbeing of looked after children (2009, 2015)	Statutory guidance for multi-professionals responsible for children's health and wellbeing who are in the care of local authorities	Recognises that looked after children are more vulnerable to the negative impact of health and seeks to mitigate the impact on children's development	Requires efficient levels of integrated working

(Continued)

Table 3.1 (Continued)

Name and date of policy	Aim	Advantages of policy/ legislation	Comment
6 Early Years High Impact Area Department of Health (2014)	Published to support and inform the transition of commissioning to Local authorities. To articulate the contribution of Health Visitors to the 0-5 agenda	6 High Impact areas are: 1. transition to parenthood and the early weeks with a focus on maternal mental health 2. breastfeeding 3. healthy weight and promoting physical activity 4. managing minor illness 5. reducing accidents 6. health, wellbeing and development of the child age 2 – 2 year review	The 6 high impact areas is aimed at promoting health and improving the use of resources Focuses on early intervention. Education of parents in how to manage illness and prevent injury will reduce hospital attendance and admission Promotes 'school readiness'
National Framework for children and young peoples' continuing care (2016) under section 26 of the Children and Families Act 2014	This Framework is intended to provide guidance for clinical commissioning groups (CCGs) when assessing the needs of children and young people (up to the age of 25) whose complex needs cannot be met by universal or specialist health services.	At the heart of arrangements for children and young people is an integrated Education, Health and Care plan (EHC plan). Aims to address the holistic needs of C and YP Provides a personal health budget	Requires efficient levels of integrated working
Integrated health and development review of 2–2½-year-olds (2015)	LAs, health visiting services and early years providers work together to review the development and health of 2-year-olds	Gives an opportunity for early years practitioners and Health Visitors to pool their expertise in order to work together to maximise children's potential	Not all 2-year-olds access services The logistics of practitioners and Health Visitors working together may be a challenge

leave a legacy of disability or, in some cases, death. Thus, there is an ethical dilemma, because the child's right to health is potentially being denied; such children are at risk of contracting a preventable infectious disease such as meningitis. On the other hand, if immunisations were enforced, parents' right to exercise their beliefs would be denied.

Continuing with the example of immunisation, consider other children in your setting – if a child has not been immunised, there is a risk that they may contract a preventable disease. In turn, they could infect a child who genuinely cannot be immunised for medical reasons, such as having chemotherapy for cancer treatment. Unlike in the USA, there is no law on this in the UK and therefore no legal obligation on parents to have their child immunised before entry to school.

REFLECTION

- What are the possible consequences for you in your setting if you have a child who is unable to be immunised and a child whose parents refuse immunisation for their child?

- Consider the risks to the child who is not protected because of medical need versus the child who is not protected because of parental choice.

- Consider your position in maintaining the health of such children.

Consider the viewpoint of the drug companies who produce the immunisations for the NHS. If immunisations were not part of the UK child health policy, their revenues would be reduced. If children were not immunised, the numbers of children affected by infectious diseases would return to pre-immunisation levels. This would result in a greater number of children developing disability. Therefore, consider the financial advantage to the country of having children immunised in order to reduce expenditure on services for children who develop a disability following a disease such as polio.

Considering how to hear the voices of children
A way of evaluating the aims and strands that make up child health policy is to keep in mind those children in our society whose voices are sometimes hard to hear, or not heard at all. Consequently, their right to health, as outlined in the United Nations Convention on the Rights of the Child (UN 1989) and in government policy, may not be upheld. As you read the summary of child health in the UK, you may notice that achieving the aims relies in some part on the cooperation of parents. However, tensions and conflicts of interest may arise as a consequence of an aim of a policy, as outlined in the previous section. Other reasons why a child's voice may be hard to hear may be to do with their families' circumstances; for example, children who live in Traveller communities, those who are refugees, or those who have parents in situations that mean they are deemed to be disadvantaged because

of mental health or drug addiction. All of these situations may present difficulties for parents and inhibit their access to health services for their child.

Context of health policy for children in the UK

In order to understand the current child health policy in the UK, it is important to examine events in the chronosystem to appreciate the complex influences that have shaped current policy and legislation.

Societal change as an influence on child health policy

Chapter 2 explored the historical perspective of child health. From reading the chapter, you will have gained an understanding that children's health is inextricably linked to their status in society and also their environment. Over the last 200 years, there have been several Acts of Parliament passed in the UK that have helped to improve the health of children. For example, making it illegal for small boys to work as chimney sweeps helped to reduce the number of males who developed cancer of the testes because of the contact they had with carcinogenic (cancer-causing) soot. However, it was the UNCRC (UN 1989) that was the start of a global initiative to recognise children as individuals in society. The Rights were not just related to health, they also examined each aspect of children's lives in a holistic way. Article 24 states that children have a right to health. (Table 3.1 summarises policies relating to children's health and wellbeing.)

Medical improvements as an influence on child health policy

Another influence on policy and legislation is the impact that medical advances have had on children's health and wellbeing. As discussed in Chapter 2, in relatively recent times there were many conditions that were a cause of death in children and this is no longer the case. Children with chronic or complex medical conditions are surviving for much longer and experiencing an improved quality of life (Brown 2009). Such conditions will probably mean that there is a need for on-going medical care to minimise the effects of these conditions. Consequently, there is a need for legislation and policy aimed at improving these children's health and promoting their inclusion in their early education and in society.

The legacy of previous governments

Child health policy is complex partly because, historically in the UK, the government has divided up health and education, each with separate departments and responsibilities. The historical legacy of this separation was a failure to bring together these two aspects of children's development. However, following the election of the Labour Government in 1997, this situation changed when in 1998 responsibility for childcare services transferred from health to education.

Moss (2014) argues that the election of New Labour was the start of early childhood education and care becoming a policy priority, thus correcting a situation where children and relevant government policy had been neglected since the end of the post Second World War period in 1945. The Labour Government was in power from 1997 to 2010 and continued to develop policy that impacted on children's health during the 13 years of its administration. Probably the most influential policy was the Every Child Matters (ECM) Green Paper (HM Government 2003). The aims of ECM placed the emphasis on an integrated and holistic way of working with children and families and brought about profound changes for the planning and delivery of children's services, including health. The outcomes in the Green Paper mirrored the Rights of the child; this included five outcomes that the government at that time aimed to achieve for children in relation to health: every child should 'be healthy'. As a consequence of the ECM outcomes, a raft of policy and initiatives has been developed in the UK. Some of the legislation is derived from previous policy and legislation.

The Conservative and Liberal Democrat Coalition Government of 2010–2015 continued to develop the work that was put in place by the previous government, although the emphasis on ECM outcomes was not as evident in its policies. One of the most notable contributions of the Coalition Government in relation to children's health was the Free School Meals initiative (DfE 2014b).

The Conservative Government that was elected in 2015 inherited a treasury that was still recovering from a worldwide downturn and a gloomy economic situation. As a consequence, budgets have been severely reduced and, in turn, services also. In particular, Children's Centres, which are regarded as being central to supporting children's health, have been closed in many areas of the country. The impact of such closures remains to be seen.

Current government departments

In England, in 2016, the two main departments that bear responsibility for delivering good outcomes for children's health are (what are currently known as) the Department of Health and the Department for Education. The recognition that children's health and education are entwined has resulted in the publication of some joint guidance, though the two departments continue to produce independent legislation, policies and guidance aimed at improving the health and wellbeing of children. Consequently, there is a range of healthcare and education professionals who have a responsibility for implementing legislation and producing policies that follow guidelines for good practice. This, in turn, highlights the need for professionals to work in a collaborative and integrated way, which is discussed further in Chapter 4. Figure 3.1 provides a summary of the structure of the Department of Health and the Department for Education, and includes some of the bodies and organisations that have an influence on children's health.

Devolution of the UK

It is important to bear in mind that the four countries of the UK may have different policies. The effect of devolution has added to the complexity of how child health policy and legislation are organised in the UK. However, what each of the countries of the UK has in common, in relation to child health policy, is the aim of reducing inequalities in health so that all children reach their full developmental potential in childhood and across the life span.

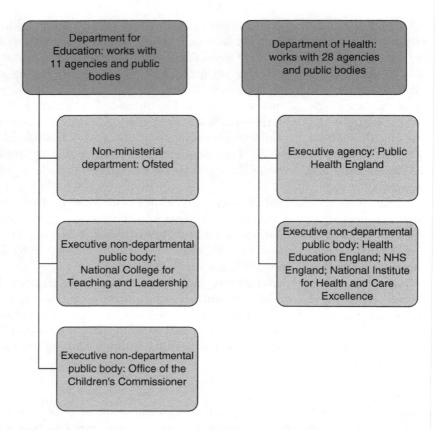

Figure 3.1   Department of Health and Department for Education

---

REFLECTION

The aim of policy relating to child health is focused on the following principles:

- universal services available to all children to prevent or reduce the effects of poor health and promote good health outcomes
- targeted services aimed at reducing inequalities in health with the provision of early intervention with targeted services to minimise the impact of conditions on children's health across the age span.

Universal services

Universal services are rooted in the principle that preventative measures should be offered to all children. An example of such a public health programme is childhood immunisation (see Chapter 8). Public Health England works closely with the Department of Health. It produces guidance relevant to early years settings aimed at preventing the causes of ill health, such as infection (see Chapter 8).

In May 2016, Public Health England (2016a) published comprehensive guidance on health promotion for children – 'Health Matters: Giving every child the best start in life'.

Children's Centres were developed following the ECM agenda and replaced Sure Start Centres. A main aim of Children's Centres was to be able to offer services that would improve outcomes, including health, for children.

Targeted services

Despite the UK being considered one of the richest nations in the world, health inequalities exist and lead to ill health in children. A major cause of inequality in health is living in poverty. The link between poverty and poor health is well documented. Underdown (2007) describes the 'social gradient' (p. 57) in child health, meaning that the lower the socio-economic group a child belongs to, the higher the risk of poor health. Professor Mitch Blair (Blair et al. 2010) describes how socially disadvantaged children have 'poorer outcomes in virtually every health indicator' (p. 177). The reasons why this is so are discussed in Chapter 5.

The Marmot public health review (2010) highlighted the health inequalities that are caused as a consequence of children living in poverty in the UK. He recommended that actions to reduce inequalities in health should offer proportionate universalism, meaning that services should be proportionate to the level of disadvantage.

In summary, the aim of child health policy is to offer services that provide the best effect in improving health for all children, such as immunisation programmes. It also aims to provide additional services for children and families who are at risk of poor outcomes.

Child health policy for specific conditions and groups

As discussed in the previous section, the collective governmental approach to children's health is to offer universal and targeted services using an early intervention approach (see Chapter 4). However, in addition to universal child health policy, it should be noted that there is legislation and policy that is relevant to other areas of children's health – for example, the National Institute for Health and Care Excellence (NICE) guidance (the significance of this is discussed below).

National Institute for Health and Care Excellence (NICE) guidelines

The aims of the Healthy Child Programme are wide ranging, but overall they are prevention and health promotion. The NICE guidance is designed to supplement the HCP.

The aim of the guidelines issued by NICE is to reduce the differences and inequalities in treatment and services available in the NHS. There are several guidelines relevant to early intervention strategies for children, young people, infants and newborn babies. An example of a group of children that is recognised as requiring particular consideration is 'looked after' children and young people (NICE 2010). In addition, NICE guidance summarises the clinical effectiveness of interventions, drugs and devices used for medical conditions. There are many conditions affecting children that require specific guidance in order to manage them. Examples are anaphylaxis, asthma, diabetes, eczema and food allergy.

Of particular importance to you as a practitioner working with children in the early years is the NICE guidance on social and emotional wellbeing for the early years (2016a). This guidance was written to complement the aims of the EYFS and makes clear links to the terms used in the EYFS. The content and relevance of this guidance is discussed in detail in Chapter 6. There is a large quantity of NICE guidance available to download from the NICE website. NICE guidelines are frequently being published and updated via the website. Reference will be made to NICE guidance where relevant in other chapters in this book.

Universal child health legislation and policy

This section summarises some of the influential pieces of legislation and guidance that have had a profound impact on the organisation of child health services in the UK:

National Service Framework (Department of Health 2004): One of the most important pieces of policy as a consequence of ECM was the National Service Framework (NSF) for children, young people and maternity services. This framework set standards of expected levels of care for the first time. This, in turn, led to the Healthy Child Programme.

The Healthy Child Programme (HCP): The most notable initiative as a consequence of the ECM Green Paper in relation to children's health was the Child Health Promotion Programme (CHPP) (DCSF and DoH 2008). The CHPP was superseded in October 2009 by the Healthy Child Programme, which is described as follows:

An effective and high-quality preventive programme in childhood is the foundation of a healthy society. This is as true today as ever. For more than 100 years we have provided a preventive health service that has protected and promoted the health of children. (p. 2)

The HCP is in three parts and is published in separate documents, comprising:

- pregnancy and the first five years
- the Integrated Review (formerly the Two Year Review)
- 5–19 years.

The aims of 'Pregnancy and the first five years' are to:

- offer universal services, at the same time as focusing on vulnerable babies, children and families
- recognise that the concept of good health for children starts at conception
- identify preventative health measures to improve children's health
- educate adults in order to promote good health in children
- ensure that Children's Centres are seen as central to promoting children's health.

The areas of health targeted in the HCP include:

- improving health and wellbeing through health and development reviews
- health promotion
- parenting support
- screening and immunisation programmes.

REFLECTION

How can the areas of focus help to improve health outcomes for children?

Integrated Review for 2-year-olds

In September 2015, the Integrated Review was introduced and this brought together two existing reviews for children aged 2 to $2\frac{1}{2}$. The central tool of the Integrated Review is the questionnaire for parents to complete – the Ages and Stages Questionnaire (ASQ3). The National Children's Bureau has produced supporting material to help you prepare for an Integrated Review (NCB 2015). In the guidance, it is advised that parents bring the child's Personal Child Health Record or 'red book' (p. 27) (which is issued to every baby to keep a parent-held record of development and health) with them to the review. The two reviews are the HCP review and the EYFS progress check.

The Healthy Child Programme review at age 2 to 2½

The HCP review is a health-focused check carried out by health visitors, encompassing the health, wellbeing and development of the child at age 2. The Department of Health has recently announced that local authorities are to take over the commissioning of children's health services. To support the transition, there have been six 'high impact areas of health' (drawn from the HCP aims) identified as a priority for health visitors to address (see Chapter 4).

The Early Years Foundation Stage progress check at age 2

The EYFS progress check is a statutory requirement where practitioners are required to assess a child's progress. The aims of the progress check are to:

- review a child's development in the three prime areas of the EYFS
- ensure that parents have a clear picture of their child's development
- enable practitioners to understand the child's needs and plan activities to meet them in the setting
- enable parents to understand the child's needs and, with support from practitioners, enhance development at home
- note areas where a child is progressing well and identify any areas where progress is less than expected
- describe actions the provider intends to take to address any developmental concerns (including working with other professionals where appropriate).

The Early Years Foundation Stage: Statutory framework for the early years foundation stage (2014)

The third version of the Early Years Foundation Stage framework (DfE 2014a) strengthened the welfare and safeguarding requirements of the 2012 framework.

Special Educational Needs and Disability (SEND) as part of the Children and Families Act 2014

The most recent legislation includes a chapter for early years providers outlining their responsibilities in relation to planning for children with special educational needs (SEN), whether or not they have an Education, Health and Care (EHC) plan. Providers must also provide for children with medical conditions. EHC plans are written where appropriate and this document helps settings to plan for care and provide support to meet the medical needs of children. Such support may include the provision of equipment or services from physiotherapists or other health professionals. Personal health budgets are available for children who require continuing healthcare.

Pupil Premium (2014)

For children with complex medical needs and/or SEN, the Pupil Premium is additional funding for publicly funded schools in England to raise the attainment of disadvantaged pupils and close the gap between them and their peers. Some children with chronic health conditions will not have specific SEN or complex medical needs, but they may need adaptations to the curriculum to make it inclusive.

First aid

Since October 2016 it has been a statutory requirement for practitioners with level 2 and 3 qualifications to hold a Paediatric First Aid qualification. This decision was taken by the government, following a campaign by the parents of Millie Thompson who died from choking whilst at her nursery in October 2012.

All Party Parliamentary groups

All Party Parliamentary Groups (APPGs) transcend party politics and work collaboratively and in cooperation with each other to produce reports aimed at informing and influencing policy. The reports are useful for several reasons. First, the reports include evidence-based recommendations that build on messages that are presented in other reports. Second, the message from APPGs is that investing in the early years must be long term and not a political issue depending on which political party is in power; therefore, the recommendations within the reports should be adopted by present and future governments. The following selected reports should prove interesting and readable; they contain many references to working in the early years and are highly relevant to your practice:

> *Conception to the Age of 2* (2013) is an inter-disciplinary approach to identifying how best to improve child development outcomes by supporting families in early childhood; includes recommendations for the workforce.

A Fit and Healthy Childhood: Play (2015) makes recommendations of ways to promote play and improve childhood development.

A Fit and Healthy Childhood: The early years (2015) is aimed at developing practical policies to reduce childhood obesity and increase health and fitness.

Implications for practice

The success of the government's child health policy relies heavily on practitioners in early years settings. The complexity of the policy presents challenges to you working in practice. As Baldock et al. (2009) point out, 'policy information and implementation is a complex process that can take a considerable amount of time' (p. 125). One of the first implications for practice in relation to developing a child health policy for your setting is to develop your own understanding of the complexities of this area of ECEC.

REFLECTION

Having gained an overview of child health policy from the content of this chapter, consider some of the following questions:

- How can you translate the aims of legislation and government policy to implement policies in settings?
- Are there any conflicts of interest in implementing government child health policy in your setting?
- Are there any ethical issues?
- How can the voices of hard-to-hear children and families be represented in order to maximise the possibility of each child's right to health?
- Not all government policy is legislated for, therefore can this mean that some important aspects of health for all children are less likely to be understood or implemented?
- What are the implications for integrated working and working with parents?

RESEARCH FOCUS

The students in my research (many of whom were experienced practitioners working in a range of early years settings) identified the following considerations and challenges related to implementing government child health policy:

- keeping up to date with government policy is time-consuming
- knowing where to look for policy announcements can be difficult because they can be in different government department web pages

(Continued)

(Continued)

- access to training to understand how to implement policy can be expensive, both in terms of attendance fees and arranging cover at their setting

- analysing the relevance to children and families in their settings

- analysing the benefits of the policy to children's health

- identifying whose voice is missing from the policy

- analysing current practice and identifying where changes need to be made to address the aims of new policy

- identifying implications for working with others, for example the health visitor or voluntary services

- evaluation of child health policies needs to be on-going

- government policy can pose ethical dilemmas if the aim is not thought to be in the child's best interests or appropriate to the needs of each child.

REFLECTION

Examine the policies you have in your settings and consider how they:

- meet the aims of government policy

- meet the needs of children, families and practitioners

- meet the needs of children with additional health needs

- may cause conflict or tension

- ensure 'hard to hear' voices are reflected in the policies.

REFLECTION

Rosie Dunn reflects on some reasons why policy is useful in her setting:

 When working in a setting that deals with children with such diverse needs, it is important to identify the current policy and legislation in place that help support children within our care. When assessing the level of care needed, the Department of Health (2016, p. 38) acknowledges that if a child 'has a medicine regime that requires daily management by a registered nurse and reference to a medical practitioner to ensure effective symptom management', this is recognised as a 'severe' level of need. This means that if the school nurse was absent, a practitioner must be trained and authorised to prescribe and deal with medical procedures in order to ensure the care was effective.

Conclusion

This chapter has summarised the aims of child health policy in the UK and out-lined some of the responsibilities in relation to children's health. The complex web of policies and legislation in place since the start of the century assumed that Children's Centres would play a key role in delivering those services designed to improve health for all pre-school children. Children's Centres were designed to provide services in an integrated and inter-professional way. This put the early years workforce at the centre of implementing healthcare. However, austerity measures have led to the closure of Children's Centres, therefore there is now greater responsibility placed on private, voluntary and independent early years providers to be aware of child health priorities.

Further reading

All Party Parliamentary Group (2013) Conception to Age 2: The age of opportunity. Wave Trust/Department for Education. Available at: www.wavetrust.org/sites/default/files/reports/conception-to-age-2-full-report_0.pdf (accessed 12 July 2016).

All Party Parliamentary Group (2015a) A Fit and Healthy Childhood: Play. Available at: www.activematters.org/uploads/pdfs/Play-Report-final.pdf (accessed 12 July 2016).

All Party Parliamentary Group (2015b) A Fit and Healthy Childhood: Early years. Available at: https://gallery.mailchimp.com/b6ac32ebdf72e70921b025526/files/APPG_Report_Early_YearsFINAL.pdf (accessed 12 July 2016).

Department of Health (2014) Overview of the Six Early Years High Impact Areas. Available at: www.gov.uk/government/uploads/system/uploads/attachment_data/file/413127/2903110_Early_Years_Impact_GENERAL_V0_2W.pdf (accessed 12 July 2016).

Department of Health (2016) National Framework for Children and Young People's Continuing Care. Available at: www.gov.uk/government/uploads/system/uploads/attachment_data/file/499611/children_s_continuing_care_Fe_16.pdf (accessed 6 March 2016).

Henry, L. (2014) The Little Red Book and the Revised EYFS 2014. Available at: www.laurahenryconsultancy.com/2014/04/04/the-little-red-book-and-the-revised-eyfs-2014/

National Children's Bureau (2015) The Integrated Review: Bringing together health and early education reviews at age two and two-and-a-half. Available at: www.ncb.org.uk/media/1201160/ncb_integrated_review_supporting_materials_for_practitioners_march_2015.pdf (accessed 26 July 2016).

United Nations (2016) Sustainable Development Goals: Ensure healthy lives and promote wellbeing for all ages. Available at: www.un.org/sustainabledevelopment/health/ (accessed 10 July 2016).

Useful websites

Information about public health priorities in England – www.gov.uk

NICE guidance – www.nice.org.uk/Guidance

Northern Ireland – www.publichealth.hscni.net

Scotland – www.healthscotland.com

Wales – www.publichealthwales.wales.nhs.uk

4

THE IMPORTANCE OF EARLY INTERVENTION AND COLLABORATIVE INTEGRATED WORKING

CHAPTER AIMS AND OBJECTIVES

- To define terms and explore the rationale for early intervention and integrated working
- To identify the roles of early intervention and integrated working in supporting children's health
- To explore implications for practice

Early intervention

Early intervention (EI) is a broad concept that is applicable to social, education and health services. It shares similar principles to the concept of health prevention, meaning that illness can be prevented using strategies that stop conditions from occurring. This means there is a reduced need for treatment with the attendant costs to the nation. In addition, and perhaps more importantly, preventing the condition from occurring is part of our responsibility in relation to safeguarding children.

Definition of early intervention

EI is defined by Graham Allen in his report (2011, p. xi) as follows:

> I wish to reserve the term Early Intervention for the general approaches and the specific policies and programmes which are known to produce the benefits described here for children aged 0–3 and for older children up to 18 who will become the better parents of tomorrow.

The concept of EI can be likened to the old saying 'a stitch in time saves nine', meaning taking action and sewing up a hole as it appears, instead of leaving it until the hole is bigger and far more stitches will be needed to repair the hole. In terms of early years practice, this is at the heart of what you do, because early intervention is about knowing your children and families, identifying where there may be a need for action and what is the action best suited to the identified need, and then putting this into action.

The quote by Frederick Douglass (1818–1895), the American slave abolitionist, supports the aim of early intervention: 'It is easier to build a strong child than repair a broken man.'

EI is not solely for children living at a disadvantage, however the approach is especially effective for children living in poverty, because their health is adversely affected by their circumstances. However, on early versus late intervention, Allen (2011, p. 3) says:

> There are now two competing cultures: the dominant one – of late intervention – and the growing one – of Early Intervention. I explore in later chapters how we can bring these two into better balance. It is not an either/or – we must continue to swat the mosquitoes but we can drain the swamp too. The bleak truth is that decades of expensive late intervention have failed. Major social problems have got worse not better: despite heroic frontline efforts tackling the symptoms, their causes often remain unaddressed.

The recommendations in the Marmot Review, *Fair Society, Healthy Lives* (2010), are based on the principles of EI, but make the distinction that some EI is most effective when resources are focused on children who are likely to benefit the most from them.

Economic benefits to the macrosystem

The Wave Trust and Department for Education report (APPG 2013) *Conception to Age 2: The age of opportunity* describes this period of a child's life as a 'critical phase of human development and is the time when focused attention can reap great dividends for society' (p. 3). This assertion is based on previous research carried out in other countries, which has calculated the economic benefits of investing money and services in the early years, which are aimed at promoting and enhancing health outcomes into adulthood. In addition, improved health is associated with crime reduction.

The economic benefits of EI have been researched in the USA. A notable example of research that supports the concept of EI includes the work of James Heckman, a Nobel prize winner and a professor of economics. His research into the economic viability of early childhood education programmes highlights the importance of practitioners' knowledge and skills as vital components that contribute to the success and effectiveness of early childhood programmes. In a similar way, the Scandinavian countries have invested heavily in early years prevention, which has resulted in financial benefits as well as improved health outcomes. The benefits include a reduced infant mortality and improvements in heart and lung function in adulthood (APPG 2013).

In the UK, the case for the economic benefits of EI is made in the Allen Report (2011, p. vii):

> Early Intervention is an approach which offers our country a real opportu-
> nity to make lasting improvements in the lives of our children, to forestall
> many persistent social problems and end their transmission from one gen-
> eration to the next, and to make long-term savings in public spending.

As a consequence of the Allen Report, the Early Intervention Foundation was
formed, the aim of which is to: 'support local agencies and national policy makers
to tackle the root causes of problems for children and young people, rather than
waiting to address issues once they are embedded' (p. 5).

Evidence-based interventions

The principle of EI is convincing for those of us who have experience and knowledge of working with children and families, especially those who are in need of
support. However, by definition, EI works by prevention rather than cure, therefore
it is necessary to have evidence that the interventions work. This is especially
important for politicians who are responsible for allocating government funding.
In order to measure the effectiveness of EI strategies and programmes, research is
carried out using random controlled trials.

Examples of evidence-based early intervention for health

Examples of programmes that have evaluated well and that have been shown to
have a positive impact on preventing injuries to babies include:

- the Healthy Child Programme (see Chapter 3)
- the Early Years Foundation Stage (2014)
- Sure Start Children's Centres.

The school readiness agenda, which starts at birth, is considered a public health
issue. The aims are to prepare children cognitively, socially and emotionally for
school in order to maximise their success. The aims are embedded in a range of
health and education policies and legislation.

The case for early intervention in the ante-natal and post-natal period

Early intervention during pregnancy (the ante-natal period) and after birth (the
post-natal period) and into infancy is evaluated positively in relation to promoting
the health of mothers and babies. The aims of EI in this period are to reduce injury
and promote attachment. Babies are especially vulnerable to injury and abuse
because of the combination of a crying baby and parent(s) experiencing excessive
tiredness, lack of support, high stress and, possibly, low levels of knowledge about
caring for a baby. Non-accidental injuries to babies can occur within any socio-
economic group and for this reason the universal services of prevention that are
available through the Healthy Child Programme (2009) are aimed at identifying
mothers who are at risk. For some families where there are complex situations
which increase the risk of non-accidental injury and poor attachment, targeted

early interventions can be offered, that is, proportionate universal services. The rationale for offering such early interventions is based on research that reveals that pregnancy and birth are regarded as teachable moments. This is because after birth, oxytocin, the so-called social hormone, is released and parent(s) can be more receptive to changing behaviour and display a readiness for change. Seizing the opportunity of this teachable moment is proving to be effective in promoting attachment between baby and parent(s). The importance of good attachment is important for children's short- and long-term emotional wellbeing and for improving mental health in childhood and adulthood, as discussed in Chapter 6. If a mother is attached to her baby, she is more likely to protect and care for him/her and prevent harm from occurring.

Targeted early intervention for health during pregnancy and infancy

Early intervention programmes during pregnancy and around birth are evaluating well. Some examples include:

- the *Family Nurse Partnership programme* aimed at vulnerable, often young, mothers, with the aim of promoting attachment
- the *NSPCC Baby Steps programme* aimed at helping to support parents and prevent child abuse and neglect.

Early intervention in the macrosystem

It is important that you understand the principles of EI in relation to health in the macrosystem, that is, as they are embedded in legislation and guidance, in order to implement the principles in practice. Having an understanding of the principles underlying the aims of policies and guidance can help you to plan in a way that is more meaningful. It may be the case that the principle of EI is not always evident – for example, an early years curriculum such as the English Early Years Foundation Stage (DfE 2014a) may appear to be simply statutory guidance that is designed to promote children's learning and keep them safe. However, the principles of EI are embedded in the EYFS statutory guidance, not only in relation to learning and safety, but also in relation to health. For example, communication and language is a prime area within the EYFS. Being able to communicate clearly and speak articulately is known to improve self-esteem, promote good wellbeing and reduce the incidence of mental health issues.

Exosystem: the influence of the local community

For early intervention to work and return positive outcomes on investment, the services and policies relating to health need to be meaningful and appropriate to the children and families in the local community and in your setting.

Early intervention in the microsystem

The factors that influence how meaningful EI is will partly be socio-cultural and socio-economic, as discussed in Chapter 5. Some of these influences can be a barrier to parents taking on board the EI and consequent long-term healthier outcomes for their children. This is where your knowledge and understanding about the rationale for EIs, combined with your skills and qualities in working with parents and children in sensitive and ethical ways, are vital. However, for EI to work, it is essential that all professionals working with children do so in an integrated and collaborative way.

REFLECTION

- What areas of your practice can be regarded as providing an EI for children's health?

- How are health EIs embedded in the early childhood education curriculum you work with?

Collaborative integrated working

Successful EI relies on a multi-agency approach and a high-quality workforce working together. This is a macro approach because the philosophy of integrated working (IW) is embedded in government policy.

Definition of integrated working

According to the (now defunct) Children's Workforce Development Council (CWDC) (2008), IW means 'when everyone supporting children and young people works together effectively to put the child at the centre, meet their needs and improve their lives'. This is especially relevant in relation to supporting children's health, because it is likely that a number of professionals will be involved in supporting health, as discussed in more detail below.

Aims of integrated working

Part of the purpose of IW is for children and families to only have to tell their story once, rather than having to repeat the background to a range of different professionals. In order for IW to be successful, the CWDC developed the 'Common Core' of skills and knowledge for all people who work with children and young people. The Common Core included effective communication; knowledge of children's development; safeguarding and promoting the welfare of children; supporting transitions; multi-agency working; and sharing information. The CWDC was closed in 2012 and this means that there is no longer a central, national body to which all professionals and volunteers can look for guidance and a shared understanding of what effective IW means in practice.

The spirit of IW continues in government policy. One especially important example of IW in the early years is the Integrated Review at age 2 to $2\frac{1}{2}$ (this is explained in full in Chapter 3). In brief, the Integrated Review draws on the professional expertise of early years practitioners and health visitors, as well as the parental perspective of the child's development, to assess health and development, the aim being to be able to offer EI for children if a need is identified.

The opposite of IW is often described as 'silo' working, meaning that professionals work in separate ways and do not share information and knowledge. This approach to working in a non-integrated way, where there is a lack of sharing of information and poor communication, is often cited as a reason for the failure to protect children, most notably in the Laming Inquiry (2003) which investigated the death of Victoria Climbié. The Inquiry recommended that professionals develop more effective ways of working together. Since then, government policy has reflected the recommendation of IW.

Who works together for children's health?

As discussed in Chapter 1, the health of our children is everybody's responsibility. The professionals providing health to children and families include services provided by a range of different roles and agencies relating to health, education and the third sector, which includes charities. The level of need for intervention by health professionals will rely on several factors, for example whether the child is in receipt of universal and/or targeted services, or whether the child has an additional health need which requires access to a range of medical services.

REFLECTION

Consider children in settings that you are working, or have worked, in and identify which health professionals were involved in identifying, assessing and meeting the health needs of the children.

Working with other professionals

The extent to which you will work with other health professionals to support children's health will depend on a number of factors, which include:

- whether children have an additional health need that is over and above universal services, for example a chronic or complex medical condition
- the level of support the family needs or wants in order to support the child's health needs
- the level of cooperation from other health professionals
- your setting, the structure and organisation of your setting, which can influence working practices – for example, private, voluntary and independent (PVI), childminders, Children's Centres and schools have different structures and timetables, all of which can influence how you work with others.

Working with other professionals and the local community

Children's universal and some targeted health needs, as well as services that are required for children with chronic and complex medical needs, are met wherever possible within the exosystem – that is, within the local community. The following professionals may be involved in providing healthcare to children:

Community paediatrician: a specialist doctor who has a broad range of experience in matters relating to children and disability, public health, safeguarding and managing on-going health conditions.

Community physiotherapist: promotes movement and mobility, to improve posture, coordination and breathing; works closely with children who have complex medical needs.

Dental nurse: assists dentists in all aspects of dental care; some dental nurses are involved in dental health education programmes.

Dentist: maintains dental health and treats any dental problems.

Dietitian: advises and guides on nutrition, plans diets for children with eating restrictions because of medical conditions, such as coeliac disease, cystic fibrosis.

General practitioner (family doctor): a qualified doctor with responsibility for supporting children's health; GPs are the central point for referrals to specialist and other health services.

Health visitor (HV): a qualified nurse or midwife whose main role is health promotion and the prevention of ill health; a HV leads on delivering the HCP. The evidence-based approach to health visiting is the 4–5–6 model of health visiting, which can be summarised as:

- *four-tiered service*: the tiers are community, universal, universal plus and universal partnership plus

- *five universal health reviews* for all children: ante-natal, birth, 6–8 weeks, 9–12 months and the 2 to $2\frac{1}{2}$ Integrated Review

- *six high impact areas*: where health visitors can impact positively on child and family health and wellbeing; they include: transition to parenthood; maternal mental health; breastfeeding; healthy weight; managing minor illness and accident prevention; and healthy 2-year-olds and school readiness.

Occupational therapist: works with children who have difficulties with practical and social skills and aims to work with children to be as independent as possible.

School nurse: a qualified and registered nurse (or midwife) with specialist graduate-level education in community health and the health needs of school-aged children; a specialist community public health nurse (SCPHN) qualification is also available. The fundamental role of the school nurse is to improve children and young people's health and wellbeing, as laid out in the HCP 5–19 (DoH 2009) by working in partnership with the child, family, colleagues and other specialists involved in supporting health.

Specialist nurse: a qualified nurse who is an expert in a specialism related to chronic health conditions, such as asthma or sickle cell anaemia, or to incontinence, gastrostomy feeding or ventilation, for example. Specialist nurses are based in the community and/or hospitals.

Speech and language therapist (SALT): assesses and treats speech, language, communication and swallowing problems. As communication and language is a prime area of learning and development in the EYFS, and ensures that children are 'school ready' (see Chapter 12) with good levels of development in speech and language, it is likely that you will work with SALTs.

Early years practitioner role in IW

The Chief Medical Officer's Report (Blair and Barlow 2012) included a chapter on health in the early years. Within the chapter, the authors reinforce the importance of the early years in shaping good health. They point out that early years practitioners can make an important contribution to supporting children's health and wellbeing. However, the recommendation that early years practitioners are well placed to play a key role depends on the knowledge and competence of the workforce.

The need for a high-quality workforce in order to improve children's early experiences and outcomes has been proven many times over. The need for a high-quality workforce for the early years in order to understand the complexities of EI and IW has never been greater. A feature of high quality is highly qualified staff, with practitioners who can, as Nutbrown (2012) recommended in her review of childcare qualifications, understand how to equip themselves to know what to ask in order to support children's health. Despite all of the evidence about the connection between better outcomes for children and a highly qualified workforce, at present there is no requirement for the early years workforce to consist of graduates. Despite the creation of Early Years Professional Status, now Early Years Teacher Status, the pay and conditions are not comparable to those of health professionals and teachers in state-maintained settings. Nevertheless, the legacy of having graduate leaders for the last 20 years and the government focus on improving childcare qualifications mean that a great number of staff in early years settings are well equipped to lead on supporting children's health.

RESEARCH FOCUS: COMMUNICATION WITH OTHER PROFESSIONALS

The findings in my study (Musgrave 2014) revealed that the level of involvement with other professionals from the health service varied widely. The data from practitioners suggested that children with complex medical needs, rather than chronic health conditions (CHCs), were more likely to receive the services of healthcare professionals when in day care. Children with CHCs are less likely to receive the services of other professionals. The most likely reason for being in contact with other professionals is for training purposes. Several respondents described how the school nurse or health visitor had been contacted for training or information. For example, training in the use of the Epipen (for the treatment of anaphylaxis) was the most quoted training need identified by respondents.

Maria, the manager in a PVI setting, had a child with cystic fibrosis enrolled. She requested that the parents ask the hospital to send copies of letters written after the child had attended for a consultation. This is an example of how the triad of parents, healthcare professionals and practitioners can communicate effectively in order to

(Continued)

(Continued)

optimise the health of children with CHCs. It is noteworthy that Maria holds the Early Years Professional Status (EYPS) qualification. The EYPS qualification was part of the Labour Government's aim for the early years workforce to have graduate-led qualifications available for practitioners so that children under the age of 5 would benefit from high levels of training (CWDC 2008). According to Lumsden (2012), they occupy new professional space at the intersection between teaching, health and social work. Therefore, Maria's initiative in requesting copies of letters may be a manifestation of how EYPS practitioners lead on considering the health needs of children so that they can adapt the curriculum to accommodate these children. The request by Maria for letters to be sent to her to keep her informed of the outcome of children's medical consultations, demonstrates high levels of thinking. The content of the letters received directly from health professionals may also help to reassure practitioners that they are getting the correct information. In turn, this may improve their confidence levels in how they approach adapting the environment to make it inclusive for children with CHCs. This may suggest that staff require high-level thinking skills in order to be able to consider ways to develop inclusive practice for children with CHCs.

REFLECTION

Identify reasons why being included in the distribution of copies of hospital letters can be beneficial to (a) children; (b) parents and family; (c) practitioners; and (d) other professionals?

Barriers to integrated working

There are real and/or perceived barriers to IW within each layer of the health service. In the macrosystem, as discussed in Chapter 3, the government departments for health and education have worked in isolation without consultation, often producing overlapping policies aimed at supporting children's health. In recent years, this situation has changed and there have been joint policies and legislation produced. This is a welcome move because this approach should lead to a greater shared understanding of how all professionals can work together to improve children's health. Blair and Barlow, in the previously mentioned Chief Medical Officer's Report (2012), recommend an integration of the Department of Health and the Department for Education to enable integrated policies to be produced.

Professionalism and professional identity

Early years work is not wholly regarded as a profession, though this does not mean that practitioners do not work in highly professional ways. The status of a profession is defined by the presence of a range of factors which include: protected entry to specific qualifications, such as nursing; belonging to a professional and regulatory body; a code of competence and professional standards; a requirement to maintain registration and demonstrate suitability and competence to remain on a register by completing continuing professional development. Being and remaining on a professional register is a legal requirement.

The early years workforce has started to develop as a profession with the emergence of the EYPS/EYTS standards, however there is still much to be done to reach the point where early years practitioners are regarded as belonging to a profession.

In contrast, many of the health professionals you are likely to be involved with in supporting children's health will belong to a profession. The Health and Care Professions Council (HCPC) is the regulatory body for 16 health professions including physiotherapy, speech and language therapy, occupational therapy and social work. The purpose of the HCPC is protecting the public and safeguarding children. In a similar way, nurses must be registered with the Nursing and Midwifery Council.

For the early years workforce, the absence of a professional body, and not being regarded as a professional, can mean there is a lack of professional identity (this is explored in Messenger 2013). A participant in Messenger's research, which was conducted in Children's Centres, remarked that according to her, 'there's a perception that if you're early years, you're only early years' (p. 144). This perception is one that we must all work to change so that the early years workforce can gain the status that the children you care for, especially in relation to supporting their health, deserve.

Having a professional identity and being a member of a profession can, paradoxically, be a barrier to professionals' ability to work in an integrated way. According to Messenger, this is because interpretations of where professional boundaries end are sometimes misunderstood. The existence of professional standards and a register can sometimes mean that professionals are cautious about engaging in aspects of their work which may be deemed as outside their level of competence. This is because a breach of standards or unprofessional conduct can mean being struck off, with the resultant lack of career and income.

An individual's ability to communicate effectively, one of the common core skills, may be inhibited by a lack of clarity about what needs to be regarded as confidentiality versus the need to share information. However, it is vital that early years practitioners work in collaborative and integrated ways with other professionals, especially health visitors.

Working with health visitors

Health visitors have a responsibility to meet and provide for the universal health needs of children, as laid out in the Healthy Child Programme (HCP) (see Chapter 3 for more on the aims of the HCP).

The commissioning of health-visiting services moved from NHS England to local authorities in October 2015, and this is an opportunity for health visitors to be 'at the heart of the early years strategy' (Fuller 2014, p. 20).

The health visitor is the professional who works most closely with early years settings to deliver universal and some targeted services. In particular, the Integrated Review at age 2 to $2\frac{1}{2}$ (see previous chapter) is designed to be an assessment that draws on the developmental and health progress of children (see section below). The Integrated Review will challenge health visitors and early years practitioners to form new professional relationships.

Emma Bailey's account of working with health visitors

Emma is an undergraduate early years teacher trainee working in a childminder setting:

We hope to work in partnership with HVs to give a bigger picture of the child, their wellbeing and their current stage of development than that which can be obtained in a short visit under unfamiliar circumstances. Initially we always sought to gain an opportunity to chat with the HV directly, either alongside the parent in the 2 year check or have them visit the setting whilst the child is present, whatever the HV may find more beneficial. We quickly realised this was not going to come to fruition, so we aimed to prepare a summary of development along with any concerns we may have in time for parents to bring this along to their health visitor appointments, but we found these were often disregarded.

I attended a 2.5 year check for my own daughter where I found there were tensions regarding some parenting decisions (e.g. my extended breastfeeding which was at this point coming to an end, and my plan to home educate) and again disregarding of the developmental summary provided by the EYT in the setting. I made it my aim to create a working document that mirrored more closely those used by HVs so that it was more familiar and user friendly for them to work with without wasting time. This came in the form of a condensed tracker.

Since then, however, we have found that the response is very mixed, having sent the same document with two families at the same time to different appointments. We found one health visitor happy to sign it and another came back without a signature, as they could not confirm we are qualified in making these judgements.

As professionals working with children in a childminding setting, we found the advice given regarding weaning practices; sleeping arrangements; behaviour management and early years education was often prescriptive and inflexible rather than tailored to the situations the families find themselves in. This often left the families we work with worried about their parenting decisions and feeling deflated in their abilities. In some cases, families were told children would 'never learn to speak with a childminder, they need to be in a nursery', leading us to believe that the understanding some HVs hold of childminders may be ill informed.

We have sometimes found there are barriers to accessing support they advise in order to support children (for example with speech delay) and they were inflexible in allowing childminders to attend drop-in sessions, even though it suits the family (in a practical sense due to work commitments but also due to the level of time we spend with the child because we could implement the support strategies).

We will continue to strive for partnership working with HVs as we feel they hold a valuable perspective due to their specialist knowledge and skill set but find at the moment we often come up against many barriers.

We have had some positive interactions with HVs, and would like to embed these in our provision so we can communicate more smoothly on a consistently integrated basis.

Student practitioners: experience of working with others

Student practitioner, Rosie Dunn, reflects on her understanding of how other professionals can benefit the health of a child with complex medical needs in her placement setting:

The setting works closely with a number of outside multi-agencies that come into the setting at least once a week to work with child A and support his learning needs. One particular agency that comes in is his main physiotherapist who helps teach practitioners new techniques to support the child with his condition. Envy and Walters (2013, p. 16) highlight that 'to improve outcomes for young children and their families, it is vital that they have access to the correct services to offer early intervention'.

Working with parents

The more services that a child requires to support their health, the greater the need for an integrated approach, which is especially the case when a child has complex needs. It is often the case that the parents of the child are the lynchpin that keeps the information about their child and, consequently, they are frequently asked to repeat their knowledge about the child to a number of professionals. This can cause 'narrative fatigue' and frustration. Rachel Wright describes in her blog, the value of a communication passport for communicating her son Sam's needs to other professionals:

Communication passport

Sam's communication passport is a ragged folder of information and facts, that go everywhere with him. It tells you what medication he is on, what time he needs to use the toilet, what he likes, what he doesn't and how you can tell he is in pain. It is now over 20 pages long and brimming with information.

It has short direct statements and lots of photos. I spend a lot of time keeping it up to date but it is worth it. Whenever Sam is in hospital, has a new carer or goes to the hospice for respite, the communication passport is thumbed through and re-read.

REFLECTION

- In what ways can you develop good communication between professionals and parents in your setting?
- What are the limitations to using a communication passport?

The opportunity to critically reflect

Eunice Lumsden reflects on one of the key findings from her doctoral research that 'A new professional space with flexible borders is developing at the intersection of education, health and social care, occupied by those with EYPS, though the title "Early Years Professional" was not being used' (Lumsden 2012, p. 304).

 You never change things by fighting the existing reality. To change something, build a new model that makes the existing model obsolete. (Buckminster Fuller)

The words of Buckminster Fuller have much to offer our understanding of the shift required in the early years to ensure a holistic approach for young children and their families. In fact, the introduction of Early Years Professional Status in 2007 afforded an opportunity to create a new model, a new profession that drew on interdisciplinary knowledge to act as a catalyst for change. Indeed, the doctoral research I completed during the first evolutionary cycle of the EYP reinforced the notion that a new space was being developed with 'flexible borders' at the intersection of health, social care and education (Lumsden 2012). The new space that was emerging embraced a new professional with a wide range of professional capabilities that enabled them to lead practice and work with families, children, staff and other professionals. This new professional was complementary to early years teachers with Qualified Teacher Status, and subsequent research (Lumsden 2014) supported the idea that those with Early Years Professional Status really believed they were impacting positively on practice. In fact, the Ofsted Early Years Report (2015) stated that 85% of early years providers that were inspected were good or outstanding. Arguably, this was a reflection of the workforce reform agenda in the early years sector and the embedding of the graduate leader.

However, there have been, and will continue to be, real challenges in creating a new reality in the early years, a reality which sees an integrated rather than a segregated approach to meeting the needs of young children and their families.

This is arguably a missed opportunity in creating a truly interdisciplinary professional that can navigate the boundaries of other professions, or is it? The answer to this lies in the standards and how the trainers, settings and early years teachers themselves interpret them. The Early Years Teachers' Standards are not just about delivering the Early Years Foundation Stage; they still shape a professional where interdisciplinary knowledge is essential. They still need the knowledge and skills to cross professional and occupational boundaries, with families, staff and children. They are the only professional that has a specific standard to meet in relation to safeguarding young children, and the importance of nurture as well as learning through a play-based curriculum framework should underpin all they do. For me, the new space still exists filled with a huge number of committed, aspirational professionals who have a holistic approach to early childhood at their heart. What we have to do is work together to ensure that this new professional model does not become 'obsolete', rather it continues to evolve as a holistic leadership profession, a catalyst for change that navigates professional boundaries and advocates for the youngest children ... what do you think?

REFLECTION

Consider Eunice's words – how relevant are her thoughts to yours?

Implications for practice

Working with other professionals is central to improving and supporting children's health. However, there are factors that can influence how settings can successfully collaborate and work in integrated ways. Some of these influences are:

- the setting – a childminder, PVI nursery, state-maintained/academy school will have different organisation, staffing and funding, all of which will affect collaborative working practices
- the health needs of children
- the level of support that parents and carers require to support their children's health
- the quality of services provided by other professionals, which includes levels of communication, access to and level of service.

REFLECTION

- Consider how you work with others in your setting and identify what is good and what could be improved about your relationship with those who provide additional health services for the children in your setting.

- What are the solutions to improving the quality of how you work with other professionals?

- How can successfully working with others to support their health help to promote inclusion for the children in your setting?

Conclusion

The success of early intervention to support children's health relies on effective collaborative IW approaches. The early years workforce has a pivotal role to play and a valuable contribution to make to implement policies that are central to supporting children's health. Part of the success relies on you working in the child's microsystem by developing good communication. This responsibility includes a need to draw health multi-agencies together so that each professional's contribution is being understood and having a positive impact on the child. Another vital responsibility is to develop good communication with parents so that health strategies are shared, understood and implemented.

Further reading

Royal College of Nursing (2014) A RCN Toolkit for School Nurses. Available at: www.rcn. org.uk/professional-development/publications/pub-003223 (accessed 24 March 2016).

Useful websites

For more about the role and work of health visitors – www.england.nhs.uk/ourwork/qual-clin-lead/hlth-vistg-prog/; https://vivbennett.blog.gov.uk/2015/03/05/the-4-5-6-model/

Baby Steps – www.nspcc.org.uk/services-and-resources/services-for-children-and-families/baby-steps/

Health and Care Professions Council – www.hcpc-uk.org/mediaandevents/pressreleases/index.asp?id=573 (accessed 2 July 2016).

Rachel Wright's blog about her life with Sam, her son who has cerebral palsy – www.bornattherighttime.com/top-6-disability-hacks/ (accessed 13 July 2016).

5

SUPPORTING THE CHILD AND THE FAMILY

CHAPTER AIMS AND OBJECTIVES

Identify your role in relation to:

- implementing universal services
- identifying the health needs of children
- adapting play to support health
- managing transitions for children who have been absent
- working with parents to support children's health.

As you read this chapter, you are encouraged to consider your role as a practitioner in relation to addressing the needs of children and their parents: what qualities, skills and knowledge do you think are necessary?

The role of the practitioner

Your role in supporting children's health and wellbeing is wide-ranging and complex. The range of health-related activities could be as simple as ensuring that correct hand-washing procedures are followed, to possibly carrying out suction on a child with complex medical needs. Before you can identify your role in supporting children and families, it is important that you examine your understanding of health.

REFLECTION

Consider your responses to some of the following questions:

- What does health mean to you? What are your perceptions and views on health?
- In what ways do you support children's health and wellbeing?

(Continued)

(Continued)

- Are the interventions driven by personal experience; policy and legislation; the individual needs of the children? Or are there other drivers that influence how you support children's health and wellbeing?

- What are the issues that affect the health of the children (and their families) in your setting?

- Are there any boundaries and/or challenges to how you support children's health?

The aim of the questions above is to provoke your thinking about the different approaches to supporting children's health. You may find that your response to question 2 reflects the broad range of ways that children's health is supported in early years settings.

Defining your role in supporting children and families

How you work with parents to support children's health, or ill health, will partly depend on the type of health issue that you are addressing or managing.

RESEARCH FOCUS

The breadth and depth of early years practitioners in relation to supporting children's health are summarised in Table 5.1. The findings draw on the views of student practitioners' and practitioners' views of how they see their role based on their experiences in practice.

Table 5.1 The extended role of practitioners in supporting children's health and wellbeing

Practitioner's role	example	considerations
Knowledge and understanding	About specific conditions	Access to training
	About supporting health by preventative strategies, health promotion, health education, maintaining health	Locating valid and correct information
Knowing the child	Carrying out observations	Observations require analysis and reflection in order to gain meaning from the data
	Working with parents and other professionals	Identify solutions to real or perceived barriers to working effectively with parents and other professionals
Understanding policy and legislation	Universal policy, targeted universal policies	Assessing parents' need
	Condition and situation specific legislation and policy	Being aware of the hard to hear voices in policy

Practitioner's role	example	considerations
Implementing policies	Ensuring policies are in place and being followed In the setting	Awareness of how legislation overlap, when does a health issue become neglect and a safeguarding matter
Working with parents	Knowing the family and identifying influences on health and health beliefs	Demonstrate cultural competence and religious awareness
	Assessing level of support needed by parents	
	To minimise the affects of negative determinants of health in the community	
Working with other professionals	Using initiative to make links with professionals	Develop professional identity to have your voice heard and accepted
Enable the environment for the child	Maintain hygienic standards for all children	How can you enable the environment for children with health issues in ways that are as inclusive as possible for all children
	Reduce triggers in the environment, for example dust, pollen for children with asthma	
Personal skills and qualities	Ability to demonstrate leadership	How can leadership help to support children's health?
	Be a positive role model for children and families	Do your eating habits represent healthy eating guidance?
Promote social and emotional wellbeing for all children	Being aware of the additional impact of health conditions on children's S and E development	Which strategies work to support S and E development
	Be able to reinforce positive behaviour in a meaningful way	The importance of understanding behaviour, not just managing behaviour
Consider other children's needs	How can you adapt activities to include all children and not disadvantage any child?	How can you adapt meals and snacks to meet the needs of all children?

Let's look at how the various terms differ from each other:

Maintain health: for example, by administering medication, offering healthy food and opportunities for physical activity, providing first aid when necessary

Educate children about health, for example encouraging them to learn about good dental care and the reasons why it is important to clean teeth regularly

Promote good health by being a positive role model and planning activities suitable for children, parents and practitioners

Preventative measures are considered, for example children and practitioners are aware of the importance of good practice in hand washing, or practitioners are knowledgeable about preventative health strategies such as immunisation

Specific health needs – it is important to bear in mind that when we talk about how we support children's health, we need to address children's *ill* health and how we respond to periods of ill health.

REFLECTION

- What are the possible consequences of not fulfilling the parts of the role?
- What perspectives should you consider in relation to your role?
- How do the different parts of your role help you to include children in your setting?
- Are there any additions you would make to your role in supporting children's health and wellbeing?

Knowledge and understanding of the condition

Understanding the impact of the health condition starts with gaining knowledge of the condition. Gaining knowledge of health issues and conditions can be a challenge. Access to training can be limited because of funding or the availability of suitable courses; this situation can be especially difficult for private day nurseries. However, practitioners in Children's Centres can find that health professionals are relatively easy to access. The participants in my research worked in a private daycare nursery and training opportunities were very limited. They worked closely with parents to understand individual children's conditions, however they did their own research which included looking at websites. These included UK charities associated with a specific condition or government websites aimed at giving guidance on how to promote physical activity for young children.

Knowing the child

In order to be able to support children's health, it is important that you know the individual child so that you can assess how the issue or condition impacts on that child. This can also be viewed the other way, because it is important to know the child in order to identify how the condition affects children in unique ways.

Children's understanding of health

More needs to be done to gain children's views on health because little is known about when children start to develop an understanding of health and healthy behaviours. Seeking their views of *ill* health, or sub-optimal health, is probably easier because children may have concrete experiences based on having symptoms caused by a chronic health condition which causes them on-going discomfort.

There have been research studies that have explored children's perceptions of health, wellbeing and illness, but the participants in such studies have been aged 4 and above. Most studies include children aged 8 and above, for example Piko and Bak (2006). Understanding children's thinking about health and illness is important since it is easier to establish positive health attitudes than change negative ones later. Eiser (1989) has explored children's understanding of experiencing illness rather than their understanding of health. She points out that this understanding is influenced by their age and stage of development.

This highlights the need to develop age-appropriate explanations of illness and preventative health problems (Piko and Bak 2006).

In relation to my research, I found that two of the young children in my study were able to make connections between the experience of applying cream and alleviating itchiness caused by eczema. DJ's mum explained how he demonstrated this ability when he was 20 months old:

DJ has got his own little kit in his bedroom ... he knows exactly what's what ... if you ask him do you want your cream on? He'll say 'yes' and he'll just go and get it. He has to be careful because the one cream is really large and heavy, but he's quite confident to just go and get it or he'll understand what we need him to do.

Freddie's Mum recounted a similar experience:

When he's scratching himself, he'll go and get his cream out of his bag 'cos we've got a bag with all his kit in, and he'll go and get it and tell us to put it on him. He was about two and a half. He brought me the suncream, I asked him why he brought me that and he was scratching and scratching and then I realised what he had done. I said 'you are the cleverest boy in the world!'– making a big thing of it.

These examples suggest that young children can become active participants in managing their health from a young age.

Observations

Observations are a valuable tool to gain a deep understanding of how children's mood and behaviour may be affected by their physical health status and the impact this may have on their wellbeing. Laevers and Heylen (2003) measure children's level of wellbeing by assessing their involvement in activities. Therefore, it can be argued that children's wellbeing can be improved by minimising the effect of health conditions on them, as well as by adapting activities to make them inclusive, thus maximising participation in early years education. It is important to allow time for reflection in order to analyse what you have seen and identify the implications for practice as a consequence of children's health conditions. Such information helps you to plan inclusive activities.

The importance of leadership

A finding from my research was that knowledge and understanding of how to support children's health gives practitioners the confidence to lead on and advocate for children's health. This is especially important for children who are looked after and possibly for those who are cared for by their kin, but not their biological parents. Messenger (2013) found that effective leadership is critical to be able to develop a culture where children's needs are met; this is even more so in order to be able to support the complexities surrounding children's health.

Determining levels of support for children and families

In the UK, the ecological approach means that supporting children's health is everybody's responsibility; this includes government, communities, professionals, parents, carers and the children themselves. The level of support will vary depending on a range of factors, as outlined below. In order to appreciate and identify the level of support that families may require, it may be helpful for you to consider the health needs of the child. The greatest negative impact on children's health is living in poverty. This is because, for many families, living in poverty means that there are inter-related negative factors, such as poor housing and poor nutrition, which impact on health. In addition, there are social and cultural behaviours that influence how families live and, in turn, may impact negatively on children's lives and their health. For example, as Chapter 3 explains, the main thrust of approaching children's health is by offering universal and preventative approaches to improve all children's health, as outlined in the Healthy Child Programme (HCP) (DoH 2009). However, the services in the HCP are expensive to offer and, in order to justify the costs involved, it is important to ensure that services are being offered to families most in need, a concept described as 'targeted universalism' (discussed further in this chapter). Conversely, some of the families most in need are sometimes those who can be 'hard to reach'.

Identifying families most in need of support with their children's health

In order to evaluate the effectiveness of the HCP, a Rapid Review to update evidence for the Healthy Child Programme was commissioned by Public Health England in order to assess its effectiveness in improving children's health in the six years since the previous update of the HCP (2015). One of the aims of the review was to help identify those families who are in need of additional support. Figure 5.1 summarises the factors in the home that impact most on children's health and wellbeing.

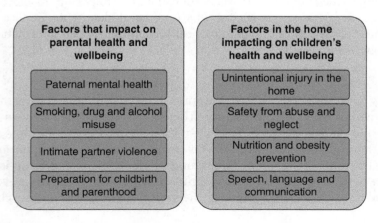

Figure 5.1   Factors impacting on children's health and wellbeing

---

REFLECTION

- How relevant are these factors to the children and families in your setting?
- What strategies and interventions can you use to minimise the impact of these factors on children in the microsystem of your setting?
- Why do you think some families are hard to reach and how can you work with them?

Working with parents

Parents are usually the adults who bear the greatest responsibility for their children's health. However, this responsibility is shared or even taken over by you when parents leave their children in your care. Therefore, you play a vital part in the child's exosystem – you are a link between home and the setting, as well as between other professionals. No matter what the health issue, you will need to build non-judgemental and inclusive relationships with parents. The Wave Trust/DfE report (APPG 2013) highlights the need for practitioners to demonstrate emotional intelligence, which is defined in the *Dictionary of Psychology* (Coleman 2006) as: 'the capacity of individuals to recognize their own, and other people's emotions, to discriminate between different feelings and label them appropriately, and to use emotional information to guide thinking and behavior'.

Knowing the child's family and circumstances

Knowing the child and their family is important to understanding why parents may behave in certain ways or hold particular views about children's health. For example, socio-economic factors, culture and religion can impact on parental choices for their children's health.

Knowing the child's circumstances can help you to gain insight and identify where there may be gaps in the provision of child health services. Children whose families move regularly from one area to another can find engaging with health services more difficult. From the health professionals' perspective, it can take time for health records to catch up with children when they move from one area to another. This makes it challenging to gain a full understanding of their health status and to identify any gaps. For example, the universal offer of immunisations for all children (see Chapter 8) requires careful record keeping to keep track of which injections have been administered. Children of military families may move areas and countries because of their parents' work. As a diverse country which is home, or a place of refuge, to people from around the world, many babies will have been born to women who will not have received the ante-natal services that are available in the UK. Mothers who belong to Gypsy, Traveller and Roma (GTR) communities are 17 times more likely to experience a stillbirth (Wilkin et al. 2009). The needs of children who do not live with their biological parents because of their circumstances can have a profound impact on the provision of health services and hence on meeting needs. For example, looked after children and children who live with kinship carers (relatives who are not the child's parents) have significant inequality in their health. There are many reasons for this, but one reason is that maternal health and the ante-natal healthcare preceding the child's birth may not have been optimal, thus leading to on-going health problems.

Including all parents

Developing positive relationships with parents can be challenging and rewarding, however children's health, or ill health, can raise sensitive issues and provoke emotions. The majority of parents want their child to enjoy the benefits of feeling physically well, but there are many factors that can influence how this aim is achieved and some factors can be barriers to ensuring the child has good levels of health. Socio-economic status is a potent influence on children's health, as discussed in Chapter 1. Parents' understanding of their children's health can be influenced by their level of education – the higher the parent's education, the better the health outcomes. Some parents have cognitive needs themselves and may have special needs or learning difficulties.

Access to health services may be inconvenient for working parents and fitting in immunisations may be challenging. Parents who have migrated to this country may have limited understanding of how the health system works; in addition, they may have limited or no English. Some parents' wishes will raise tensions and may challenge the line between what is ethical or even possibly legal, and what is not.

Ethical considerations can arise when parents' decisions or lack of action about their children's health are in conflict with what is accepted as being a good choice for children's health. Most commonly, cultural and religious influences can create such dilemmas. In the main, parents' beliefs need to be respected. However, it is important to be able to recognise actions that are a safeguarding issue, or even illegal.

Cultural influences

Cultural and religious influences can sometimes be entwined and the terms can be used interchangeably. Therefore, it is important that you do not make assumptions about the origins of certain practices in relation to children's health. Practices may have evolved culturally rather than from a religious edict. This is why part of your role in supporting children's health is to develop cultural competence and to be informed about the reasons why families may be influenced by practices that can conflict with your beliefs.

It can be difficult to work with parents when their views, beliefs and actions are in contrast to yours. Sometimes, working with parents can raise ethical issues – this is especially the case when what parents want to do is not illegal but challenges what you believe is right for the child. On occasions, health choices can be illegal, such as the practice of witchcraft and female genital mutilation.

There is migration into the UK of people from cultures who maintain traditions, such as that of *witchcraft*, which would be viewed as questionable here in the UK, but where such beliefs are not reported. It is therefore important to be aware that, as Tedam (2014) reports, the belief in witchcraft can mean that harm is caused to children. She further warns that witchcraft is a growing practice in the UK. Tedam cites the example of Victoria Climbié's great-aunt who believed that Victoria had been possessed by evil spirits. This belief led to the torture Victoria had inflicted upon her and contributed to Victoria's death. Relatedly, some African cultures believe that children who have epileptic fits are possessed by evil spirits, and this belief has been the cause of child abuse and death (Tedam 2014).

Female genital mutilation (FGM) is a deeply held cultural tradition, mainly in sub-Saharan Africa. FGM is illegal in the UK, however it is a procedure that is carried out on girls as young as 3 (FGM is discussed further in Chapter 12).

Parents' knowledge of their child's health

Becoming unwell can change children's behaviour and such changes can become obvious a couple of days ahead of signs and symptoms appearing. Parents are often the first people who will notice that their child is behaving differently and recognise that they may 'be coming down with something'. Children with chronic and complex medical conditions may become unwell with greater frequency. For example, children with a chronic health condition, such as asthma, may come into contact with a trigger, such as pollen, which provokes the symptoms of asthma and can result in an emergency situation where an asthma attack occurs. Children with complex medical needs are more prone to infections, and the added complication for some children is that they may not be able to verbalise how they feel. Consequently, parents are usually those who understand their child best, and, in particular, the parent of a child with a chronic or complex medical condition is likely to be the one who knows the best way to manage a child who is unwell or who requires management of their condition. In my research, John's mum explained why it was important that she worked closely with the practitioners in John's day-care setting:

 I know little things that they don't know about John and just because he has got diabetes, it might be slightly different to another child's diabetes.

John's mum demonstrated her level of knowledge about John's diabetes and how she adjusts his insulin dosage:

 He is having a growth spurt and they go higher in the day and lower at night so we can give him 30–40% more insulin in the day and 30% less at night. When he is growing, we have to decide how much to give him, it's not the hospital, we have to judge.

REFLECTION

John's mum is motivated to care for John and has high levels of understanding about his diabetes:

- What about children who do not have parents who are willing and able to become experts and advocates for their children with chronic health conditions?

- If children do not have parents like John's, what if practitioners/teachers are not willing or able to lead staff and work in partnership with parents to support children's health?

Impact of on-going health conditions on the family

In order to be able to understand how to manage children's on-going health conditions, it is important to understand how the condition(s) may impact on the family. Two of the most common ways that a child's health condition can adversely affect the family are sleep disturbance and financial implications.

Sleep disturbance can occur during acute infectious diseases, especially when children have a high temperature; fortunately, this is usually a short-term event and can be treated as described in Chapter 8. However, children with complex medical needs who have reduced mobility may need to be turned at night to prevent pressure sores from developing. Rachel Wright writes in her book, *The Skies I'm Under* (2015), about looking after Sam, her son with complex medical needs:

> I clearly remember crawling into bed early one night feeling physically and emotionally exhausted. I lay and wept. Living had become relentless and unpredictable, so in exhaustion I cried out 'I can't do this anymore. It is too hard. I'm too tired. I'm too stretched. I'm at my limit. Enough is enough.' (p. 107)

Clearly, sleep deprivation can impact greatly on the child and the family. Children can be irritable and their behaviour can be difficult to manage. This, combined with parental sleep deprivation, may mean children can be irritable and not so easy to work with.

Working parents who have children with on-going health problems may find it difficult to continue working if they have unsympathetic employers, and this may have *financial implications* for the family.

RESEARCH FOCUS

The findings from my research revealed that from a parent's point of view, part of your role is to show love and affection to a child who has an on-going health condition that can affect wellbeing. John's mum summarises her feelings about what she would welcome from practitioners caring for her son:

> I would want them to be thorough, to fully understand. Firstly, John's illness and if they don't understand, I want them to be able to talk to me to call me up and say I don't understand and ask me rather than pretending they do understand. So, honesty, I guess to be loyal and loyal to John as well, not just me. And to be warm and loving towards John especially if he is really high or his sugars are low, John wants cuddles and lots of love. So that's it really, I want them to be honest and say if they understand it or don't understand it because that is going to have an effect on John if they don't understand it, which is what happened.

REFLECTION

- What are the benefits to children like John of taking this approach?
- Thinking about the role of the key person, what are the possible implications for other children in John's key group?

Including the child

Probably the most important part of your role in supporting children's health is adapting activities in order to include children in their early childhood education and care. One of the most useful definitions of inclusion is: 'Inclusion may be seen as the drive towards maximal participation and minimal exclusion from early years settings, from schools and from society' (Nutbrown, Clough and Atherton 2013, p. 8).

This definition provokes thinking about how you can adapt activities for children with health conditions, the symptoms of which may preclude them from full inclusion.

The Supporting Pupils at School with Medical Conditions guidance includes a statement that makes inclusion a statutory requirement: 'No child with a medical condition should be denied admission or prevented from taking up a place in school because arrangements for their medical condition have not been made' (DfE 2014c, p. 7).

Including children here requires understanding of how to minimise the physical and emotional impact of health conditions on children. Therefore, broad and deep knowledge of the signs, symptoms and causes is essential. It should be borne in mind that full inclusion can be a challenge and sometimes plainly unsafe for children. For example, children who are allergic to foods or animals cannot be included in activities that involve those triggers because of the potentially life-threatening consequences of the symptoms associated with allergy and anaphylaxis. Careful thought needs to be given to how such activities can be adapted in ways that create a balance between inclusion on some level and keeping children safe.

As part of our inclusive approach to addressing children's health, it is vital to remember that we are living at a pivotal moment in the world's history, at a time when the impact of war and economic factors have resulted in mass migration. Some of you may be working in settings where you are educating and caring for children who are refugees. In this case, consider the implications for practice – in particular, what might be some of the differences/challenges/solutions in relation to children's health and wellbeing? (See Chapter 12 for more about refugee children's health).

Policy and legislation

Part of your role in supporting children's health and wellbeing is to have knowledge and awareness of government policy and legislation relating to children's health. In turn, legislation needs to inform the policies in your setting (Chapter 3 discusses policy and legislation in more detail). It is especially important you're your policies for children with on-going health conditions have robust systems for creating and updating education, health and care plans. Such documents are key to good communication in relation to children's health needs.

The role of the student practitioner in supporting children's health

The ability to respond in a way that causes no harm and gives support to a child in an emergency situation is vital for all practitioners. Kelly Wilcox explains how she responded in an emergency situation that arose at her setting.

CASE STUDY 5.1 THE ROLE OF THE STUDENT PRACTITIONER IN SUPPORTING CHILDREN'S HEALTH

'As a student, you will experience a lot of situations which are new and unfamiliar and one in particular which I found interesting yet very difficult was when children have to receive first aid medication or anything related to health when I have been attending placements. This was an interesting scenario because as a student I was not allowed to get involved with confidential issues such as the child's records or contact numbers and this proved to be a barrier to me in my role in supporting a child's health and wellbeing as it results in one less pair of hands to help the child. Because of this restriction, I found it difficult to be 'part of the team' when supporting a child's health. However, this does not mean that I was not responsible for less confidential situations such as calming, cooling or warming the child as well as preoccupying them whilst making them feel safe and secure in a familiar environment. As a student practitioner, I believe that this is the most important role any practitioner can carry out because if a child is feeling unwell or is suffering from an allergic reaction, then they must be reassured and kept composed. I have been in a situation where the staff were panicking, thus making the children become overwhelmed because of the confusion, upset and worry.

The example from my practice was when I was on placement at a nursery and we discovered a wasps' nest after a child disturbed it and the wasps swarmed. I became aware of the nest when I saw a few children running away from the bushes where the nest was situated. I then noticed that one child had a wasp stuck in their neck. I called to the other practitioners that the children were being stung and that I had discovered a nest. At this point the practitioners shouted for the children to go inside and I helped by escorting the children to a safe environment. I noticed that the children became very upset when the young members of staff starting screaming and running into the room shaking their clothes.

As I student I was not allowed to be left on my own with the children, yet there was a shortage of staff for a period of time as they were locating the nest, gathering all of the children, calling parents and treating the children who had been stung. But I started to take the lead and used my knowledge of how to treat allergic reactions. I sat with the children (and some staff members) and started checking the children's hands, necks and faces. I saw that a few children had been stung and were starting to have a reaction and therefore discussed what the procedure was with a staff member. I was told to collect the ice packs from the freezer and apply them to the area of inflammation to keep it cool. Once I had achieved this, as a group, we started to sing nursery rhymes and songs. The children participated and waited patiently for their parents to collect them to take them to hospital.

Reflecting on this situation, I think it is clear to see that even as a student I played an important role in managing this situation by supporting the staff and children. I supported the staff by ensuring that all of the children were in a safe, wasp-free environment. I distracted the children by initiating the songs, as well as comforting the children who were distressed by giving them a reassuring embrace. Therefore, as a student, I believe that even though we are not allowed to be left alone with children, I was able to play a part in the team by offering support, encouragement and reassurance to support children's health. The skills I used in this example can be applied to other situations. I have learnt that even as a student I was able to offer my help emotionally rather than physically via communicating with the children and offering my reassurance, support and playful spirit to ensure that they were kept calm.

REFLECTION

- Consider situations where you have played a contribution in supporting children in a first aid situation. What was helpful or unhelpful about the situation?

- How did Kelly's leadership skills help to calm the situation?

Working with other professionals

Working with other professionals is key to your role in supporting children's health. This role can be a key one in the mesosystem – that is, the linkage between hospital and community-based professionals. The Integrated Review means that health visitors and practitioners working with 2-year-olds will be required to work closely together (the benefits and challenges of this are discussed further in Chapters 3 and 4).

Play as health promotion

Part of your role in supporting children's health is to be aware of the value of play in improving children's health. Play can be regarded as a health-promotion strategy for all children. The benefits of physical play to children's health, for example in reducing obesity and promoting wellbeing, have been reported on by an All Party Parliamentary Group (APPG 2015).

Giving children the opportunity to play outdoors helps them to assess risk and avoid accidents: 'more children are taken to A and E having fallen out of bed than having fallen out of trees' (Moss 2015, EECERA conference). This quote highlights how children's outdoor play has been curtailed and, as a consequence, opportunities to climb trees that help them to develop their gross motor skills and spatial awareness are reduced. In turn, this is likely to mean that they are not as able to move competently and avoid accidents. In addition, giving children outdoor play experiences helps them to use up more energy which can help to reduce obesity levels. Therefore, outdoor play can be regarded as health promotion. Adapting outdoor activities for children with a chronic condition, such as asthma, requires careful thought. For example, outdoor play in cold weather or on days when there is a high pollen count could trigger an attack.

The value of play to children's learning is well recognised; in the same way, play is a valuable source of therapy for children coping with the impact of a health condition. According to Piaget (1951: 167), 'we can be sure that all happenings, pleasant or unpleasant, in the child's life will have repercussions on her dolls'. Therefore, it stands to reason that play opportunities can help children to manage their response to the symptoms of a health condition. There are many health events where play opportunities can be helpful to give children an outlet for their curiosity and help to alleviate their emotions, for example following bereavement. Play as therapy can help to reduce children's anxiety and lead to greater emotional security. Hospital play therapists use play as a diversion tactic for children who need painful clinical procedures. If children have a condition that means they are going to be admitted to hospital, planning activities that will familiarise them with equipment, a hospital environment and the types of people they will meet will be useful to them. Setting up the home corner as a hospital or planning small world play provide helpful and achievable play opportunities.

Children with chronic health conditions often experience emotional disturbance and sometimes behaviour changes as a consequence of having on-going symptoms. Imagine what it must be like to have a constant itch because of eczema, an itch that is only alleviated by scratching, sometimes to the extent that the skin bleeds. Having play activities that can engage the child's concentration and absorb them is a helpful diversion. Similarly, imagine what it must be like to experience the on-going pain of arthritis; again, an absorbing play activity can help to take a child's mind off the pain.

Howard (2010) states that the vast majority of children who face significant challenge, may not need therapy if they have the ability and opportunity to play.

Thinking about the plight of refugee children who have experienced unimaginable adversity, many of whom are living unaccompanied in refugee camps where there are no play opportunities, it is not difficult to comprehend reports of increasing mental health problems in those children. However, it is important to be aware of cultural differences and views about play which may reduce the therapeutic and helpful benefits.

Driessnack's (2006) research revealed the therapeutic benefits of giving opportunities to children to draw their feelings. In a similar way, Brown's (2007) work with young children with life-limiting conditions revealed how drawings helped them to articulate their feelings about death.

REFLECTION

- How can you balance the risks associated with outdoor play and giving maximum health benefits to children?

- Consider how you may adapt sensory play to make it inclusive for children with eczema.

Making transitions

Children who need to attend or go into hospital because of their health needs will be absent from the setting and part of your role will be to support them to make transitions between the setting and hospital.

Preparation for hospital

It will depend on the level of understanding that the child has in relation to their health how much of a role you will have in helping to prepare children for hospital visits, especially when they are going in for a medical procedure. Children's hospitals produce information that is available on their websites about preparing children for going into hospital (see further reading section).

No matter what level of understanding children have, a hospital admission is a source of anxiety for the child's family and is an unwelcome interruption to the child's routine. In order to help the family feel included, it is important that you let them know you are thinking of them whilst the child is away from the setting.

Returning to the setting

Children with complex and chronic health conditions have a high risk of being unwell and are more likely than other children to be away from the setting as a consequence of their health. Being absent from the setting because of illness or an admission to hospital, for what may have been a painful procedure, interrupts the child's routine and can be unsettling, especially if their absence has been prolonged. Returning to the setting can also be unsettling and the child will need support to make the transition back into their daily routine. This sense of feeling unsettled may manifest itself in unusual or different behaviour. Rosie Dunn draws on her placement experience to explain the effect of absence on Jake.

CASE STUDY 5.2

As Jake has complex health needs, he often has to attend appointments and routine check-ups with the GP. However, the duration of time taken out and the return of the child to the setting are not always successful, as children may suffer complications. If the child returns to the setting after having an operation, they can often appear lethargic or uncomfortable and have difficulty controlling emotions. Spending time out from the setting can also impact on the child's social development. Being out of the setting for some time takes the child away from their peers and social interactions, often leaving the child feeling different from their peer group when they return.

REFLECTION

How can you support children to make their transition back into your setting following a hospital admission?

Looking after yourself

Supporting children's health and wellbeing and working with parents to do so is a significant responsibility, and can take its toll on your energy levels and emotions. This is especially so if you are caring for a child who has on-going health needs. For example, children with asthma will require you to be vigilant and tuned in to the child's environment in order to identify possible triggers of the symptoms which could provoke an attack. In my research, one of the participants described the impact on her and her staff of ensuring that a child who had anaphylaxis to nuts remained safe: 'It was more emotionally draining for staff because it was more of a life-threatening condition. We were always double-checking things.'

Such a response is understandable and perhaps unavoidable, because the majority of practitioners are hard-wired to keep children safe. The level of anxiety in keeping children healthy and safe can be greater or lesser, depending on the child's age and stage of development and understanding of their condition. The findings from my research indicate that practitioners are acutely aware of the responsibility and take it in their stride. However, it is important that practitioners recognise that this responsibility can have an impact on their own wellbeing. Solutions for how to alleviate the impact on individuals' wellbeing can be mitigated by strong leadership from all practitioners. Translated into practice, this can mean that sharing the responsibility, rather than it being solely a concern of the child's key person, can help to reduce the impact on practitioners.

Infectious diseases are common in early years settings and Chapter 8 makes suggestions for some of the ways that you can look after yourself and reduce the risk of becoming unwell.

It is also important to be conscious of how you protect yourself when handling and lifting children in order to avoid injuries to yourself. This can be especially important in special schools where older and larger children may have a physical disability. It is important that training is given to all staff, including student practitioners.

Conclusion

This chapter has encouraged you to consider your role in supporting children and families in relation to their health. You have been encouraged to consider health in its broadest sense. In addition, you have been asked to think about the range of knowledge and skills that you think are necessary to acquire and develop in order to manage such health issues. Supporting children's health is challenging but it can be very rewarding, and maximising children's health maximises their participation in their early education and gives them a fair chance of being able to flourish and succeed.

Further reading

Billingham, K. and Barnes, J. (2014) The role of health in early years services. In G. Pugh and B. Duffy (eds) *Contemporary Issues in the Early Years.* London: Sage.
My thesis includes further details that focus on your role in supporting children's health:
Musgrave, J. (2014) How do practitioners create inclusive environments for children with chronic health conditions? An exploratory case study. Thesis for Doctor of Education, University of Sheffield. Available at: http://etheses.whiterose.ac.uk/6174/1/Jackie%20Musgrave%20-%20 Final%20Thesis%20incl%20Access%20Form%20for%20submission%2019-5-14.pdf (accessed 24 July 2016).

6
SOCIAL AND EMOTIONAL WELLBEING AND MENTAL HEALTH

CHAPTER AIMS AND OBJECTIVES

- To discuss the links between social and emotional wellbeing and mental health
- To identify interventions to promote social and emotional wellbeing

As you read this chapter, you are encouraged to consider:

- Your role in promoting good wellbeing in children
- Ways you can work with parents

Introduction

Promoting positive wellbeing and preventing mental health problems are a public health issue. At the macro level, the universal services that are available for children's health in the UK aimed at educating adults about promoting good wellbeing and preventing mental health issues are embedded in government strategies. In May 2016, the UK Department for Education appointed a minister with responsibility for mental health. Strategies to address and improve children's mental health go beyond the national picture and extend to global strategies such as the work of Unicef (2013, 2016). At a time of mass migration of people and reports of unaccompanied and displaced children moving around the world, a global awareness of the importance of promoting good wellbeing has never been greater.

In the microsystem, the contribution to children's wellbeing that can be made by practitioners in relation to this area of health is important in helping to minimise the impact of poor mental health on children and on society. Positive social and emotional development and the impact this can have on children's overall development have been a focus of early childhood academics, policy makers and practitioners for many years. In more recent times, the legacy of children not having the ecological system to develop socially and emotionally has become an area of concern. There is a link between impaired social and emotional development and an increased risk of mental health issues, both in childhood and into adulthood. Padmore (2016) reminds us that delays or disruptions in children reaching the expected developmental milestones can be a sign that something is amiss. Therefore, your knowledge about children and observations of children can be a useful tool in identifying developmental delay which can impact on wellbeing and mental health.

Definitions

It is important to have an understanding of the terms used in relation to children's wellbeing and mental health. The task of defining terms in order to understand their meaning is made even more challenging because of the many different definitions that are offered. A look at the definitions may help to appreciate the links between social and emotional wellbeing and children's mental health:

> *Emotional development*: emotional expression, attachment, personality and temperament

> *Mental health*: An interpretation of illness and the medicalisation of behaviours considered to be beyond the norm (Burton et al. 2014, p. 4). The term 'mental health' is an umbrella term for a wide range of conditions. Such conditions include: eating disorders, anxiety disorders, psychosis, depression, conduct disorders, neuro-developmental disorders such as attention deficit hyperactivity disorder (ADHD), autistic spectrum conditions (ASC), separation anxiety disorder and selective mutism

> *Social development*: understanding of 'self', relationships with others and sociability (Doherty and Hughes 2009)

> *Wellbeing*: 'the state of being comfortable, healthy or happy' (*Oxford English Dictionary*, 1998, p. 2096); Statham and Chase (2010, p. 2) define wellbeing as 'generally understood as the quality of peoples' lives … it is understood in relation to objective measures, such as … health status'.

Rationale for promoting positive social and emotional wellbeing

The rationale for improving the wellbeing and health of children was outlined in Chapter 1 (see Figure 1.1). In brief, the effort made to improve children's wellbeing in the early years is a financially sound investment both for the individual and for society. Not only does childhood set the foundation for a well-functioning and healthy adulthood, but children ought to be able to experience life in a positive way and flourish as children. On the other hand, children who do not have the foundations for good social and emotional wellbeing are more likely to experience poor wellbeing both in childhood and adulthood.

As Rutter is quoted as saying in Cuthbert, Rayns and Stanley's (2011) NSPCC publication *All Babies Count*, 'early adversity casts a long shadow over children's development'. This assertion is reflected in NICE (2012) health guidance which states that 'a complex range of factors have an impact on social and emotional

Table 6.1   Factors that influence good versus poor wellbeing (from NICE 2012)

Good wellbeing	Poor wellbeing
A good pregnancy	Prematurity and/or light-for-dates babies
Infant mental health	Parental drug and alcohol problems
Love and attachment	Parental mental health problems
Positive parenting	Parents with low educational attainment
Self-regulation	Parents with SEN
Opportunities to play	Parents who were looked after as children
	Family relationship problems, including domestic violence
	Criminality
	Poor communication and language difficulties
	Physical disability

development. Knowledge of these factors can help encourage investment at a population level in early interventions to support health and wellbeing' (p. 7).

Similar NICE guidance (2016a) is directed at helping all professionals, including early years practitioners who work with children who are 'vulnerable' (p. 3), to address poor social and emotional wellbeing.

Ingredients of good emotional wellbeing

Sue Gerhardt writes compellingly about *Why Love Matters* (2004) in her book of the same name. Her work reports on the neuroscientific research that explains how affection and love help to develop pathways in babies' brains which assist in laying the foundations for how we respond to stress in later life. In the 1980s, the plight of the Romanian orphans who were left socially isolated without love and interaction, taught us that babies who have such early experiences are more likely to develop poor social and emotional wellbeing. Chugani et al. (2001) reported that those Romanian babies who had been deprived of love during the first three years of life had little chance of recovering from the lack of brain development, leading to impaired social and emotional development and poor wellbeing. Babies who experience trauma and lack of attachment are at more risk of developing psychiatric disorders in later life. It is important to bear in mind that the factors that contribute to poor wellbeing are not necessarily experienced in isolation. It is often the case that children have overlapping and multiple disadvantages that predispose them to develop poor wellbeing.

A good pregnancy for the mother includes a good diet, no smoking, no alcohol or drugs, low stress levels, being in a positive relationship with good levels of support from those around her, not being socio-economically disadvantaged and being in good physical and emotional health. Babies born prematurely or who are light in weight frequently require medical treatment at birth. Early removal from the womb can be a stressful and negative experience for babies which may mean they are more at risk of poor wellbeing.

Positive infant mental health is partly developed by *love and attachment* between baby and parents and is seen as a vital ingredient of good mental health for children. Again, premature babies may be disadvantaged because of the need to be incubated and the consequent removal from physical contact with the mother. Interventions such as kangaroo care (skin-to-skin contact) are proving effective in helping to pro-mote infant/parent bonding and attachment, and therefore wellbeing in premature babies (Penn 2015). In addition, premature babies are more likely to need painful and uncomfortable treatments, which are likely to be traumatising for them.

Positive parenting

As well as providing love and developing strong attachments, positive parenting includes supporting children to develop resilience. Resilience is the ability to recover quickly from negative events – it is the protection that is learned from hav-ing adverse life experiences.

Children's ability to withstand adversity is influenced by how capable they are of developing deep pockets of resilience. The factors that help children to develop good wellbeing can help them to face adversity and overcome what may be negative events in their lives.

Self-regulation is the skill of regulating emotions, so that children 'are not hos-tage to their impulses and emotions, it makes it easier for them to develop friendships, persevere and concentrate, and cope with the stresses of everyday life. Researchers believe it also helps them to do better at school' (Tassoni 2016, p. 34).

Pain and wellbeing in children

Children with chronic and/or complex medical conditions may experience physical pain and this could have an impact on their wellbeing. There is limited literature available about, for example, the effect that the administration of ceaseless injec-tions has on young children. Clark (2003) studied children at 5–8 years of age and her findings report children's experiences of pain as a result of injections. However, she stressed that the pain children experience is not only physical, but also emo-tional. She claims that emotional pain is experienced because 'injections do violence to the boundaries of self' (p. 31). This could mean that children who experience pain are at greater risk of developing 'poor' emotional wellbeing (NICE 2012, p. 18).

Measuring children's wellbeing

There are other measurements of wellbeing in relation to children's health using child mortality statistics and rates of immunisation uptake. The research does not explore how these objective measurements impact on the quality of children's lives. Unicef (2013) reports objective measurements of children's wellbeing. In the UK, the Office for National Statistics (2016, p. 15) shows how

> children are faring in the arenas of life that are important to them, for exam-ple, school, family and peer relationships, having autonomy and aspirations for the future. There is a mixed picture, with children reporting relatively high levels of personal wellbeing, and positive relationships with parents. However, there are still areas of concern, such as the proportion of children who report being bullied frequently and the proportion of children reporting symptoms of mental ill-health.

The Children's Society Good Childhood Report (2015) includes qualitative data of well-being as reported by children. However, the participants are older children and the views of much younger children in the early years are not reported. What is reported as being important to children's wellbeing is having positive relationships. This finding is probably even more relevant to children in the early years in out-of-home childcare settings.

Laevers and Heylen (2003) measure children's level of wellbeing by assessing their involvement in activities. This highlights the need for practitioners to promote children's wellbeing by minimising the negative effects of health conditions on them, as well as by adapting activities to make them inclusive, thus maximizing participation in early years education. This is particularly important for children with chronic health conditions (discussed in Chapter 9).

The range of perspectives from which the concept of wellbeing can be viewed, and the lack of research into young children's views about wellbeing mean that it is unclear exactly what you need to do in order to promote children's wellbeing. However, what we do know is that relationships are important for young children's wellbeing. The roles of practitioners in relation to promoting positive wellbeing and managing mental health issues bear some similarities. Effective interventions that are currently used in early years settings are discussed below.

Research and children's wellbeing

There is limited research available which can form the basis of developing good practice for practitioners in supporting very young children's health and, therefore, supporting wellbeing. According to Piko and Bak (2006), this is partly because little is known about very young children's understanding of health and wellbeing. In turn, the challenges associated with the ethical issues relating to conducting research with very young children may be a barrier. This highlights the importance of practitioners taking the lead in identifying ways of supporting health and wellbeing.

Whitington et al. (2015) carried out the Wellbeing Classroom Project in Australia. Their participants were 6–8 years old with a range of issues that were impacting on their wellbeing, such as living in poverty and/or the presence of a chronic medical condition, such as asthma. The children's poor wellbeing manifested itself in behaviours causing concern, such as disruptive behaviour or being withdrawn. The aim of the project was to 'evaluate an innovative approach to building an inclusive early years classroom supportive of children's social and emotional development'.

The strategies used in the Wellbeing Classroom Project were to:

- build a classroom community that is safe, inclusive and built on trust
- provide the teacher with professional development, enabling them to model emotional self-regulation
- teach social and emotional skills using play opportunities and soft toys
- provide regular support from a community outreach worker
- enable deep teacher reflection
- involve parents in after school sessions.

The findings showed that by adopting a community-building approach, where children felt a sense of belonging, their academic progress improved.

REFLECTION

Consider the implications of this research for your practice.

Mental health in children

The imperative is to improve children's wellbeing in order to prevent the increase in the number of children who are exhibiting signs and symptoms of mental health problems. In order to identify your role in understanding and recognising such concerns, the following sections summarise key points in relation to this issue.

Defining mental health conditions in children

A mental health disorder can be defined as 'a clinically recognisable set of symptoms or behaviours associated with personal functions' (WHO 1992). A mental health condition is not only defined or diagnosed by identifying a set of signs and symptoms, the condition also has an impact on social functioning. The presence of a mental health condition will cause distress and an inability to function within the norms of society.

Diagnosis of mental health conditions in children

The diagnosis of mental health in children is not straightforward because children's behaviour and the presentation of symptoms can change over time. The diagnosis of a mental health condition can be viewed as a medical model of health and this can be regarded as a stigma for children and their families. However, a diagnosis of a condition can help to understand how to manage the signs and symptoms of the condition and, where appropriate, medication can be prescribed. An important point for you to bear in mind is that if a specific diagnosis is made, this can mean that a child may be eligible for helpful services.

Reasons for increased incidence of mental health conditions in children

Early childhood should be a time for firm foundations to be built for future good mental health and wellbeing, and, for the majority, this happens successfully. However, some children find the periods of growth and change though the life stages difficult. Children who are denied the opportunity to develop 'good' wellbeing are those who are at greater risk of developing mental health issues.

Children who are vulnerable to 'poor' social and emotional wellbeing, and are therefore predisposed to mental ill health, are more likely to have experienced adversity. Such adverse experiences include:

- being born prematurely
- living in poverty
- being 'looked after' (according to the NSPCC, half of children who are looked after are thought to have mental health issues)
- being a refugee
- being affected by certain cultural practices (e.g. witchcraft, genital mutilation)
- having SEN
- living with domestic violence.

The impact of on-going stress

The body's physiological response to the experience of a stressful situation is to release cortisol. Studies have shown that children who live with domestic violence have high levels of circulating cortisol because of the anxiety and trauma that can accompany the unpredictability of living with a violent person, even if the abuse is not directed at the child. The exposure to domestic violence has implications for children's development and attainment (APPG 2013) and for their long-term health into adulthood.

Recognising mental health disorders

Mental health problems can present as physical symptoms in children. Such symptoms include: headaches, bed-wetting (enuresis), faecal soiling (encopresis), headaches, tummy aches and sleep disturbance. Changes in children's behaviour may also be indicative of emerging issues, for example isolation and withdrawal, attachment and relationship difficulties. Developmental delay can be a significant sign of mental disturbance.

Depression is a symptom that can affect young children, however it can be hard to detect because the effects on the child's behaviour can be put down to life events such as friendship difficulties and parental separation. Young children with depression may find it difficult to concentrate or cry easily. Depression is not only limited to young children – babies as young as 4 months can experience depression (NSPCC 2016).

Treating mental health disorders

After diagnosis, the relevant treatment will be decided on. Such treatment can include medication and therapy. An education, health and care (EHC) plan will be an important tool in understanding the aims of treatment and management. As with all medication that is administered in a setting, it is important to understand the aims and side-effects and to follow the administration of medication policy.

Legislation and policy

Since the start of this century, research from neuroscience has informed child and mental health policy. As outlined in Chapter 3, the Department of Health and the Department for Education are now more frequently issuing joint policy documents. The following are examples of policy and guidance aimed at improving social and emotional wellbeing and preventing mental health problems in children:

- *The Healthy Child Programme: Pregnancy and the first five years of life* includes universal and targeted early interventions to promote the social and emotional wellbeing of babies and young children
- *The Healthy Child Programme: From 5–19 years* includes priorities to promote emotional health, psychological wellbeing and mental health
- *Early Years Foundation Stage*: personal, social and emotional development is a prime area and the key person approach is a statutory requirement of the framework
- *The National Curriculum*: personal, social, health and economic education (PSHE) is included at each key stage
- *Children and Adolescent Mental Health Services* (CAMHS) is a multi-agency approach to meeting the needs of children with mental health issues; services include voluntary and statutory providers
- *Social and Emotional Wellbeing of Children and Young People in Primary School* (NICE 2008)
- *Future in Mind* (Department of Health/NHS England 2015) government taskforce report on the strategy for improving children's mental health and wellbeing.

Implications for practice

In contrast to a physical health condition, where a child may display a range of specific signs and symptoms, children with 'poor' emotional development and/or mental health issues can create challenges for practitioners. Their behaviour can be negatively affected, as in Anna's account of Joe (in Case study 6.1).

CASE STUDY 6.1

Joe was 6 and I was on placement at his setting. Joe's dad was in prison and his mum was receiving treatment for alcohol problems and she wasn't coping. Joe was withdrawn a lot of the time and found it difficult to concentrate, but on occasions he would be really angry and become destructive, hitting out and throwing things around. I had been observing him at break and realised that he loved being outdoors. I realised that taking him outside calmed him down; he would shout and run around with his arms out wide, and this opportunity meant he could let off steam. When he went back in, he was much calmer and was able to engage with the activities. I suggested that I could take him outside regularly for a few minutes before he started becoming destructive. This worked and Joe was much happier.

REFLECTION

- Consider how Anna's intervention helped Joe, the teacher and the other children in Joe's class.
- What are the implications of Joe's response to his situation for Joe's inclusion in his education?

Impact on practitioners

Page (Nutbrown and Page 2008) discusses her notion of 'professional love' (p. 184), which she describes as the emotions that practitioners have for the children with whom they work. This is a notion that goes beyond the regulatory requirements of the role of the key person. Increasing numbers of children with emotional and mental health problems mean that the key person may be the one who knows the child best and may be the only one who shows them love. This raises important issues for you to consider because there is an emotional cost that accompanies loving children. This is especially relevant to children who have emotional difficulties and mental health conditions.

Setting approaches

The ethics and values of many early years settings lend themselves to developing an environment that can nurture positive social and emotional development. Consistent approaches and reliable adults do much to give children confidence and promote a sense of security. Some of the approaches that can be beneficial in promoting social and emotional wellbeing and improving mental health are as follows:

Knowledge and training

In order to be able to promote the social and emotional wellbeing of babies and children, it is important that you have an understanding of this aspect of children's health. The Wave Trust/DfE report (APPG 2013) highlights the importance of practitioners having knowledge of child development in pregnancy and early infancy to 'develop awareness of how the first two years of life are critical to a child's development' (p. 7). The report goes on to recommend that at least one practitioner should have additional competence in infant mental health.

Implementing the key person approach

The importance of children experiencing positive relationships with adults has been outlined above. In the absence of their parents when in out-of-home settings, it is vital that there is the opportunity for those taking the place of parents to develop positive, loving relationships with the children. Such relationships are even more important for those children who are living in disadvantaged circumstances and who do not benefit from having loving family bonds at home. Therefore, it is vital that the key person approach is implemented in a meaningful way that serves the needs of the child and helps children to develop positive social and emotional wellbeing.

Taking a holistic approach to promoting positive mental health

Promoting positive social and emotional wellbeing can start by addressing the basic needs of children. Maslow (1954) pointed out that if humans do not have their physical needs met, it becomes difficult to address and meet their emotional needs. The universal approach to promoting good social and emotional wellbeing is embedded in the aims of the EYFS. For example, promoting physical activity, especially in an outdoor environment, is helpful to the development of good wellbeing in children.

Considering related aspects of physical health

When addressing poor mental health, it is important that aspects of physical health are taken into account as well, for example a child who is experiencing pain because of poor dental care is likely to have a reduced sense of wellbeing.

Sleep

Sleep is important for children's overall development. Therefore, children who experience sleep disturbance may be prone to developing mental health problems. For example, this may be the result of living in a chaotic home where routines are not in place, or experiencing sleep disturbance as a consequence of coughing at night because of uncontrolled asthma.

Diet

A good diet is important for promoting good wellbeing. Missing out on eating breakfast and feeling hungry means that concentration will be difficult, achievement may be less and children can feel deflated and develop low self-esteem and poor wellbeing. Practical solutions to ensuring children are well nourished, such as breakfast clubs and the provision of free school meals, can be considered as important interventions to maintain good wellbeing and positive mental health.

Communication

Providing opportunities to develop their speech and communication is essential for children's wellbeing. Frustration caused by a lack of communication can have a negative impact on children's emotions. The reasons why a child may have poor communication need to be identified, for example poor dental hygiene may be a source of embarrassment (see 'dental caries' in Chapter 12). Such opportunities for children to speak and be heard include circle or golden time.

Therapeutic interventions

A student's view

Emma Rhymer gives her reflections on therapeutic interventions:

The provision of emotional support within early years settings is a vital component of ensuring high quality experiences for children and their families. This is of particular interest to me, as through my previous placements and through my current professional role supporting a young child with additional needs I have been exploring emotional development and support and seen its positive impacts on the quality of practice.

Goleman suggests a well-rounded person experiences a myriad of emotions, ranging from joy to despair. Being able to recognise and understand your own feelings helps you 'tune into' and recognise and empathise with the feelings of others; equally, if you struggle to understand your own feelings you will find it difficult to understand those of others (Goleman 1995). Therefore, the more a child can understand their own feelings, the more likely they are to be able to anticipate how their actions may make others feel.

Fink et al. (2015, p. 502) state in their research ... 'emotional problems are on the rise'. This was also indicated by the head of my setting's Thrive team. This team is dedicated to 'prepare children and young people for life's emotional ups and downs' (The Thrive Approach 2016 online). In conversation with the head of the team, when discussing emotional wellbeing, she said: 'More children are coming through the school suffering from anxiety and a range of emotional issues, the most I have seen in my professional career'.

Within practice, I have seen practitioners ensuring high-quality emotional support. The above-mentioned Thrive team has collaborated with class teachers to create 'calm boxes'. These are sensory boxes for the children to use when they are feeling anxious or upset. The team shared its knowledge and expertise with the teachers, and together the practitioners (myself included) reflected on what in the box went well and whether certain items appeared more effective than others. Through sharing our reflections, we may extend our knowledge and understanding (Appleby 2010).

REFLECTION

- What are the difficulties that some parents may face in meeting the basic needs of their children?

- How can you work with parents who do not have routines that provide for their children's basic needs?

Play and play therapy

The place of play and your role in providing opportunities to support children's health and wellbeing is discussed in detail in Chapter 5. A health condition, whether physical or mental, can create anxiety for children, consequently play opportunities in childhood are important. However, not all children have the chance to play and they may only get such opportunities having developed significant mental health problems. Play therapy interventions may be necessary and can be a valuable tool to help children to process emotions. Play therapists are specialists in working with children who have emotional difficulties and mental health conditions. Puppets or empathy dolls can be useful too.

Reading stories

Reading stories to young children can be an opportunity for them to relax and allow them to enter an imaginary world which can have a positive impact on their wellbeing. Jessica Kingsley Publishers have a range of books for children who are experiencing events that are likely to impact on their wellbeing and mental health. For example, *Little Meerkat's Big Panic* (Evans 2016) is an illustrated storybook for children aged 2–6 who are experiencing stress, anxiety and panic. The book offers easy strategies for children and guidance for parents to follow to reduce anxiety.

Conclusion

This chapter has given a brief overview of reasons for poor wellbeing and mental health in young children. Your role in promoting good wellbeing by creating a nurturing environment for children where they experience a sense of belonging is vital for all children, but especially those who are experiencing high levels of stress. It should be remembered that it is not possible to compensate for children's experience at home, but there is much that can be done while they are in your setting.

Further reading

Burton, M., Pavord, E. and Williams, B. (2014) *An Introduction to Child and Adolescent Mental Health.* London: Sage.

Cuthbert, C., Rayns, G. and Stanley, K. (2011) All Babies Count: Prevention and protection for vulnerable babies. Available at: www.nspcc.org.uk/services-and-resources/research-and-resources/pre-2013/all-babies-count/ (accessed 26 July 2016).

Davies, L. (no date) Ten Ways to Foster Resiliency in Children. Available at: www.kellybear.com/TeacherArticles/TeacherTip25.html (accessed 6 July 2016).

Gerhardt, S. (2004) *Why Love Matters: How Affection Shapes a Baby's Brain.* Hove: Routledge.

MindEd (2016) Elearning to Support Young Healthy Minds. Available at: www.minded.org.uk/mod/page/view.php?id=22 (accessed 6 July 2016).

National Center for Infant and Early Childhood Health Policy (2005) Clinical Interventions to Enhance Mental Health: A selective review. Available at: http://files.eric.ed.gov/fulltext/ED496852.pdf (accessed 3 July 2016).

NICE (2012) Social and Emotional Wellbeing: Early years. Available at: www.nice.org.uk/guidance/ph40/resources/social-and-emotional-wellbeing-early-years-1996351221445 (accessed 23 March 2016).

NSPCC (2015) Looked after Children. Available at: www.nspcc.org.uk/services-and-resources/research-and-resources/2015/achieving-emotional-wellbeing-looked-after-children-whole-system-approach/ (accessed 11 July 2016).

NSPCC (2016) Looking after Infant Mental Health. Available at: www.nspcc.co.uk/preventing-abuse/child-protection-system/children-in-care/infant-mental-health/ (accessed 11 July 2016).

Useful websites

Jessica Kingsley children's books – www.jkp.com/uk/products/?audience_codes=17

PIPUK Infant mental health awareness week – www.pipuk.org.uk/our-story/infant-mental-health-awareness-week

7
NUTRITION IN CHILDHOOD

CHAPTER AIMS AND OBJECTIVES

- To identify contemporary issues in children's nutrition
- To give an overview of infant nutrition options
- To explore implications for inclusive practice in relation to children's nutrition

Contemporary nutrition for children

We now live in a country where there is a vast range of food available, although it must be remembered that an availability of food does not mean that all children are nourished adequately. Because of poverty or neglect, some children are regularly hungry. With the increased availability of food, there is also increased choice, which can make it difficult to make the *right* choices. There are many factors that influence parental decisions about their children's diet. The socio-economic and socio-cultural factors that can influence children's diet include parental income, parental time available, religion, culture, dietary restrictions for a medical condition and lack of awareness about healthy eating. Therefore, food and nutrition is a complex area and the consequences of changes in children's diets pose many considerations for your practice.

The Children's Food Trust (2016) points out that children spend a great deal of their lives in childcare and school. With the introduction of 30 hours of free childcare for working families, and an increased number of working parents requiring out-of-home care for their children, the need for you to be aware of how to support healthy eating for all children has never been greater. As you read this chapter, you are encouraged to consider the influences on children's eating, such as advertising. In addition to appraising your role in supporting good nutrition for all children, you are encouraged to consider your responsibility in role-modelling good eating habits for children.

The content of this chapter includes the issues that emerged in my research with practitioners in relation to children's nutrition.

Historical perspective

As outlined in Chapter 2, it is useful to examine the historical perspective of the influences within the chronosystem (Bronfenbrenner 1979) to understand the contemporary conditions relating to children's nutrition. The Industrial Revolution initiated a move into cities, and the growing population and the need to earn money in order to eat meant that many children and families were hungry or had diets that were nutritionally deficient. The public health initiatives outlined in Chapter 2 aimed to improve children's nutrition and the 20th century brought about a revolution in relation to food and nutrition.

Up until the Second World War, there was limited choice of available food and the main foods eaten were those available locally such as meat and vegetables. Until about the middle of the last century, the availability of food was governed by the seasons. For example, strawberries were only ripe and edible for a short time. Consequently, they were a welcome treat available only in June. Rationing of food continued in the UK until the 1950s. As already mentioned in Chapter 2, even though food was not easily available, and there were shortages of items like butter and sugar, this meant that people's diets were low in fat and sugar. Before this time, people ate what was locally available and could be kept fresh in the home. Until the 1960s, food was preserved by methods such as drying or salting. The processing of food underwent a revolution in the 1960s and ready meals became available and popular. Fridges and freezers were not common in homes so food had to be kept chilled using alternative methods such as cold marble slabs in larders. The transport of food was limited by a lack of road links; commercial air transport has only become widespread for the delivery of food over the last 40 years or so.

Changes in society that have changed how we eat include:

- efficient and improved transport
- advances in food technology that have extended the shelf life of food
- a wider range of imports from abroad
- changes in women's role in society that have meant more women work and are not free to spend hours preparing food
- competition amongst food suppliers
- increased travel abroad which has made people more adventurous with food choices.

Working with parents

Children's nutritional status can be a sensitive issue for you to address. You may have children in your setting whose nutritional status raises a cause for concern. The areas highlighted by practitioners as being sensitive include the following examples:

- obesity
- food allergy/intolerance
- fussy eating
- unhealthy lunch boxes

- children being hungry and underweight
- children being vegetarian or vegan.

All of the examples above require you to use a great deal of tact and diplomacy in order to address the concerns. The approach that you take will depend on the issue. Some of the issues may be approached using an inclusive approach, for example in order to encourage parents to provide healthy lunches your setting may need to have a healthy eating policy. Such a policy needs to be developed in partnership with parents rather than imposed on them.

The participants in my research revealed that parents of children with dietary restrictions, such as a potentially fatal food allergy or diabetes, found it difficult to relax when their child was away from their supervision. A similar finding was previously identified by Gillespie, Woodgate and Chalmers (2007) when they researched mothers' experience of having a child with food allergies. Their finding sheds light on the experience of being a parent of a child who could become very unwell or even die as a consequence of coming into contact with something they should not be eating. Parents are reassured about your ability to keep their child safe if you have robust policies and good knowledge and can demonstrate that you empathise with their anxieties. (See the section on allergy in Chapter 12 to see the extent to which one setting addresses managing children's food in order to keep them safe.)

In addition to anxiety, in a study that explored parents' perspectives on living with their child's nut allergy, parents described the restrictions caused by their children's dietary needs when eating away from home as akin to 'a form of social exclusion or discrimination' (Pitchforth et al. 2011, p. 10).

REFLECTION

Consider the implications for working with parents as a consequence of the points raised in this section.

Healthy drinking for babies and children

If we think of Maslow's Hierarchy of Needs (1954), the most fundamental needs that must be fulfilled in order to enable us to be equipped to develop in other areas, including emotional and cognitive development, are our physical requirements. A basic fundamental need of healthy bodies is the need for hydration in order to avoid thirst and dehydration. Public health nurses from Devon (2015) have filmed a useful video which outlines the reasons why healthy drinking is important to children's health (see the link in the further reading section). Ensuring that children receive adequate hydration is very important for improving concentration and, in turn, maximising children' ability to engage with activities. In addition, ensuring that children drink regular amounts during the day, helps them to gain good control of their bladder and can help them to avoid binge drinking when they get home, which can impact on their night-time bladder control. Adequate hydration helps to avoid constipation. Therefore, it is important to consider what babies and young children drink, as well as what we give them to eat. As outlined by the participants who made the video, there are several ways that you can encourage good practice in relation to managing children's hydration.

Good practice for healthy drinking

Babies are likely to gain sufficient hydration via their milk, whether formula or breast. Babies who are being weaned will gain extra hydration through pureed and rehydrated foods. However, introducing supplementary fluids when weaning commences is helpful to them in developing their own understanding of the differentiation between hunger and thirst. In warm weather and when babies are unwell, fluids are important to avoid dehydration.

Water is the ideal drink for children; this is because sweetened drinks, such as fruit juices, can cause dental caries and carbonated drinks can cause bladder irritation, which may mean children need to empty their bladders more frequently. Only offering milk as a drink may mean a child experiences fewer feelings of hunger and this can lead to reduced appetite. This, in turn, can lead to malnourishment and possibly a failure to thrive. It should be remembered that babies are not born with a taste for particular drinks and their preferences are formed in their early months and years. However, parental choices in relation to drinks may mean that children are reluctant to drink water. You may find that your own behaviour, for example by having your own bottle of water to drink from, will help to shape an acceptance that water is a healthy option.

Ensuring that settings meet the EYFS requirement to provide water requires some thought. On one hand, it is important to encourage hydration by having access to water. However, students report that children can become obsessive about drinking and this can have an impact on the routines of the setting. It is also important to reduce the possibility of cross-infection by avoiding the sharing of drink containers between children. Another consideration is that the containers used for children's drinking are cleaned thoroughly on a regular basis.

Legislation and policy

Concern about the increase in childhood obesity and the long-term implications of a poor diet has led to numerous policies and legislation by government departments that focus on improving children's nutrition. Healthy Start vouchers available for buying basic foods like milk or fruit for parents who are pregnant or have children under the age of 4 reflect the Healthy Child Programme aim of improving maternal and early nutrition.

The following policies and legislation are those that are reported by practitioners as being influential in how meals are planned in their settings:

The *Early Years Foundation Stage* states that 'meals, snacks and drinks must be healthy and nutritious' and fresh drinking water must be available at all times (DfE 2014a, p. 26).

The *School Food Standards Food Plan* is promoted on government web pages (see further reading section). These standards came into force in January 2015 and include recipes that have been checked with School Food Standards. There is a recipe hub which includes recipes that have been tried and tested on children. The 100 recipes in the hub have been designed to make it easy for cooks to plan imaginative and achievable meals for children.

Free school meals were introduced for England and Wales by the Coalition Government in 2011 as a response to concerns about the nutritional status of some children. Details of how to apply for free school meals can be found on government web pages (see further reading section).

The *Food Standards Agency* is a government agency, and legislation in December 2014 requires all menus in early years settings to have common allergens listed. This is to help settings ensure their menus are safe for children with allergies to foods (see below).

Healthy eating for babies and children

Good nutrition and healthy eating for children start at conception. The foundations of the adult's approach to and relationship with food are shaped in the early years.

The options for infant nutrition are breastfeeding or formula milk which is bottle fed; babies who cannot swallow, for example those who are premature, may require feeding via a tube.

Weaning is the process of introducing pureed food and supporting the transition to solid foods.

Breastfeeding

Breastfeeding is regarded as the nutrition option of choice for newborn babies. This is a view that is globally upheld by the World Health Organization and by Unicef in their guidance, which advises that babies should be exclusively breastfed for the first six months of life. In England, the Department of Health also promotes breastfeeding as the best start for babies. The Conception to Age 2 report (APPG 2103) claims that breastfeeding 'increases children's chances of leading a future healthy life' (p. 13). This is reflected in the Millennium Cohort Study which found that breastfed children had better cognitive development and higher attainment than children who had not been breastfed.

The benefits of breastfeeding to babies include a reduced incidence of:

- infections: lower respiratory tract infections; urine and ear
- wheezing
- non-infective gastroenteritis
- otitis media (ear infection)
- lactose intolerance
- asthma
- infant feeding difficulties

- gastroenteritis
- eczema
- infant feed intolerance
- obesity in later life
- diabetes mellitus in later life.

In addition to the physical health benefits, many mothers report feeling that breastfeeding was a good way of bonding with their baby.

Despite the benefits cited above, the rates of breastfeeding around the world vary and many countries report low levels of breastfeeding. Considerable investment is made in collecting data about the rates of breastfeeding. In January 2015, the statistics in England (NHS England 2015) show that 73.8% of mothers initiated breastfeeding. However, there is a dramatic drop in the number who are still breastfeeding by the time their baby is 6–8 weeks old, to 45.2%.

Reasons why mothers may not breastfeed

Breastfeeding has become fraught with complexity. What used to be regarded as a natural bodily function has now become a topic of debate and is an emotive subject. Again, examining the historical perspective, breastfeeding was the only safe way to nourish babies. If mothers were unable or unwilling to breastfeed, as became the norm for aristocratic mothers, a wet nurse would be employed to share her milk with another mother's baby.

As mentioned above, breastfeeding remains the only safe nutritional option for many babies in some areas of the world. There are many reasons given for the reduction in numbers of breastfeeding mothers. Research by Sloan et al. (2007) found that their participants preferred not to initiate breastfeeding because it was an unattractive option. One mother who participated in their research said, 'it just didn't appeal to me' (p. 288). Other mothers started and then stopped because of the pain associated with breastfeeding. The most common reason given for either not choosing or stopping breastfeeding was that the mother was returning to work. (For more discussion and reflection on breastfeeding, see Chapter 12.)

Weaning

Department of Health (DoH) guidance recommends that babies are introduced to solid foods at 6 months. The process of weaning is another aspect of baby care that has become a source of anxiety and mystique for parents. As part of your role in supporting the nutritional aspect of children's health, it is good practice to familiarise yourself with the current DoH guidance (see further reading section). At the start of weaning, it is recommended that pureed foods are introduced one at a time, in case of a reaction. Babies can be offered pureed selections, such as meat, vegetables and fruit from older children's meals. Milk should continue to be offered after pureed foods. Processed baby foods are convenient and may be preferred by parents; clearly it is important to respect parental choice. However, you may wish to consider how you can ensure a healthy diet for weaning babies in the same way as you do for older children.

Weaning is an important phase of laying down eating habits for life, as this is a time when a baby's likes and dislikes can be shaped.

CASE STUDY 7.1

Gemma is a young mum who lives in a tower block in a council estate. She regularly attends the Children's Centre with Jayden who is 2 and Abby who is 6 months. Gemma has mentioned that she is struggling to feed the children because the cooker in the flat is not working. She said that she was aware that babies could have mashed vegetables, so she had mashed up some peas and chips from the fish and chip shop for Abby.

REFLECTION

How can you sensitively support Gemma at the same time as addressing the need for children to have a healthy diet?

Baby-led weaning

Baby-led weaning is where the baby takes the lead in feeding themselves using their hands rather than being fed by an adult. According to Rapley (2015), the practice is thought to help babies to recognise when they are full and helps them to express their likes and dislikes. It is important that babies are introduced to the sorts of foods that are recommended for weaning, as laid out in government advice.

CASE STUDY 7.2

Alicia is almost 6 months and her mum wants to use a baby-led weaning approach. This is the first time Corinne, the baby room leader, has had such a request and she is keen to ensure that this is achieved successfully.

REFLECTION

- What information will help Corinne to ensure that the setting develops a policy that will meet the needs of Alicia and her mum? How does this link to government policy?

- Who in the setting (and how) can Corinne work with to develop the policy?

- What are the benefits of baby-led weaning for all stakeholders?

- What are the possible barriers to success?

Global perspective

It is important to consider that the changes in food and nutrition, as described above, are not applicable to all countries in the world. Many countries in the world are affected by war, inhospitable climates that cause drought and lives led in poverty that make access to food difficult or impossible. The result of living in absolute poverty can be hunger and malnourishment. Many countries in the world do not have access to safe drinking water, which can mean that children become dehydrated. In addition, the preparation of food can be hazardous.

A personal reflection from my work in an African country has made me real-ise that gaining access to food and water can be an on-going daily challenge for many people. Gambia is on the west coast of Africa and, unlike many African countries, it has access to water for irrigation because of the river which runs through the middle of the country. To help reduce hunger, citizens are encour-aged to have a smallholding where they grow fruit and vegetables for their family. Babies are predominantly breastfed because there is no other option. Formula milk is expensive and a lack of safe water means that bottle feeding is dangerous. I spent some time in the baby room at a crèche attached to a college and mothers would breastfeed their babies before lectures and return at lunch-time to feed them again.

Whilst travelling around in the country, it was not uncommon to see adverts for weaning foods for babies. This was unsettling because I had been warned not to drink water from taps and to only drink bottled water. If mothers decided to give their babies the commercially produced weaning foods that require the addition of boiling water to make them nutritionally safe and suitable for babies, they could be putting them at risk of an infectious disease or infestation because of the parasites that can be present in unsafe water. This was an ethical dilemma that troubled me and to which there is no easy answer.

Dietary restrictions

It is important to bear in mind that what is considered healthy eating for most children may be unhealthy or even life-threatening for some. Navigating dietary restrictions can be a minefield because there is a great deal of confusion about the various descriptions of dietary restrictions. The following definitions will be helpful to clarify the differences:

> *intolerance*: when the body cannot metabolise certain foods efficiently, the body cannot tolerate the product

> *allergy*: a response to an 'antigen' (an allergy-causing substance) that may be inhaled (into the lungs), ingested (eaten) or inoculated (through the skin); the reaction to the antigen may be localised to one area of the body or generalised and affect the whole body

> *anaphylaxis*: a severe, potentially life-threatening allergic reaction.

Conditions that require dietary restriction

There are many conditions which require dietary adjustments in order to make food healthy for the affected person. The following are the most commonly encountered conditions that affect children, as reported by practitioners (Musgrave 2014):

Anaphylaxis and/or allergy: the most common foods that cause allergic reactions are nuts, but children can be allergic to egg, shellfish, fish, lactose, kiwi, strawberries and sesame. The list of foods that have been reported as causing allergic reactions is growing. Children can be unique in their reactions to allergenic food substances. For example, it may be the case that a child is highly allergic to raw egg, but can tolerate cooked egg.

Coeliac disease is present when the small bowel cannot digest and absorb food because of sensitivity to gliadin, a protein which is found in wheat, barley and rye. A diagnosis of coeliac disease is made by taking a blood test and a biopsy of the small bowel. The treatment for coeliac disease is to remove gluten from the child's diet. Gluten is found in the cereals wheat, rye and barley.

Cystic fibrosis (CF) is a genetic condition for which there is no cure. An important aspect of caring for a child with CF is managing their diet. One of the signs of the condition is a lack of enzymes for digesting foods, therefore each meal needs to be accompanied by enzyme supplements in the form of powders or capsules to enable digestion. Children with CF require a high-calorie and high-protein diet. Each child's dietary requirements will be unique, and close collaboration with parents and other professionals will be key to supporting these children's nutritional needs.

Diabetes mellitus is a chronic condition where the child's pancreas produces inadequate supplies of the hormone insulin. Insulin is required to metabolise carbohydrate. Key to managing diabetes, so that blood sugar levels are kept within normal limits (4–7 mmol/litre of blood), is calculating the right balance of carbohydrate intake with insulin dosage and output of physical activity.

Galactosaemia is a rare inherited condition where babies are born without the enzyme that metabolises galactose, which is a sugar in milk and milk products. There is no cure for this condition and management of it involves the exclusion of milk and milk products.

Lactose intolerance: lactose is the natural sugar in milk. Some children have inadequate production, or none, of the enzyme lactase that is required for the metabolism of lactose. Consequently, children must have lactose removed from their diet. Lactose can also cause anaphylaxis in some children (see Chapters 9 and 12).

Contemporary issues

Despite the legislation, research and health education and promotion activities that are widely accessible by professionals and parents, there are a number of concerns related to children's nutrition. Many of these areas of concern are for children's long-term physical and mental health, however early years practitioners are well placed to be able to prevent and/or improve some of these conditions.

Anaemia

Anaemia is caused by a reduction in the number of red blood cells that carry oxygen around the body. As a consequence of low-circulating oxygen levels, children can become very tired, breathless and less resistant to infection. Iron-deficiency anaemia is caused by a lack of iron in the diet. Babies are born with sufficient iron to last for six months; after that period, iron needs to be obtained from dietary sources. According to Blair and Barlow (2012), 30–40% of pre-school children are anaemic due to prolonged breastfeeding or insufficient weaning.

Obesity

The number of children who are being diagnosed as obese is reaching epidemic proportions. As much as 20% of children are obese by the age of 4 (WHO 2015d). Blair and Barlow (2012), in the Chief Medical Officer's Report, recommend that breastfeeding is an important strategy in the primary prevention of obesity. The National Child Measurement Programme (Public Health England 2016b) is aimed at measuring school children's height and weight in order to monitor rates of obesity. In addition, the programme, it is claimed in the guidance, will 'help to raise parents' awareness of ... obesity' (p. 3).

The effects of obesity in childhood are not to be underestimated because being overweight can provoke conditions such as asthma and diabetes. Excess weight can mean that children are excluded from parts of the curriculum, such as physical activity. (Read how Lily's obesity impacts on inclusion in Chapter 12.)

Vitamin deficiency

Vitamin D is a fat-soluble vitamin found in dairy products and oily fish. Sunlight is also a source of vitamin D and it can be absorbed through the skin; it is essential for the formation of strong bones and teeth. Insufficient amounts of vitamin D can cause fractures and a condition known as rickets. In order to prevent rickets, the APPG(ND) has urged NICE to examine the effectiveness of a universal approach to vitamin D supplements being made available to children. For further discussion of the impact of vitamin D deficiency in children, see Bentley (2013).

Dental caries

Dental caries, or decay, is when the enamel of the teeth is broken down and the most common cause is when acid is formed by the bacterial breakdown of sugar in the diet. If there is no prevention of dental decay, or there is a lack of treatment, teeth can continue to be damaged and a tooth abscess and extreme pain can be the outcome. This is obviously an unnecessary source of suffering for children. However, the incidence of dental decay is increasing, with 40% of 5-year-olds shown to have active tooth decay. Children are entitled to free dental care in England, however only 60% of 3–5-year-olds are registered with a dentist.

Eating and drinking sugar are the cause of the increased incidence of dental decay, and some of this increase may be linked to the consumption of sugary drinks. Such is the extent of the problem that the government has issued a strategy designed to reduce the amount of sugar consumed (see further reading section). Heads et al. (2013) draw our attention to the link between dental caries and a sign of maltreatment or abuse. (See Chapter 12 for an example from practice of dental caries.) Howell and Brimble (2013) highlight the difficulties associated with promoting oral health for children with conditions such as cerebral palsy, Down syndrome and congenital heart conditions. Such children are especially vulnerable to dental caries because of a combination of influences. Some anti-epileptic medications have side-effects which can lead to gum disease. Howell and Brimble suggest that the inadequate training of professionals in being able to treat children who may have communication difficulties can mean that dental checks and treatment are challenging.

Implications for practice

Inclusion

As already discussed, routines of providing meals for children are important for their nourishment, to optimise physical health in both childhood and adulthood. However, mealtimes are important social events and it is important to provide children with a sense of belonging when providing food. Inclusion at mealtimes for all children with exactly the same food can be a challenge and will require you to have deep levels of knowledge and the ability to apply criticality to adapting diets to make them safe and acceptable.

REFLECTION

Consider the following scenarios which practitioners have encountered in practice:

- Alicia is 4 years old and has coeliac disease. She is attending a birthday party of another child. However, the mother of the child has just become aware of Alicia's dietary needs and is reluctant to provide a gluten-free diet.

- Charlie is 6, he has diabetes and is staying on at the after school club where he will be playing football.

- Ella is 7 and classified as obese, and the contents of her lunch box from home contain high-fat and high-sugar food.

- Amarjit is 6 and is vegetarian. He is a very active boy and likes to be outdoors during play time.

- Archie is 2 and is allergic to raw egg.

(Continued)

(Continued)

- Ishmel is 5 and does not eat pork. You are planning a school bonfire party. What food restrictions do you need to think of and what alternatives can you suggest?

- Georgie is 7 and has coeliac disease. You are working with Year 3 in the Roman Catholic school to prepare the class for their first Holy Communion. This involves children receiving a wheat-based wafer communion host.

1 What are the adaptations you are going to need to consider in order to include children with the dietary restrictions in these scenarios?

2 How can you work with parents to achieve maximal participation?

RESEARCH FOCUS

Ensuring that children experience maximum participation in the social aspects of eating, whilst keeping them safe, raises some considerations for practice. Janet explained the attention to detail required in removing food debris to keep a child with an allergy safe:

 Making sure when you are clearing away that the child (with allergy) stays sitting down until everything is cleared away because it would be quite easy for them to think 'oh, there is some food on the floor'. They don't have food in the rooms, because children could quite easily take something up, things like bibs, tables, chair supports, making sure they don't come into contact with the food or the allergen.

John has diabetes and his mum describes her response when she took him to a birthday party and was attempting to calculate the amount of carbohydrate in the food that was being served, so she could then work out how much insulin to give him:

 It is a nightmare, just a nightmare. We can't say to John, you can't have this, you can't have that, and the boxes are gone with all the carbohydrates written on them.

Sharon (the manager of a setting) described how the responsibility for providing alternative foods that made an activity inclusive for a child with an allergy, extended to her chef:

 My chef is brilliant, she has managed to find dairy-free chocolate so that he can be involved in making crispy cakes and there is nothing different for him.

REFLECTION

Consider who in the setting (and how) can make food experiences more inclusive for children with dietary restrictions.

Tube feeding

Some children with complex medical needs are unable to eat food orally for a variety of reasons. For example, they may have a malformation of their digestive system or they may not have a swallowing reflex, which means they are at risk of inhaling food into their lungs and choking. Therefore, they have to be nourished with commercially prepared liquids, which are administered via a tube into the stomach, via a gastrostomy tube or via a tube inserted into the nose which is passed into the stomach, called a nasogastric tube (this is discussed further in Chapter 10).

Including tube-fed children in mealtimes

The exclusion of a child from the social act of eating can have a significant impact on parents because they feel a sense of guilt and loss about what their child is missing out on. As a consequence, some parents have introduced blended diets, that is, a tube feed for pharmaceutically prepared feeds, and oral 'normal' food that has been liquidised to the consistency of single cream. Read Sian Thomas's (2016) account of the research she conducted about the support they gave to a school who were investigating the feasibility of introducing blended diets.

RESEARCH FOCUS: BLENDED DIETS – A CHALLENGE AT THE COAL-FACE (THOMAS 2016)

Children who require gastrostomy feeds sometimes find the prescribed commercially produced feed is difficult for them to tolerate. For this reason, some parents have introduced blended diets, that is a combination of the prescribed feed with 'normal' food. Sharing food is a social experience and in many cultures the sharing of food is a significant event. Children who require gastrostomy feeding are excluded from sharing food and this can impact on their quality of life. The use of blended diets can be viewed as controversial because this approach is not supported by the manufacturers of the commercial feeds due to the conflict of interest and uncertainty about nutritional advice on the subject.

In order to overcome such barriers, some health organisations have developed guidance that address professional concerns and are working in partnership with families and multi-agency colleagues (education in particular) to enable non-healthcare professionals to administer a blended diet via gastrostomy in the school setting.

One health organisation has taken steps to support the administration of a blended diet to children via their gastrostomy through the development of a protocol (which includes taking a risk assessed approach) and a multi-agency bespoke package of care.

Part of the reluctance on the part of some professionals is that there has been very little research carried out into blended tube feeding. To explore the suitability of blended gastrostomy feeding for each child, we used a risk-assessment approach. we found that blended diets are not suitable for every child. The school staff were nervous at first, but they were fantastic and were well supported by health staff. Anecdotal reports suggest that the benefits to children of having a blended diet include improved bowel function, improved mood, improved skin and hair and a reduction in gastric reflux. It is possible that there is an increased risk of blocking the tube or infection of the tube.

Reducing the amount of sugar in children's diets

Public Health England (2015) has drawn attention to the threats to children's health of excessive sugar intake. It was speculated that in 2018 the government will introduce a tax on soft drink products in order to reduce consumption and, in turn, reduce obesity and dental caries. The Children's Food Trust (2016) states that there is a need to reduce the amount of so-called free sugar, such as that added to food and drinks, plus naturally found sugar, such as that found in honey, syrups and unsweetened fruit juices. Naturally present sugar such as that found in milk and fruit and vegetables does not need to be reduced. The current guidance is that we should get no more than 5% of our daily energy intake from free sugars.

Tips to reduce sugar include:

- Avoid the use of ready-made sauces that can be high in sugar.
- Limit confectionery and sugary soft drinks.
- Limit the amount of cakes, desserts and biscuits available.

Evaluating safe and healthy diets in your setting

The London Early Years Foundation realised that it had to tackle the problem of childhood obesity in its nurseries. One of the strategies it developed to help embed healthy eating was to assess the knowledge of the chefs. As a consequence of this initiative, the Foundation contributed to developing a qualification accredited by CACHE for chefs working in early years settings. The qualification is Food Procurement and Cooking for Early Years (Level 2). The qualification aims to equip chefs to be able to view food from a child's point of view so that food is served in attractive ways that suit children's appetites. The qualification therefore helps chefs to play a key role in contributing to children's health and wellbeing, not just working in the kitchen but also developing ways of working with parents.

Outdoor play and nutrition

Outdoor play where children can move around freely and are encouraged to use gross motor skills is a useful preventative and curative role in reducing obesity. Access to the outdoors is also a helpful way to reduce cases of rickets because of the opportunity for exposure to sunlight, which is helpful for vitamin D absorption. However, it is important not to block out the sunrays by using sunblock.

Safeguarding and children's nutrition

A child's nutritional status can be an indication of the level of care and attention they receive from their parents. We have learned from Daniel Pelka's Serious Case Review (Coventry LSCB 2013) that a child who is underweight should raise your suspicions. As is well documented in the report into Daniel's death, he was so hungry that he would take discarded food out of waste bins. The staff at Daniel's school did raise their concerns about Daniel's behaviour. However, his mother was so convincing with her explanations about the medical reasons for his eating habits and loss of weight, it appears that the staff were unable to take their concerns further.

A rare example of how dietary neglect contributed to a child's death is illustrated by the case of 8-year-old Dylan Seabridge from Wales. He was diagnosed with scurvy, a condition that is caused by a lack of vitamin C, which is available in citrus fruits. It can be surmised from the case that his diet was inadequate and, consequently, he developed the condition. His parents thought that he had growing pains and gave him painkillers. The coroner in Dylan's case stated that scurvy is an easily preventable condition. The other factors that contributed to Dylan's death were that he was educated at home and access to Dylan was limited. In addition, his mother had mental health issues.

The point of including details of these two children's cases is to highlight that a child's appearance can indicate a lack of nutrition caused by neglect, which, in turn, is a safeguarding consideration.

On the other hand, it is important to be aware of a nutritional issue that may give rise to inaccurate safeguarding concerns. For example, consider the case of the Webster children who were removed from their parents' care because their fractures were diagnosed as being non-accidental rather than due to rickets as a consequence of vitamin D deficiency.

REFLECTION

- What policies or procedures do you have in place to observe children's eating habits?
- What behaviours in relation to eating would raise your suspicions?

Conclusion

The contents of this chapter have given a broad overview of a range of ways that you can support children's nutrition. It is important to remember that what is healthy eating for some children may not be healthy, and may even be life-threatening, for children with dietary restrictions.

Further reading

Albon, D. and Mukherji, P. (2008) *Food and Health in Early Childhood*. London: Sage.

All Party Parliamentary Group (APPG) (2013) Conception to Age 2: The age of opportunity. Wave Trust/DfE. Available at: www.wavetrust.org/sites/default/files/reports/conception-to-age-2-full-report_0.pdf (accessed 12 July 2016).

APPG (2015) A Fit and Healthy Childhood: Food in schools and the teaching of food. Available at: https://gallery.mailchimp.com/b6ac32ebdf72e70921b025526/files/FoodIn SchoolsBroJune2015AwFinal.pdf (accessed 12 July 2016).

BBC News (2009) We're Classed as Child Abusers. Available at: http://news.bbc.co.uk/1/hi/uk/7892809.stm

Food Standards Agency (no date) Are You Allergy Aware? Available at: www.food.gov.uk/the-website-of-the-food-standards-agency

GOV.UK (2015) Free School Meals. Available at: www.gov.uk/apply-free-school-meals (accessed 23 July 2016).

Pollock, I. (2016) 'Concerns' Raised before Dylan Seabridge Died from Scurvy, BBC News, 21 January. Available at: www.bbc.co.uk/news/uk-wales-35361261

Public Health England (2015) Sugar Reduction: The evidence for action. Available at: www.gov.uk/government/uploads/system/uploads/attachment_data/file470179/Sugar_reduction_The_evidence_for_action.pdf (accessed 29 June 2016).

Public Health England (2016) National Child Measurement Programme 2016: Information for schools. Available at: www.gov.uk/government/uploads/system/uploads/attachment_data/file/531904/NCMP-information-for-schools.pdf (accessed 23 July 2016).

Public Health Nurses (Devon) (2015) The Importance of Fluid Intake. Available at: www.youtube.com/watch?v=WyLBntO9FQQ&feature=youtu.be (accessed 29 June 2016).

Unicef UK (2014) The Baby Friendly Initiative: Breastfeeding in the UK. Available at: www.unicef.org.uk/BabyFriendly/About-Baby-Friendly/Breastfeeding-in-the-UK/ (accessed 29 October 2014).

Unicef (2014) Baby Friendly: Baby led weaning. Available at: www.unicef.org.uk/BabyFriendly/News-and-Research/News/UNICEF-UK-and-Baby-led-Weaning/ (accessed 29 October 2014).

Useful websites

CACHE Level 2 Food Production and Cooking in the Early Years – www.cache.org.uk/Qualifications/CYP/CYPL2/Pages/CACHE-Level-2-Diploma-in-Food-Production-and-Cooking-in-Early-Years-(QCF).aspx

Children's Food Trust – www.childrensfoodtrust.org.uk

Food a fact of life: national curriculum support – http://foodafactoflife.org.uk/Sheet.aspx?siteId=20&sectionId=118&contentId=747n

NHS Healthy Start – www.healthystart.nhs.uk

NHS Children's teeth – www.nhs.uk/Livewell/dentalhealth/Pages/Careofkidsteeth.aspx

NHS Baby teething symptoms – www.nhs.uk/Conditions/pregnancy-and-baby/Pages/teething-and-tooth-care.aspx#close

School Food Standards School Food Plan guidance – www.schoolfoodplan.com/actions/school-food-standards/

8

INFECTIOUS DISEASES, INFESTATIONS AND THE ACUTELY ILL CHILD

CHAPTER AIMS AND OBJECTIVES

- To identify the causes of infections and infestations
- To examine ways of removing and reducing the spread of infections and infestations
- To identify the implications for practice in reducing the impact of infections and infestations on children
- To learn what is good practice in caring for an acutely ill child

Introduction

As discussed in Chapter 2, life-threatening infectious diseases are less of a threat to children than they were in the past. However, infections in children remain a significant cause of ill health. This is especially so in early years settings because of early socialising (Kelmanson 2015) as a consequence of a large number of humans being together in close proximity, thus creating the ideal conditions for the spread of infectious diseases and parasites that can cause infestations. Infectious diseases and infestations are commonplace and regarded as an inevitable occurrence of childhood. Some infections can result in what is regarded as a minor illness. However, the effect of infections, such as recurrent respiratory infections in children, can be underestimated. Kolak et al. (2013) highlight the impact of what can be regarded as minor illnesses on children, citing decreased levels of activity, increased irritability, reduced emotional competence and a reduced ability to engage with those around them, thus impacting on their social development. They go on to state that:

> Even though illnesses that are relatively minor and of short duration may not necessitate visits to the doctor, it seems plausible that children who experience minor illnesses on a reoccurring basis may be at an increased risk for poor developmental outcomes. (p. 1234)

Infections can result in episodes of short-term and sudden illness in children, and recognising that a child is acutely unwell and knowing the actions to take require you to have a wide range of knowledge and skills as well as meaningful policies in order to be able to respond appropriately. It is also important to be aware that some infections, such as bacteria that cause meningitis, remain potentially life-threatening.

In a similar way to infections, infestations can have a negative impact on children's health and, in turn, their wellbeing. Head lice is a common infestation, which can result in persistent head scratching, interrupting sleep and resulting in tiredness during the day and lack of concentration. The effects of infections and infestations on children are unwelcome and, therefore, it is vital that you are aware of your role in managing the reduction of these conditions in your setting.

Causes of infections

Infections are caused by micro-organisms, so called because they are living organisms that are invisible to the naked eye:

- viruses, for example the common cold, chickenpox
- bacteria, such as salmonella, staphylococcus, streptococcus, which cause diarrhoea and vomiting, meningitis
- fungi, for example candida 'thrush'.

Infections are acquired in the following ways:

- ingesting – by swallowing, for example bacteria in food
- inhaling – by breathing in a virus
- inoculation – by puncturing the skin which allows the micro-organism to enter the blood stream.

Prevention of infection

Preventing the spread of infection requires some logical thought. As outlined above, infection is caused by the spread of micro-organisms. Therefore, inhibiting their spread is the first step to take in reducing or preventing the impact on children's health. The reduction of the spread of infection has been a focus of public health activity for many years and it is important that we all understand our role in minimising the spread of infection, especially when working with children.

Public Health England (2014) list three main ways of preventing infection:

1. High standards of personal hygiene, particularly hand washing
2. Maintaining a clean environment
3. Routine immunisation

1. High standards of personal hygiene, particularly hand washing
The single most effective way of avoiding the transfer of infection is by hand washing. The practice of hand washing is widely accepted, however it is possible for

ineffective hand washing to take place. It is important that we are consciously competent in how we approach hand washing. As a student nurse, I can remember learning how to wash my hands thoroughly with warm water, soap and drying with disposable towels using the Ayliffe et al. (1978) hand-washing technique (see link in further reading for a diagram). In reality, the time and attention that this method requires can be a barrier to effective hand washing, especially in a busy day-care setting. The use of hand sanitisers is a quick and safe way of ensuring that hands are less likely to transmit infections.

The important times when hands should be washed include after using the toilet, before and after personal and/or intimate care, such as giving first aid or administering medication, and before eating.

Part of the school readiness agenda is that children in the early years are taught how to manage their personal care. In most cases, this will begin in the child's home and attendance at a pre-school setting will often be a seamless continuation of the hand-washing and personal hygiene practices that are regarded as commonplace. Depending on their age and stage of development, children need a great deal of support to teach them how to maintain hygienic standards. However, it is worth considering that some children and their families have a range of different circumstances that may influence their approach to such matters.

Considerations for practice

For people living in parts of the world where toilets, sewerage systems, running water and soap are plentiful, and good hand-washing techniques are learned and followed, it may be difficult to understand that access to such facilities is not the norm. The practice of open defecation has not been the norm in developed countries for more than 150 years. However, in countries where the resources associated with toileting that we take for granted are unavailable, there is no other option. Along with the obvious risks associated with this practice, the climate and presence of insects and animals add to the risk of the spread of infection.

The effects of open defecation are devastating for children's health causing a range of infectious diseases as well as the spread of infestations, such as worms, when the faeces contaminates drinking water. As a consequence, children are prone to developing diarrhoea, which is the third biggest killer of children under 5 in sub-Saharan Africa. The World Health Organization is campaigning to stop the practice of open defecation; however, in order to achieve this, countries need to be able to afford to develop safe disposal of human waste.

Bearing in mind the above context, consider children who may come to your setting who have not experienced the facilities that are the norm in the UK.

2. Maintaining a clean environment

The decrease in cleaning in hospitals in previous years as a cost-cutting exercise has had a profound impact on the safety of hospitals for patients. The emergence of hospital-acquired infections was a partial consequence of reduced cleaning. The lessons learned from this situation are transferrable to early years settings. There are a range of areas within settings that require consideration and a policy to ensure that they are attended to, in order to maintain cleanliness, and these are outlined later in this chapter.

An essential aspect of maintaining a clean environment is considering how to manage the bodily fluids that you can come into contact with as a consequence of working with children. This can raise some tensions when working with young children where part of your role is to promote independence in self-care, at the same time as minimising the spread of the micro-organisms that spread infection. Another barrier to minimising the spread of infections through bodily fluids is that it can be time-consuming and there are often many tasks to be completed at what seems like the same time. The winter months mean that many children are prone to developing common colds and no self-respecting practitioner would overlook the runny noses that need cleaning up. The use of hand sanitiser, when it may be less convenient to use soap and water after using a tissue and disposing of it straightaway, is an acceptable alternative.

Managing bodily fluids can be a distasteful aspect of your role, as Sophie outlines in her account.

RESEARCH FOCUS: SOPHIE

I had worked in several early years settings and felt that I had eventually overcome my initial difficulties associated with nappy changing and wiping messy noses. I then went on placement to a SEN school where the majority of the children had complex medical needs. Some of the children were older and had global developmental delay. Two of the boys were immobile and spent their days on bean bags. They had to have all of their personal care attended to by the practitioners. It was a very different experience for me to adjust to managing adult-sized males' toileting. I was also shocked to discover that one of the boys frequently masturbated and ejaculated. I discussed this with my mentor who explained that the boy had been seen by a psychologist and, after a great deal of discussion, it was felt that accommodating his need was better for him than preventing him from masturbating. My mentor explained how the staff had developed an approach whereby they provided as much privacy as possible. They ensured that disposable towelling was used and careful washing of his hands was carried out when he had finished. I found it shocking because as an early years student, I had never considered that this would be part of my experience. He was only a couple of years younger than me. However, I realised that this action helped to keep him calm and the staff had really worked together, with his parents and other professionals, to come to the approach they had developed.

---

3. Routine immunisation

In the UK, as one of the aims of the Healthy Child Programme (DoH 2009), all children are entitled to free immunisations for a wide range of infectious diseases. Immunisations are available from health professionals, such as a general practitioner, a practice nurse or a health visitor based in a medical centre. The schedule of immunisations available in the UK is aimed at stopping children

Table 8.1 Childhood immunisations available for children under 5 in the UK – taken from NHS immunisation schedule (Public Health England 2016d)

Age Due	Diseases Protected Against	Administration
8 weeks old	Diphtheria, tetanus, pertussis (whooping cough), polio and haemophilus influenzae type b (Hib)	Thigh
	Pneumococcal (13 serotypes)	Thigh
	Meningococcal group B (MenB)	Left thigh
	Rotavirus gastroenteritis	By mouth
12 weeks old	Diphtheria, tetanus, pertussis, polio and Hib	Thigh
	Rotavirus	By mouth
16 weeks old	Diphtheria, tetanus, pertussis, polio and Hib	Thigh
	MenB	Left thigh
	Pneumococcal (13 serotypes)	Thigh
1 year old	Hib and MenC	Upper arm/thigh
	Pneumococcal (13 serotypes)	Upper arm/thigh
	Measles, mumps and rubella (German measles)	Upper arm/thigh
	MenB	Left thigh
2–8 years old (including children in school years 1, 2 and 3)	Influenza (each year from September)	Both nostrils
3 years 4 months old	Diphtheria, tetanus, pertussis and polio	Upper arm
	Measles, mumps and rubella	Upper arm

from contracting a large number of diseases that are caused by viruses or bacteria. These conditions can cause death to children, or they can leave a legacy of disability. (For a summary of the immunisation schedule that is currently available (as of August 2016) for children aged from 2 months to 3 years 4 months in the UK, see Public Health England 2016d and Table 8.1 above.)

Considerations for practice

The success of immunisations rests largely on the principle of what is known as herd immunity, meaning that in order to be effective, it is important that the majority of people are immunised in order to protect as many people as possible.

It is important to note that 100% herd immunity is not possible. In rare cases, immunisation does not work and children may develop the condition for which they have received an immunisation. However, it is likely to be a mild dose. In addition, some children are unable to receive immunisations for medical reasons. Such children include those who are receiving medication that suppresses the body's immunity, for example those receiving cancer treatment or immunosuppression after an organ transplant.

Children who were born prematurely should be immunised in the same way as full-term babies because their immunity is lower and they are more prone to infection.

Bearing in mind the benefits to children's health and wellbeing, it is not surprising that most parents choose for their child to have the programme of immunisations. However, there are a number of children who do not benefit from being immunised against these conditions for a variety of reasons, which include:

- religious or cultural influences
- hard-to-reach families who may not access health services
- working parents who may have difficulty accessing immunisation clinics because of their working hours
- parental concerns about 'overloading' their child's immune system
- concerns that immunisations are unsafe
- lack of knowledge about how immunisations work.

Personal reflection

As a practice nurse, I used to give the injections for immunisations to children in the general practice where I worked. For very small babies, this was fairly straightforward; although they cried when they experienced the needle going into their leg, they were quickly comforted by their parent with a feed or a dummy. It was different with babies who were over a year old who came to receive their MMR injection. At this age, they were interacting happily and usually smiling, until the needle went into their skin and they registered the stinging of the medication entering their tissue. The look of betrayal they gave me when they made the connection that I was the cause of their pain always pulled at my heartstrings. The babies' responses made me understand why parents sometimes found it difficult to bring them for immunisation. It also made me think that for parents who come from countries where immunisation is not part of a highly structured health service, as in the UK, or for parents who do not understand English, injecting a baby and upsetting them so much must be a very strange thing to do.

Protecting yourself from infection

Protecting yourself from the possibility of contracting an infectious disease is important for your wellbeing as well as for that of the children. Staff absences due to sickness create a burden on all involved.

REFLECTION

Consider some of the everyday practices that you do in order to prevent infection spreading.

If you work with very young children, it is likely that you use gloves to prevent the spread of infection when changing nappies. However, gloves can create a false sense of security and, depending on when you remove them, they may do more harm than good. For example, do you remove the gloves immediately after you have cleaned the nappy area and wrapped up the soiled nappy? Or do you remove them at the end of the procedure when you have ensured the baby is safe, and whilst doing so you will have touched the baby's clothing and other surfaces and in the process spread bacteria?

As well as being aware of the immunisation requirements of the children you work with, it is important to consider how you can protect yourself against infectious diseases that are largely preventable. It is worth pointing out that even though immunisations have been available for many years, some young adults may have missed out on the measles, mumps and rubella (MMR) triple vaccine. This is because of the uncertainty about the safety of the vaccine that followed the publication of research by Andrew Wakefield, which claimed that the vaccine caused autism and other conditions. The research has since been discredited, however the uncertainty caused widespread lack of confidence among parents and significant numbers of them chose not to have their children protected against MMR by not having their children immunised. Consequently, this created an immunisation gap, which means that many people who are now young adults are not protected. This has resulted in an increase in these conditions, especially measles. If you did not receive two immunisations of MMR as a child, consider discussing your immunisation status with your GP and arrange to have any from the schedule that you have not received.

Coming into contact with some of the common infectious diseases if you are pregnant may require some caution, mainly because a high fever during pregnancy may cause miscarriage (Public Health England 2010).

Infection in early years settings

As this chapter has discussed so far, there are interventions that can be implemented to avoid and minimise the impact of infection in settings. The nature of early years settings means that this infection can spread widely. However, it is unlikely that infection can be completely eradicated and it is likely that you will encounter infectious diseases in children, causing periods of ill health and creating a need for absence from the setting. Clearly, infectious diseases can also impact on staff health and result in staff absence, which, in turn, can create extra pressure because of the additional workload. Therefore, there is a need for you to be vigilant in preventing infection as well as being able to recognise diseases that can cause significant illness in children.

Vulnerable children

Avoiding infectious diseases in all children is extremely important and should be regarded as part of your safeguarding responsibility to the children in your setting. However, some children are more vulnerable to the effects of infectious diseases. In this context, vulnerable children refer to those who are more likely to have a negative impact from the effect of an infectious disease. Such children include those with a range of pre-existing conditions such as asthma or diabetes, or those who are receiving medication that suppresses the body's immunity, for example those receiving cancer treatment or immunosuppression after an organ transplant. In addition, babies are more vulnerable to the affects of dehydration, which is a common symptom of infectious diseases. Many infectious diseases affect the skin and can cause itchy rashes; children who already have eczema and then become infected with chicken pox are vulnerable to developing complications because of their already delicate and damaged skin.

Incubation periods

Once you have come into contact with an infectious disease, there is a period of time before the disease appears – this is known as the incubation period. This means that children may become unwell and be infectious before the symptoms of the specific condition appear.

RESEARCH FOCUS: INFECTIOUS DISEASES ENCOUNTERED IN SETTINGS

Table 8.2 summarises some of the main points from information that is available on the NHS Choices website about the most common infectious diseases seen in early years settings as reported in my research. (Further information on this can be obtained from the NHS Choices website.) For most of these conditions, there is no vaccine available, and minimising the incidence of these conditions is based on the good practice outlined above. However, as pointed out, reduced uptake of immunisations means that a disease such as whooping cough occasionally occurs.

Less common infections

In addition to the conditions in the list below, there are other less common causes of infectious diseases that can make children ill. For example, some children may not have been immunised against infections, such as polio. This may be as a result of parental choice or because they have moved to the UK from a country that does not offer childhood immunisations (or children may have been in a country where malaria is prevalent). Medical advances have resulted in more children living with complex medical needs, and managing their health needs can mean that they require numerous hospital admissions. This may result in them getting a hospital-acquired infection such as methicillin-resistant staphylococcus aureus (MRSA).

Malaria

Malaria is an infectious disease which affects 400 million people around the world and causes the death of a million people each year. It is passed on by bites from mosquitoes infected with malaria. Malaria is not a common cause of illness and death in the UK. However, as a theme of this book has highlighted, not every child

Table 8.2 Commonly seen infectious diseases in early years settings (adapted from NHS Choices website, NHS 2015b)

Condition and cause	Symptoms	Treatment	Special considerations
Chicken pox: highly contagious, for most children a mild illness caused by varicella zoster	Rash of red, itchy spots that can appear over the whole body, the spots become fluid-filled blisters which burst and crust over and form scabs which eventually drop off	Children should be away from the setting until the blisters have crusted over, usually 5–6 days after the appearance of the rash, plus reduced fever and itching	Children with chicken pox must not be given ibuprofen
Virus commonly occurs in March–May	Fever during the first few days		90% of adults are immune
Most common in children under 10	A persistent cough can develop because of blisters forming inside the airway		Pregnant women; children with a weakened immune system or who have eczema should be protected from coming into contact with the virus
			A cough or pain in a child's chest or infected blisters require medical advice
Common cold: a viral illness considered to be mild	Sneezing, runny or blocked nose, sore throat, headache	Treat with paracetamol or ibuprofen	Medical advice is needed if a child complains of severe pain or sensitivity to light, or if symptoms occur in a newborn baby
Conjunctivitis: common condition causes redness and inflammation of the covering of the front of the eye; can be caused by an infection or allergic reaction to pollen or other trigger; most cases are not a cause for concern	Inflammation causes the tear glands of the eye to produce more mucus and fluid	Careful cleaning and the use of a cool compress are usually sufficient and the infection usually goes away after 2 weeks	
	Infected symptoms: stinging and gritty feeling in the eye, sticky discharge in one eye that usually progresses to both eyes, enlarged gland in front of the ear	Occasionally antibiotic drops, such as chloramphenicol, are prescribed	
	Allergic symptoms: itchiness of the eye	Allergic conjunctivitis may require antihistamine drops, but cold compresses can soothe discomfort	

(Continued)

Table 8.2 (Continued)

Condition and cause	Symptoms	Treatment	Special considerations
Diarrhoea and vomiting: can be caused by a bowel infection such as norovirus or a bacteria such as salmonella	Sudden projectile vomiting and watery diarrhoea	No treatment available but important to treat symptoms Especially avoid dehydration	Babies are especially prone to dehydration Exclude for 48 hours after symptoms have cleared Avoid swimming pools for 2 weeks after last episode of diarrhoea
Foot and mouth: caused by coxsackie virus	Mouth ulcers and spots on the hands and feet (not related to foot and mouth disease which affects farm animals); fever; coughing; sore throat; blisters	No treatment Treat symptoms	Usually clears up after 7–10 days
Fungal infections: athlete's foot, ringworm	Itchy, red	May be prescribed steroid cream	Can be spread via bedding and towels Fungus thrives
Impetigo: skin becomes infected by bacteria, staphylococcus or streptococcus, entering the skin via a cut or insect bite	Non-bullous impetigo typically affects the skin around the nose and mouth, causing sores to develop that quickly burst to leave a yellow-brown crust Bullous impetigo typically affects the trunk (the central part of the body between the waist and neck), causing fluid-filled blisters that burst after a few days, leaving a yellow crust Sores are not painful but are itchy	Symptoms may not appear until 4–10 days after contact with the bacteria Children should stay away from setting until 48 hours after the start of treatment Treatment is with antibiotics, which can be cream or medication	Complications are rare Some cases of psoriasis have been associated with impetigo Children with a weakened immune system or eczema may be affected by the bacteria and there is a small risk of septicaemia occurring

Condition and cause	Symptoms	Treatment	Special considerations
Influenza ('flu'): caused by different viruses Annual flu vaccine nasal spray is available to 2-, 3- and 4-year-olds and children in years 1 and 2	Fever; tiredness and weakness; headache; aches and pains; dry chesty cough	Treat symptoms	Rest is necessary
Mumps: a viral illness against which the majority of children will be immunised Immunisation available	Painful swelling at the side of the face and under the ears, giving the appearance of a hamster face; fever; headache and joint pains Can cause a testicle to swell and result in a reduction in fertility in males	Reduce fever Adapt the child's diet to softer food	Symptoms can be similar to glandular fever or tonsillitis If mumps is confirmed, this is a notifiable disease Remain away from the setting for 5 days after the symptoms start Rarely, viral meningitis, which is much less serious than bacterial, can occur
Norovirus: a viral illness lasting 1–2 days Most common in winter months Can be virulent in settings	Diarrhoea and vomiting	Avoid dehydration	Children should not attend for 24 hours after symptoms have stopped
Rotavirus: a viral illness, can be immunised against it at 8–12 weeks	Diarrhoea and vomiting	Avoid dehydration	

(Continued)

Table 8.2 (Continued)

Condition and cause	Symptoms	Treatment	Special considerations
Scarlet fever: caused by streptococcus bacteria Can follow an infection such as impetigo There are increasing numbers of children being affected by scarlet fever	Sore throat, headache, fever, flushed face and swollen tongue Pink-red rash develops on the body 12–48 hours later Rash can feel rough and looks like sunburn Rash turns white when a glass is pressed on it	10-day course of antibiotics	Can return to setting 24 hours after starting antibiotics Rarely, ear infections, abscesses and other complications can occur
Slapped cheek: caused by paro virus Normally a mild infection	Can start with symptoms of a cold – highly infectious period Bright red rash on cheeks Sometimes a light pink rash may appear on the trunk and limbs a few days later	Normally gets better without treatment Treat symptoms	Risk of miscarriage in early pregnancy
Whooping cough: serious and highly infectious, caused by bacteria bordetella pertussis which infects the trachea (windpipe) Immunisation available	Distressing bouts of dry coughing The gasping for air after such a bout causes a distinctive whooping sound Fever, runny nose and vomiting follow coughing Cough can last for 3 months	If diagnosed within 3 weeks of the infection starting, antibiotics may be prescribed	Prolonged bouts of coughing can mean there is a risk of choking Babies under 6 months need protection from contact with whooping cough Babies under 1 may be hospitalised because of the risk of breathing difficulties Return to setting 5 days after antibiotics have been started

who lives in this country was necessarily born here. The reasons for the increase in the incidence of malaria include:

- increasing numbers of people who travel long haul to areas where malaria is endemic
- increasing numbers of immigrants entering this country from areas of the world where malaria is a common cause of illness and death; this includes countries in sub-Saharan Africa
- an increase in the incidence of malaria in tropical countries.

Malaria is largely preventable with the use of a course of medication, however failure to take preventative medication for malaria is very common, especially with children. Another effective way of preventing mosquito bites in malaria-infected countries is the use of nets over beds. Both of these preventative methods are not widely available in affected areas, therefore it would be usual for children not to be protected, consequently there is a higher chance of children who have emigrated from affected areas, or returned to visit family, to be unprotected and vulnerable to mosquito bites.

Malaria can be difficult to diagnose. Children who are infected with malaria can develop a high fever and, as the disease progresses, they can start to have epileptic seizures. This can lead to respiratory failure and death.

Septicaemia (also referred to as sepsis)
Sepsis is blood poisoning caused by an infection. It has attracted a great deal of attention in the media because sepsis is difficult to identify in babies and young children, consequently there have been deaths associated with sepsis (see NICE 2016b for help with identification and treatment).

Sexually transmitted diseases (STDs)
STDs are obviously a very sensitive and possibly controversial area, but they may need to be considered if a child has a discharge or symptoms that raise suspicion about the cause. Consider your setting's safeguarding policy and discuss with your manager if you have concerns.

Aims of treatment
Many infectious diseases do not have treatment available and the condition has to run its course. However, as you can see from the conditions in Table 8.2, many of them have common symptoms. Therefore, an aim of treatment is to reduce the symptoms of the condition in order to make the child feel as comfortable as possible and avoid side-effects that may occur as a consequence of the condition. Children's responses to the symptoms of infectious diseases will partly depend on their age and stage of development. Small children who have not developed language will express themselves by becoming irritable or crying and may be difficult to please. As mentioned above, infectious diseases have an incubation period when the infection is 'brewing' and symptoms of the specific disease may not yet be evident. Children's behaviour can change as a consequence of the discomfort they are feeling.

Medication

Antibiotics can be prescribed for some infectious diseases that are caused by bacteria and they can be administered either in a cream applied to the affected area of the skin or orally. Gloves should be used to apply cream. It will be necessary to ensure that this is done following the administration of medicines policy in your setting.

Medication can be given to reduce high temperature (fever) and reduce pain. Suitable medication is paracetamol, which can be bought over the counter. It is important that the correct dosage is given and recorded. It is important to note that aspirin must not be given to children under the age of 12. Neither should ibuprofen be given to children with chicken pox. Medication must be given in accordance with the policy of the setting which has been written to comply with legislation.

Reducing common symptoms

Reducing fever

Children behave differently when they are unwell and changes in their behaviour will be apparent to those who know them well. However, illness also presents itself in clinical signs, such as a high temperature, or fever.

Normal body temperature is 37.5–37.7 degrees. A high temperature can cause children to become lethargic, tired and pale and have a decreased appetite. When a child develops a high temperature, there is a risk that it can rise rapidly and may cause a febrile convulsion (see Chapter 12). Therefore, an aim of treatment is to reduce the child's temperature, which can be achieved in two ways:

- applying cold compresses – this can be a flannel that has been soaked in cold water and then placed on the child's forehead; it should be left in place until the compress becomes warm, and then the process repeated
- administering medication that reduces fever, such as paracetamol in medicine form.

Reducing febrile convulsion

This is caused by an immaturity of temperature control in children's nervous system; it is most common between 6 months and 5 years of age. As the body temperature rises, there is neurological disturbance, which can cause a seizure or febrile convulsion. This event normally lasts for up to 15 minutes and, although it is distressing, it usually does not produce complications for the child. First aid advice on how to manage this is included in Chapter 12.

Reducing aches and pains

Administering medication to reduce pain and fever will help to keep a child comfortable.

Avoiding dehydration

This can be done by giving plenty of fluids to replace the fluids being lost from the body. There can be grave consequences of severe dehydration such as organ failure, therefore preventing dehydration from occurring is a vital aim of treatment. Encouraging babies and children to drink when they have a sore throat can be challenging and requires you to persevere. A baby should be offered their usual milk feeds, supplemented with boiled, cooled water. For older children, diluted apple juice can encourage them to drink. Signs that children are becoming dehydrated include dark urine; if dehydration is more advanced, skin will feel cold and look mottled.

Reducing itching and scratching

Some infectious diseases result in rashes and an aim of treatment is to try and reduce the itching in order to prevent scratching. Calamine lotion or cooling gels can be applied to reduce pain and itching – this is especially important for children who have eczema, are pre-verbal or have a reduced ability to communicate. Itching can be intensely uncomfortable and can affect children's participation in activities as well as disturbing sleep. Scratching can cause long-term scarring. For some children, it will be appropriate to administer an antihistamine (obviously in consultation with their parent/carer). For babies, cotton mittens may be used. For older children, gentle distraction techniques could be used.

Providing rest and sleep

Infectious diseases can cause lethargy and exhaustion and thus create a need for more sleep. Excessive tiredness can go on for some time after the initial period of the illness, so providing extra nap time and restful activities will be helpful to children as they recover.

Legislation and policy

As discussed in Chapter 3, the aim of the government child health policy is to promote children's health and wellbeing by preventing some of the causes of ill health. Infectious diseases are a significant cause of ill health in children. Reducing the incidence of infectious disease is one of the areas of prevention that is included in the aims of the Healthy Child Programme (HCP) (see Chapter 3 for more details).

> *The Early Years Foundation Stage (2014)* addresses the need for children to manage their own basic hygiene and personal needs successfully, including going to the toilet independently.

> *Public Health England (2014)* has produced guidance on infection control in schools and other childcare settings which contains useful information which is helpful in informing policies in your setting.

> *Health Protection (Notification) Regulations (2010).* If a child is diagnosed by a doctor as having a 'notifiable' disease, such as mumps, malaria or polio, settings have a legal responsibility to report this to Public Health England. Notifiable diseases are contagious, can be life-threatening and can cause epidemics. Outbreaks of infectious and, in some cases, notifiable diseases have increased because of the rise in travel abroad and reduced uptake of childhood immunisations.

Implications for practice

Preventing the spread of infection has implications for practice and requires a great deal of logical thought, hard work and sensitivity.

To prevent or minimise the spread of infection, *policies in settings* need to address how to maintain a clean environment, by managing bodily fluids, teaching children good personal hygiene and avoiding the spread of infection by having sickness policies which give guidance about absence from the setting.

The following areas of practice require consideration and development of policies for all to follow in order to minimise the potential for infection.

Managing bodily fluids:

- a policy for dealing with soiled laundry
- first aid responses to minimise contact with blood
- clinical waste needs to be kept separate from domestic waste; used nappies/pads, gloves aprons and soiled dressings should be stowed in dedicated clinical waste bags and stored in foot-operated bins; clinical waste bags should only be two thirds filled and should be kept in a secure area until collection by a registered waste contractor
- the disposal of sharps such as needles for children with chronic health conditions such as diabetes needs to be into sharps bins that conform with BS7320 and UN 3291.

Laundry and equipment:

- a routine that sanitises toys and equipment regularly in a way that reduces the possibility of cross contamination
- preventing the sharing of flannels and bedding
- laundry facilities for bedding and other items.

Managing risk from animals:

- consider hygiene in relation to handling them and managing waste to avoid infections
- many animals, such as frogs, carry salmonella and are not suitable for early years setting.

Other perspectives

Illness is an inconvenient and unwelcome event and children becoming unwelcome can create difficulties and consequences for all involved. Some of the perspectives of those involved include parents, other children and practitioners.

Working with parents

Avoiding the spread of a preventable infectious illness is good practice and part of your responsibility in supporting children's health and wellbeing. However, implementing a sickness policy can create a source of conflict with parents, especially for those who work and have to miss going to work, or need to make alternative arrangements, because their child needs to be excluded from the setting because of illness. It is important to work in partnership with parents to gain their understanding of, cooperation and compliance with your policies about exclusion whilst children are infectious with an illness.

Considering the health needs of other children

Children with chronic and/or complex medical conditions can be vulnerable to the effects of infectious diseases. All children can experience reduced wellbeing as a consequence of an infectious illness. Children who return to the setting when under par may require more of their key person's attention, which can mean other children do not get an equal share of time.

Consequences for practitioners

Becoming unwell is an inconvenience that can have wider implications in terms of staffing. Relief staff may be unknown to children and this can be unsettling for the youngsters. Childminders can find illness especially difficult to manage.

Your role in managing infectious diseases

As always, understanding your role depends on your level of knowledge of managing the identification and spread of infection. It is important to have a breadth of knowledge of policies in the macrosystem, such as childhood immunisation schedules. It is also important to have a depth of knowledge about infections, especially in relation to those reported in the media, such as MRSA, which can be misunderstood and cause distress to parents and staff. Knowing where to find accurate and current information, such as via government and NHS websites, is important.

It is also important that you understand that the universal preventative measures designed to reduce the spread of infection that are embedded in policies, are made explicit to children, staff and parents – for example, teaching children about personal care, as laid out in the EYFS. On occasions, there may be sensitivities associated with practices related to controlling infection. For example, colleagues may not adhere to effective hand-washing techniques. Ensuring that practitioners are aware of being a positive role model for children may be an issue that you have to lead on making clear to colleagues. On occasions, there may be conflicts between families' levels of hygiene and those at your setting. It will require tact and diplomacy to ensure that children maintain the levels of hygiene set without causing embarrassment to the child or friction with the parents.

RESEARCH FOCUS

Fiona had recently been appointed manager of a day-care setting. She was spending some time getting to know the setting and one of the concerns she identified was the high number of absences as a consequence of staff and children being ill. The absences had led to a great deal of unrest; children were unsettled and practitioners

(Continued)

(Continued)

were exhausted and finding work a chore. The level of illness was impacting on parents too, as they were becoming unwell and many were missing work. At the same time as becoming the manager, Fiona was studying for her top-up degree and as part of her research module she needed to identify an area of practice to carry out a piece of action research on. At a staff meeting, Fiona expressed her concerns about the impact of illness on children, parents and families. Following the discussion with her colleagues, it was decided that the focus of the action research could be to explore the reasons why there had been an increase in illness and look at ways of reducing it.

Fiona started by looking at the records relating to the causes of absence and noted the following:

- diarrhoea and vomiting
- hand, foot and mouth
- 'colds' and upper respiratory tract infections
- asthma attacks
- conjunctivitis
- suspected mumps.

Fiona identified that the causes of illness were mostly infections. Initially, she was surprised at the number of asthma attacks reported, but as she acquired more knowledge she made the connection that rotavirus was a trigger for asthma symptoms which could provoke an attack. Therefore, she realised that by addressing the incidence of infection, she would also be improving the health of children with asthma.

Fiona made a list of the actions she felt she needed to take to reduce the incidence of illness and improve the wellbeing of children, families and practitioners:

1 Review practice and policies relating to preventing and treating infection.

2 Promote, maintain and educate about health.

3 Consider the implications for practice.

4 Critically reflect on how children with infectious diseases are included in their ECEC.

REFLECTION

What ways have you identified that you can improve policies and procedures for better hygiene and to prevent cross-infection in your practice?

Infestations

Infestations, such as head lice, are caused by parasites that live in or on humans and survive by feeding off their host. Parasites thrive in densely populated areas where

Table 8.3 Most commonly seen infestations in early years settings

Type of infestation	Signs and symptoms	Treatment
Head lice: parasitic insects that live in human hair	Intense itching caused by an allergy to the lice	Detection combing
Nits are the remains of the hatched lice	Not all people are allergic to lice, therefore itching may not be a sign	
Scabies: caused by tiny mites that burrow under the skin, passed on by skin-to-skin contact or, rarely, by sharing bedding	Intense itching, especially at night	Permethrin 5% cream or malathion 0.05% lotion
Worms (threadworms, roundworms): symptoms begin 4–6 days after swallowing the eggs	Ingestion of soil contaminated with roundworm eggs	Over the counter medication Strict hygiene measures

humans are in close bodily contact with each other, so early years settings are hotbeds for infestations to thrive. Therefore, it is a good idea to develop an awareness of infestations and recognise them so that parents can be informed and treatment can start.

An inclusive approach to preventing infection and infestation

Preventing infection requires a great deal of thought and effort. It is important to consider how the policies can be implemented in a consistent and fair way, so that all children can be protected from unnecessary episodes of ill health and be included in their ECEC. It is also important that children do not experience prejudice because they have an infection or infestation. Bear in mind that not all infectious diseases or infestations will present with signs and/or symptoms. For example, a child may have been born with Human Immunodeficiency Virus, but they may not have symptoms. Or a child may have an infestation which is not evident. Therefore, they are a source of infection or infestation. Preventing and managing infectious diseases and infestations can be emotive experiences, but applying the policies and procedures in the same way to all children is an inclusive approach.

Conclusion

Infections and infestations are responsible for absences from settings of children and practitioners, as well as causing the absence of parents from work. The consequences of absence for largely avoidable infections mean that children lose valuable opportunities for learning and development and can experience poor wellbeing as a result of illness. Absence from work causes a loss to the economy as well as being a source of anxiety to parents when they are faced with the difficulty of trying to find alternative childcare.

Infestations can cause itching and disturbed sleep and can have an impact on cognitive development because of tiredness and lack of concentration. However, you can do a great deal to prevent and contain infections and infestations within your setting and, in turn, maximise children's attendance.

Further reading

Ayliffe, G.A.J., Babb, J.R. and Quoraishi, A.H. (1978) Six Stage Hand Washing Technique (poster). Available at: www.ahpo.net/assets/handwashing-poster-.pdf (accessed 26 July 2016).

GOV.UK (2016) Pre-school Immunisations: A guide to vaccinations (from two to five years). Available at: www.gov.uk/government/uploads/system/uploads/attachment_data/file/522119/PHE_9809_Preschool_A5_28p_2016_02_web.pdf (accessed 16 May 2016).

NHS (2014) How to Prevent Germs from Spreading. Available at: www.nhs.uk/livewell/homehygiene/pages/prevent-germs-from-spreading.aspx (accessed 14 July 2016).

NHS (2015) A Quick Guide to Childhood Immunisations for the Parents of Premature Babies. Available at: www.gov.uk/government/uploads/system/uploads/attachment_data/file/522123/PHE_9809_Premature_quickguide_2016_02_web.pdf (accessed 7 June 2016).

NICE (2016) Sepsis: Recognition, diagnosis and early management. Available at: www.nice.org.uk/guidance/ng51/resources/sepsis-recognition-diagnosis-and-early-management-1837508256709 (accessed 14 July 2016).

Public Health England (2010) Guidance on Infection Control in Schools and other Childcare Settings. Available at: www.gov.uk/government/uploads/system/uploads/attachment_data/file/522337/Guidance_on_infection_control_in_schools.pdf (accessed 1 April 2016); poster available at: www.publichealth.hscni.net/sites/default/files/A2%20Schools%20poster_1.pdf

9

CHILDREN WITH CHRONIC CONDITIONS

CHAPTER AIMS AND OBJECTIVES

- To define what is meant by chronic health conditions

- To identify contemporary chronic health conditions

- To explore management of chronic health conditions

- To discuss inclusion of children with chronic health conditions

As you read this chapter, you are encouraged to consider the children you work with who have chronic health conditions.

Defining chronic health conditions

A chronic condition can be defined as one that is of long duration (*Concise Medical Dictionary*, OUP 2010). Brown, Krieg and Belluck (1995) state that a chronic condition is one that is 'on-going, lasts for longer than three months, is incurable and can affect everyday life'. Unpacking the terms used in this definition illustrates some of the implications for children and their families of having an on-going condition. As Edwards and Davis (1997, p. 3) put it, 'although chronic conditions vary in severity and the extent to which they affect a child's life, what they have in common is that they do not go away'. Consequently, because the conditions are incurable and do not go away, the child and the family face a situation where they have to make adjustments in order to minimise the impact of the condition on their lives.

The most common chronic health conditions that affect children in the UK are listed in Table 9.1. These chronic conditions are all very different and are characterised by a range of **signs** and **symptoms**.

The *Concise Medical Dictionary* (OUP 2010) offers the following definitions:

Sign: an indication of a particular disorder that is detected by a physician while examining a patient but is not apparent to the patient

Symptom: an indication of a disease or disorder noticed by the patient

Table 9.1 Contemporary chronic health conditions affecting children

Chronic condition and incidence	Description of condition	Signs and symptoms relevant to practitioners	Typical triggers in a setting	Possible impact on inclusion	Treatment
Anaphylaxis 6% of children diagnosed (NICE 2011)	Severe allergic response (potentially fatal in rare cases) High incidence of children having other allergic conditions such as asthma and eczema	Rash, breathing difficulties, swelling of airway, lips and eyes, runny nose, vomiting	Foods (commonly nuts, kiwi, egg and lactose), animal dander and hair, latex	Managing the environment in order to remove the risk of contact with known allergens may impact on some activities, e.g. contact with certain foods and animals	Avoidance of the allergen Antihistamine or adrenaline auto-injector (Epipen) if allergy triggered
Asthma 10–15% of children affected (NICE 2013b)	An inherited condition which causes inflammation of the breathing airways Can be associated with allergy Often exercise induced Attacks can be fatal	Wheeze, cough and difficulty in breathing	Contact with allergens can trigger an asthma attack Common triggers include dust, animal hair and saliva, pollen, chemicals, aerosols, physical activity, moving between contrasting temperatures Emotions such as crying, excitement and laughter can trigger a response	Avoiding contact with an allergen can result in a child not taking part in certain activities Reduced physical exercise Reduced outdoor play in cold weather and during pollen season	Reliever inhalers (blue) are frequently prescribed to be administered via a spacer device to give extra relief if a child is in contact with a trigger for their asthma Preventer inhalers (typically brown, orange or purple) are usually prescribed for twice-a-day use and can be given at home

Chronic condition and incidence	Description of condition	Signs and symptoms relevant to practitioners	Typical triggers in a setting	Possible impact on inclusion	Treatment
Coeliac disease 1:100 affected	Sensitivity to gliadin which is a protein found in gluten which is in wheat, rye and barley A gluten-free diet is required	In the short term, eating gluten can cause diarrhoea and discomfort Long-term damage includes an increased risk of cancer	Food containing gluten, drinks containing barley, playdough made with wheat flour	Can create challenges for those responsible for menu planning	Gluten-free diet
Cystic fibrosis 1:3000 newborns affected	A genetic condition that affects breathing and digestion	Sticky mucous builds up in the lungs Enzyme replacement	Prone to infections	Dietary restrictions Shortness of breath may make physical activity difficult	Physiotherapy and breathing exercises to prevent mucous build-up
Diabetes mellitus 26,500 children affected with type 1 500 with type 2 (NICE 2015)	The pancreas fails to produce adequate amounts of insulin Type 1 requires insulin injections Type 2 requires weight management and possibly medication to stimulate the body's own stores of insulin	Children may experience high (hyper) or low (hypo) blood sugar levels	Physical activity; eating excessive carbohydrates; physical (in) activity; warm/cold weather	Dietary restriction; missing out on routines of the setting for blood sugar tests and insulin injections	Balancing carbohydrate and insulin intake with physical activity.
Eczema Exact figures are not available but estimated to affect 11% of children Eczema is the most common reason for children aged 0–2 years to consult a family doctor (NICE 2007) Eczema is the most common skin condition that affects children (WHO 2007)	An inherited inflammatory skin condition Eczema comes from the Greek word 'to boil'	Itchiness and scratching Bleeding from lesions Tiredness from disturbed sleep	Can include pollen, house dust mite, sand, water, animal hair, soap, modelling dough, food (tomatoes)	Reduced sensory play, e.g. sand play Tiredness can lead to lack of concentration Unsightly skin can be a barrier to social interaction	Regular use of emollient creams to moisturise skin Avoid contact with triggers where possible Vinyl gloves are sometimes used to help children access activities that can trigger a reaction

(Continued)

Table 9.1 (Continued)

Chronic condition and incidence	Description of condition	Signs and symptoms relevant to practitioners	Typical triggers in a setting	Possible impact on inclusion	Treatment
Epilepsy 1:279 children affected (0.4%) (NICE 2013)	Electrical impulses in the brain can trigger seizure. There are many causes of epilepsy, including: brain damage as a consequence of trauma or infection (such as meningitis) or a genetically inherited condition. Sometimes there is no known cause	Seizures, tiredness	Emotional responses; lighting are common but trigger can be unique to each child	Tiredness, lack of concentration, a need for more sleep	Medication Avoiding triggers First aid knowledge when a child has a seizure
Sickle cell anaemia Affects 1:2000 live births but can impact 1:300 children in some areas	An inherited disorder where red blood cells develop abnormally. mostly affects. African-Caribbean children. Risk of stroke in childhood	Anaemia can cause shortness of breath, delayed growth and development Painful joints	Injuries, dehydration Cold or hot weather Viruses	Physical activity may be painful, injuries can provoke a reaction	Avoid dehydration. Risk assess physical activities

NICE (2015) Diabetes (type 1 and type 2) in children and young people: diagnosis and management. Available from https://www.nice.org.uk/guidance/ng18/chapter/introduction accessed 16 January 2017.

Chronic conditions are characterised by a range of signs and symptoms that are incurable, meaning that they cannot be made to go away.

Signs and symptoms of conditions can be provoked by the presence of 'triggers' in the child's environment.

Trigger: a substance that can exacerbate signs and symptoms of chronic health conditions – for example, dust can exacerbate the symptoms of asthma.

Difference between a chronic and an acute condition

As discussed above, a chronic health condition is on-going, however chronic conditions can have acute flare-ups. The symptoms of an acute exacerbation can appear suddenly; they may be triggered by an infection. For example, children with asthma or diabetes can have acute illness and/or symptoms provoked by a common cold virus. Children with sickle cell anaemia can have an acute crisis provoked by dehydration. Anaphylaxis is considered a chronic condition because it is on-going, however children can have an acute exacerbation of the condition as a consequence of coming into contact with an allergen, such as a food to which they are severely allergic.

Managing chronic health conditions

Signs and symptoms can be reduced or removed in order to lessen the impact of the condition on children. A chronic condition can result in the child experiencing pain, anxiety and exclusion from activities. Therefore, your role is critical in reducing the signs, symptoms and triggers in order to enable a child to be free of pain and anxiety and included in activities. The main ways that symptoms can be managed or reduced are by:

- *administering medication* – this includes medicine by mouth or via a nasogastric tube; the application of creams for skin conditions; the use of spacers to give asthma inhalers; the injecting of insulin to control blood sugar levels in children with diabetes mellitus, either injections into the skin or via an insulin pump; and the rectal administration of diazepam, which is sometimes needed for children with severe epilepsy
- *the use of measuring devices*, as well as therapies to keep children healthy and to ensure that the symptoms of their condition are kept under control – for example, the measurement of blood sugar for children with diabetes; this involves piercing the child's skin with a fine needle to draw a droplet of blood which is applied to a glucose monitoring strip and inserted into a machine
- *physiotherapy* – for example, for children with cystic fibrosis
- *managing the child's environment* to reduce or minimise the presence of triggers – for example, avoiding contact with furry animals in children with asthma and/or eczema
- *dietary restrictions* to keep children with conditions such as coeliac disease, allergy or cystic fibrosis healthy.

The use of clinical interventions, as listed above, which are necessary to support and maintain children's health, requires practitioners to develop the necessary clinical skills in order to manage chronic health conditions. The practitioners who participated in my research had developed a wide range of skills, as above, that equipped them to be able to meet the medical needs of children with chronic health conditions.

Legislation and policy

The Early Years Foundation Stage (DfE 2014a) seeks to ensure that 'every child is included and supported' (p. 5). In relation to managing chronic health, there is guidance about the administration of medicines, food allergies and first aid requirements.

Supporting pupils at school with a medical condition

Section 100 of the Children and Families Act (DfE 2014a) included statutory guidance aimed at maintained schools, academies and pupil referral units. The document replaces the 2005 Managing Medicines in Schools and Early Years Settings. The aim of the legislation is to give responsibility to schools to set out arrangements for how they will support children with medical conditions in terms of both physical and mental health. The legislation aims to strengthen the links between education, health and care settings. One of the requirements of the guidance is that children with chronic conditions have an education, health and care (EHC) plan.

When the Supporting Pupils at School with Medical Conditions guidance came into force, a ministerial statement excluded children in early education who were not in school, saying 'this will not apply to early years provision as there is already sufficient coverage of this issue in the statutory Early Years Foundation Stage'. However, as there is no specific guidance in the EYFS about chronic health conditions, you may find that this guidance contains useful information that is applicable and useful to practitioners in early years settings that are not schools.

Policy for management of asthma

Since 2014, schools are allowed to purchase salbutamol without a prescription to be used in emergency situations by children with asthma. The Department of Health (2015a) has written guidance for schools about the emergency use of salbutamol inhalers in school.

Written records

It will be vital that policies designed to improve and maintain the health of children with chronic medical needs include written records. Such documentation needs to include parental consent for the administration of medication. The Department for Education has useful templates available to adapt for writing these records, as well as a template for writing an education, health and care plan. (See Further Reading for details).

Medication policy

Implementing the Supporting Pupils at School with Medical Conditions statutory guidance (DfE 2014c) means that policies in schools must address the following points:

- Ensure there is understanding of the medical condition: its triggers, signs, symptoms and treatments.
- Assess the pupil's resultant needs: medication and other treatments, time facilities, equipment, testing, access to food and drink where this is used to manage their condition, dietary requirements and environmental adaptations.
- Specify support for the pupil's educational, social and emotional needs.
- Assess the level of support needed (including emergencies) according to age and stage of development.
- Identify who will provide the support (including cover, school trips and school activities outside the normal school timetable) that will ensure the child can participate.

RESEARCH FOCUS

My doctoral research (Musgrave 2014) examined how practitioners created inclusive environments in day-care settings for young children with the chronic health conditions asthma, anaphylaxis, eczema, diabetes and epilepsy. The total number of children in the 19 settings who participated in my research was 1,053 and of that number 11% had one, or more, chronic health condition(s). The most common conditions that affected children were asthma, allergy and eczema; indeed, some children had a combination of all three. These findings concurred with statistics that give estimates of the number of children who have asthma (10–15%). There is no exact figure for the number of children who have eczema, but it is thought to be 11%. The number of children with anaphylaxis in my research was 3%, which compares to a predicted figure of 6% of children nationally who have this serious allergy. The least common conditions reported were diabetes and epilepsy.

The reasons for the low figures for anaphylaxis, diabetes and epilepsy are speculative. It may be that diabetes is less common in very young children, although the number of children with this chronic condition is increasing. Another reason may be that parents encounter difficulties in finding suitable day care. The suggestion that parents of children with chronic conditions may find it difficult to find suitably motivated and skilled practitioners, who are willing to take on the responsibility of caring for such children, was borne out by John's mum who had taken him away from his setting because of the manager's lack of insight into the care John needed to manage his diabetes.

The findings from my research are summarised as follows:

- The symptoms of chronic health conditions have a profound effect on children and their families.

- Eczema is especially common and (depending on its severity) can create challenges to inclusion.

- Practitioners and parents working together is crucial to maximise the child's inclusion in their day-care setting environment.

- The leadership skills of practitioners are critical to creating an inclusive environment and minimising exclusion.

Impact of a chronic condition on children

My research revealed that chronic health conditions affect children in the following ways:

- Asthma and eczema symptoms cause sleep disturbance to children (and, in turn, their families).
- Receiving medication and other interventions to manage the symptoms of their condition can interrupt children's activities.
- Children with chronic conditions experience discomfort and pain.
- Children with a chronic condition are more likely to be unwell and absent from their setting.
- Children notice when they are given different food.

The impact of the symptoms on children and your role in minimising the impact will be discussed throughout the chapter.

Sleep disturbance

Children with on-going conditions may experience sleep disturbance on a regular basis and this is troublesome for children and their families. For example, children with eczema often experience sleep disturbance because of the need to scratch. Even if they have had a night-time routine of therapeutic baths, emollients and steroid creams applied and possibly bandages, as the effect of the cream wears off during the night they can still become itchy and need to scratch. Similarly, if children with asthma are going through a period of experiencing symptoms, or are recovering from an attack, it is common for them to have coughing spells at night. The mothers who were participants in my research described how their sons' chronic condition affected their sleep patterns:

 My boyfriend and I take it in turns to go to bed, he would stay up with Freddie until 6am, when I would get up. That's the way we had to work it so that we had some semblance of sleep. [Freddie's mum]

DJ's mum also commented on a similar arrangement:

 We do shifts, I go to bed early … he [her partner] stays up later because he knows that DJ will get up at some point, he's awake every 2–3 hours.

Disturbed sleep during the night can lead to tiredness and irritability during the day, which can have an impact on social, emotional and cognitive development. Part of your morning handover from parents should include questions about sleep and whether naps and quiet times are needed. The impact of lack of sleep can be problematic when children start school.

Impact on development

The symptoms of chronic health conditions need to be viewed holistically in order to assess the potential impact. Eczema can have a profound impact on children's wellbeing as well as on their learning. Children's hands may be so badly affected that they find it difficult and/or painful to hold a pen, thus their fine motor skills and pre-writing development can be harmed. Children with sickle cell anaemia, asthma or cystic fibrosis may be discouraged from exerting themselves because of the risk of triggering symptoms, consequently the development of gross motor skills may be impaired.

Resilience

It is important to point out that the impact of having an on-going health condition is not always negative. Alderson (2011) notes that children who have experienced long-term ill health or disability, can show early maturity because of having to cope with adverse experiences. Children can develop responsibility for their health at an early age. In addition, the challenges they face can mean they create deep pockets of resilience, which can help them to respond with maturity to other life challenges.

The role of the practitioner

Your role in supporting children with chronic health conditions includes:

- gaining knowledge about conditions
- developing your skills relating to managing the symptoms of conditions
- working with parents and other professionals
- maximising inclusion in activities and minimising exclusion.

Gaining knowledge about chronic conditions

Knowledge about a chronic condition is key to understanding how you can plan for a child's education and care. The main sources of knowledge are likely to be from parents, healthcare professionals and other sources such as the internet. The internet is a good place to seek out such knowledge – try consulting NHS websites and UK-based charities' pages that aim to inform people about specific conditions (some examples are given in the further reading section). Highly recommended is the National Institute for Health and Clinical Excellence (NICE) set of guidance on several chronic health conditions (see Chapter 3 for more details about NICE's role, and also the further reading section for links to relevant guidance).

Learning about conditions needs to be in-depth and it needs to be borne in mind that ethnic origin can be significant. For example, because of physiological differences between black and white skin, eczema in children with black skin can be more severe than the visual appearance indicates (Kelly and Taylor 2009).

Accessing training from health professionals is especially helpful, but there are challenges such as getting time away from your setting and funding of courses.

Liaising with health professionals and working together in an integrated way is a recommended way of gaining knowledge and developing skills (there is more on integrated working in Chapter 4). In my research, there were many examples of excellent practice where the manager had taken the initiative and, with the cooperation of parents, liaised with health professionals about the on-going health needs and management of conditions. One practitioner had improved communication by requesting that she was copied in on letters between hospital health professionals, parents and the family doctor.

Sadly, there are some children who are unable to access early childhood education and care because of the reluctance of, and lack of knowledge demonstrated by some practitioners, as illustrated by John's mum who reported the following experience:

> He was 13 months when he started at the nursery, he was there when he was diagnosed with diabetes, they were the first people to look after him. They had a new manager ... I wasn't happy, I didn't feel comfortable with her looking after John for the whole day because of some of the things she was saying ... she made me feel uncomfortable [to John's dad] you probably remember what she was like and what she was saying.
>
> She said she couldn't understand what all the hassle was about, and it was easy to see when diabetic children were poorly. Then, on another day, they phoned up because he wasn't very well, the machine (insulin pump) wasn't working, when we went in the pump had become disconnected [John's dad].
>
> She had messed up basically, his sugar was going high.

Knowing the child

As well as finding out about the condition, it is important to find out how the condition affects the individual child; this is where observations of the child are useful.

RESEARCH FOCUS

An extract from my observations demonstrates how one practitioner, responsible for DJ (24 months old, with severe eczema on his hands), helped him to play in the sand:

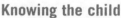

13:45 The practitioner explains to DJ that she needs to put his cream on and to wait for her before touching the sand. She quickly locates his cream and joins DJ at the sandbox, where he has started to gently pat the sand. DJ puts his hand in the practitioner's hand, one at a time, patting the sand with his free hand. He remains engaged with playing alongside his friend as the practitioner applies cream rapidly, but gently.

14:05 DJ is still playing in the sandbox. He has had a sustained period of engagement with the sand. He has been scooping sand into a colander and making animated noises, not speaking words. He has been smiling. He has been taking handfuls of sand from the sandbox to another box repeatedly. After 20 minutes of engaging with the sand, he moves on to another activity in the outdoor play area.

REFLECTION

- How did the practitioner's actions help to enable DJ to play in the sand?
- What are the potential consequences to children's development of not engaging with sensory play?

Developing skills to manage chronic conditions

The most common way the practitioners in my research learned how to carry out the clinical skills was from parents or from health professionals. This was especially the case in relation to administering inhalers for asthma. The situation arises partly because in privately owned nurseries, practitioners often find access to training a challenge and, for this reason, parents often teach them how to carry out the procedures. This practice is not always the best approach because parents may have developed their own interpretation of the skill and there is a possibility that an important aspect of the recommended approach to the procedure is not adhered to. This comment is not intended to undermine parents' skills or knowledge, but it is important to be aware that procedures have been developed using an evidence base and health professionals are acutely aware of the need to follow recommended procedures. If they do not do so, they may find that they are not meeting the competencies of their profession and this can lead to them being struck off the register relating to that profession. It is also important to bear in mind that not following the recommended approach may be harmful to the child.

An important skill to develop is to learn from the child how you can minimise the pain that accompanies some procedures, especially when needles are being inserted for blood monitoring or injections of insulin.

Including children with chronic health conditions

Full inclusion for some children with some conditions may be challenging and unrealistic. However, careful planning can maximise their participation and minimise the activities and situations that may exclude them. Inclusion is discussed in greater depth in Chapter 5. It is important that you have a good understanding of the causes and triggers of conditions so that you know how to adapt activities to make them safe and comfortable for those affected.

Enabling the environment

One of the main aims of supporting children with chronic health conditions is to minimise or remove the possibility of the child coming into contact with a 'trigger', that is something that will provoke the symptoms of the condition. Table 9.1 has a column that includes a range of different triggers for some of the contemporary chronic health conditions considered in this chapter. Avoiding nuts for a child who is allergic to nuts may seem relatively straightforward – many settings have a policy that bans nuts in order to reduce the risk to the anaphylactic child. However, when the allergen is a staple food such as milk, minimising the risk to a child with lactose allergy is more problematic because it is not feasible to ban milk. This situation requires careful thought about how you can enable the environment and make it safe for a child who is allergic to milk. You will have to think about how you can reduce the cross-contamination caused by spillage or by contact with other children.

Enabling the environment for children with asthma also requires some thought. Asthma symptoms can be provoked by emotion and/or physical activity. Trying to balance the requirement for children to be physically active, but not so much that they become wheezy and over-excited, can be challenging.

In addition, the outdoor play area can be a source of triggers for asthma. In winter, cold air can provoke wheeziness, and in summer, pollen can trigger symptoms. The effect of seasonal influences combined with physical activity and excitement can be a potent and dangerous mix. A quiet zone for outdoor play may be necessary to allow children with asthma to engage with the outdoors whilst minimising the impact of triggers. One practitioner described how they had to plan ahead for a child with diabetes:

> We had to think, if he was going outside to do exercise he would probably need a biscuit or something ... he would have Ribena (high in carbohydrate) and we would take an extra (blood sugar) test just in case.

Animals can play an important role in children's learning, however one practitioner commented on how the guinea pig was a trigger for children with asthma and eczema.

Avoiding infection is important for all children, but is particularly important for children with chronic conditions. For example, children with sickle cell anaemia are more prone to infections. Eczema should not be underestimated; one practitioner in my research told me that 'one child had severe eczema and needed to be hospitalised as the eczema was infected'.

As discussed in Chapter 8, hand washing is the single most important way of avoiding infections, but for children with eczema this may be a painful experience, consequently they may avoid doing it. Therefore, it is important that children with eczema are enabled to hand wash using equipment that does not trigger their symptoms. As one practitioner said, 'He uses an emollient to wash his hands because the soap was aggravating his hands. We've got paper towels which seem to be OK...'.

Adapting activities

Sand and water play can be potent triggers for eczematous skin. Respondents to my research described the ways that they adapted sand play for children with eczema by using lentils. One practitioner explained how she adapted a shaving foam activity for Freddie who has eczema:

> We had shaving foam the other week and we had it on trays and we let the children, particularly the 2–3 year olds, explore it and my colleague was doing it with

me and said 'oh, what about Freddie's skin?' So I said 'put some clingfilm over it and do it quite loosely so that he's not messing with the foam but he can poke it and press it and feel that it's soft and do what the other children are doing, not the wetness, but he can still explore it in that way'.

Absence from the setting

Children with chronic health conditions are more likely to experience absence as a consequence of their chronic health condition. Absences can be due to the symptoms of the condition or as a consequence of being susceptible to infections. Closs (2000) points out that frequent, short absences can be detrimental to children's development. Closs goes on to say that this can be as a consequence of disruption to friendships or an inability to understand schoolwork, both of which can reduce self-esteem. How young children respond to returning to their setting after absence because of ill health will depend on their age and stage of development, and the reason for the absence. An important part of your role will be to support children to make the transition back into the setting after a period of absence.

Working with parents

The symptoms of chronic health conditions can have a profound impact on parents. Sleep disturbance can leave parents feeling desperate. Some chronic conditions are life-threatening and/or life-limiting. Management of chronic conditions is improving and life expectancy for many conditions is increasing. For example, Trueland (2014) states that, in the 1970s, people with sickle cell anaemia lived on average to 14.5 years, however people are now living into their 70s because of improvements in treatment and management. Still, chronic health conditions that are not going to go away, can impact on parents' emotions because of a sense of loss, or concern about the impact of the condition on their child. Bowes, Lowes, Warner and Gregory (2008, p. 992) state that the 'chronic sorrow in parents of children with type 1 diabetes is so profound that it was likened to a grief reaction akin to a bereavement'.

RESEARCH FOCUS JOHN AND HIS FAMILY

John has been attending your setting since he was 6 months old. John's mum, Jane, is working full-time at a local college. His dad, Sam, is a paramedic. John has an older stepsister who lives with Sam's ex-wife.

John is now 18 months and he has recently been diagnosed with diabetes. He requires insulin injections to keep his blood sugar within normal levels. It is essential that he has the correct amount of insulin: if he has too much, he can become 'hypo'; and if he doesn't have enough, his blood sugar can go high, which can cause him to feel very unwell. High blood sugar can cause long-term damage and, if untreated, even death.

John's mum is anxious about leaving him at the setting, she says that she finds trusting somebody 'nerve-wracking'.

(Continued)

(Continued)

REFLECTION

- How are you going to plan for John's healthcare?
- How are you going to work with his parents?
- What are the likely concerns of John's parents?

Working with other children

Having children with chronic health conditions in your setting may impact on other children. For example, a child who is in pain or experiencing discomfort or behaviour changes because of the symptoms of their condition will require extra attention from their key person, thus reducing the time available for other key children.

Children are very curious about difference and this can extend to questions about why some children cannot eat certain foods, or need medication, or why a part of their body looks different. In order to support children affected by a chronic health condition, teaching all children about conditions can help them to develop understanding and tolerance. There are books available that can help to teach children about living with a chronic condition – for example, the Anaphylaxis Campaign has published the *Cyril the Squirrel* story to inform children about the condition (www.anaphylaxis.org.uk/product/cyril-squirrel-book/). In addition, charity websites relating to the condition may contain helpful resources.

Bullying is more common in school-aged children, although it is not exclusive to older children. Reunamo et al. (2014) report cases of bullying in day-care and pre-school settings involving children as young as 3. Children with chronic conditions can become victims of bullying, therefore vigilance is required to reduce bullying behaviours towards such children.

Conclusion

This chapter has highlighted the importance of you having a good level of knowledge and understanding about chronic conditions and how the signs and symptoms can impact on children's holistic development. This knowledge and understanding will in turn help to encourage your thinking about your role in supporting and including children with chronic health conditions.

Further reading

Department for Education (2014) Supporting Pupils at School with Medical Conditions: Statutory guidance for governing bodies of maintained schools and proprietors of academies in England. Available at: www.gov.uk/government/publications/supporting-pupils-at-school-with-medical-conditions—3 (accessed 6 July 2016).

Department of Health (2015) Guidance on the Use of Emergency Salbutamol Inhalers in Schools. Available at: www.gov.uk/government/uploads/system/uploads/attachment_ data/file/416468/emergency_inhalers_in_schools.pdf

Musgrave, J. (2014) How do Practitioners Create Inclusive Environments for Children with Chronic Health Conditions? An exploratory case study. Thesis for Doctor of Education, University of Sheffield. Available at: http://etheses.whiterose.ac.uk/6174/1/Jackie%20 Musgrave%20-%20Final%20Thesis%20incl%20Access%20Form%20for%20sub mission%2019-5-14.pdf (accessed 24 July 2016).

NICE (2007) Atopic Eczema in Under 12s: Diagnosis and management. Available at: www. nice.org.uk/guidance/cg57 (accessed 24 July 2016).

NICE (2011) Food Allergy in Children and Young People. Available at: https://pathways. nice.org.uk/pathways/food-allergy-in-children-and-young-people (accessed 14 October 2011).

NICE (2013) Quality Standard for Asthma. Available at: www.nice.org.uk/Search.do?x=- 994&y=- 200&searchText=asthma+young+children&newsearch=true (accessed 6 June 2013).

NICE (2013) Quality Standard for Epilepsies in Children and Young Children. Available at: http://publications.nice.org.uk/quality-standard-for-the-epilepsies-in-children-and- young-people-qs27 (accessed 6 June 2013).

NICE (2014) Sickle Cell Disease. Available at: www.nice.org.uk/guidance/qs58/resources/ sickle-cell-disease-2098733894341 (accessed 24 July 2016).

NICE (2015) Coeliac Disease: Recognition, assessment and management. Available at: www.nice.org.uk/guidance/ng20/resources/coesliac-disease-recognition-assessment- and-management-1837325178565 (accessed 24 July 2016).

NICE (2015) Diabetes in Children and Young People. Available at: www.nice.org.uk/guidance/ ng18/resources/type-1-diabetes-in-children-and-young-people-3224306721733 (accessed 24 July 2016).

Vize, A. (2011) *Meeting Special Needs: A Practical Guide to Support Children with Coeliac Disease and Gluten Intolerance*. London: Pre-school Books.

Useful websites

Anaphylaxis campaign – www.anaphylaxis.org.uk; videos on YouTube at: www.anaphylaxis. org.uk/hcp/what-is-anaphylaxis/resources/our-films/

Asthma UK – www.asthma.org.uk

Cystic fibrosis – www.cysticfibrosis.org.uk/about-cf/what-is-cystic-fibrosis

Diabetes UK – www.diabetes.org.uk

Eczema UK – www.eczema.org

Education for Health: Supporting Children's Health – Asthma. Available at: www.supporting- childrenshealth.org

Epilepsy – www.epilepsysociety.org.uk; www.epilepsy.org.uk

Sickle cell anaemia – http://sicklecellsociety.org/wp-content/uploads/2015/01/Dyson- School-policy-sickle-cell.pdf

10
CHILDREN WITH COMPLEX MEDICAL NEEDS

CHAPTER AIMS AND OBJECTIVES

- To define causes of and reasons for complex medical needs
- To identify skills for working with children with complex medical needs

Introduction

As a consequence of improved ante-natal care and improved medical success in preserving life, more and more children are surviving with conditions which not so many years ago would have resulted in early death, either at birth or shortly afterwards. Consequently, there are more children with complex medical needs who are accessing out-of-home education and care settings, such as playgroups or special schools. As a result, many practitioners are becoming involved in the care of such children. The conditions that can give rise to complex medical needs can be life-threatening or life-limiting and are defined as follows:

Life-threatening conditions are those for which curative treatment may be feasible but can fail, such as cancer. Children in long-term remission or following successful curative treatment are not included.

Life-limiting/life-shortening conditions are those for which there is no reasonable hope of cure and from which children or young people will die. Some of these conditions cause progressive deterioration, rendering the child increasingly dependent on parents and carers.

Causes of complex medical needs

There are many reasons why a child may have complex medical needs, so it is important that you understand the reasons and causes in order to be able to plan for the child's needs and work effectively with the family and/or carers. The conditions that are most common include:

- premature birth and 'light for dates' babies
- congenital disabilities
- trauma, either at birth or following an injury.

Premature birth

Neonatal care has developed as a specialism since the first special care baby unit was set up in the 1950s. I remember the newspaper headlines in the 1970s: 'Baby born weighing less than a bag of sugar survives', when the first baby who weighed less than two pounds at birth was discharged from hospital. Forty years later, babies can be born and, with intensive support, survive at 22 weeks of a 40-week pregnancy period. The success in keeping premature and tiny babies alive is not without cost, both to the NHS and to the child and their family. Children who are born at just over half the expected gestation period frequently face a life of disability because vital areas of their bodies have not had the time to grow in the uterus. The human gestation period starts at conception when the embryo develops and after 12 weeks becomes the foetus. During the foetal period, the major organs of the body develop and during the third trimester of pregnancy, these organs mature. Early birth and reduced gestation reduce the time period for these processes to occur. Consequently, babies who are born early do not have the advantage of being nurtured by their mother's body in the womb. As a result, babies are frequently born with physical disadvantages. For example, their body temperature regulation mechanism can be under-developed, hence the need for them to be nursed in an incubator. Depending on the stage in the pregnancy that babies are born preterm, their lungs may be immature and not equipped to support breathing. Therefore, they will need a range of breathing support, from a supply of oxygen to ventilation on a machine. The interruption to their development and maturation can leave a legacy of physical disability which lasts throughout their life.

As well as physical disability, being born early can lead to social and emotional development problems. We are aware of the importance of the mother and baby bonding after birth and how the bonding process is enhanced by physical contact straight after birth. A midwifery practice is to deliver and place the newborn baby on to the mother's tummy. The skin-to-skin contact, or kangaroo care (Penn 2015), and eye-to-eye contact can trigger the process of bonding that attachment theory has taught us is so important. However, babies who are born early are frequently small, often weighing less than two pounds, versus the average seven pounds, therefore holding babies at the time of their birth is not feasible. In addition, premature babies often require immediate life support because their breathing system is under-developed and they are incapable of breathing independently and need to be put on ventilation.

Government figures (APPG 2013) tell us that there is a higher incidence of premature babies born to mothers who live in disadvantaged circumstances. For example, mothers who live in poverty and experience the attendant factors associated with poverty, such as poor nutrition, are more likely to have premature babies.

Implications for practice

Children who are born prematurely have a 10% risk of developmental delay. The earlier the baby is born, the greater the risk of delay. Therefore, if a child's chronological age is not adjusted to reflect their developmental age, it will appear that development is even more delayed than it really is. In turn, this reinforces a deficit view of the child and their developmental achievement. It is important to know if a child was born premature so that specially adjusted weight and development charts can be used.

REFLECTION

- At registration, do you ask parents if a child was born prematurely?
- Why is it important to do so?

Light-for-dates babies

Babies who are 'light for dates' are born weighing less than would be expected for the stage of gestation. There is an increased chance of babies born to poor mothers weighing less than the average weight.

Congenital disabilities

Congenital means present at birth. As a student nurse in the 1980s on a special care baby unit, we received many newborn babies who had been born with conditions such as spina bifida or malformations in their major organs. Many of the conditions that affected babies at that time are now identified by ante-natal screening. Therefore, the conditions are corrected while the baby is still in utero or, depending on the parents' wishes and the severity of the condition, babies are aborted.

Two contemporary causes of congenital disabilities are foetal alcohol syndrome and genetic conditions as a consequence of consanguinity.

Foetal Alcohol Syndrome (FAS)

Dr Carolyn Blackburn has researched FAS, and the following contribution from her summarises some of the main points about the impact of this growing cause of children being born with complex medical needs. Blackburn writes:

Prenatal exposure to alcohol can lead to intellectual and developmental delays and differences which impact on children's learning and development throughout life. Possible physical disabilities include facial differences, growth deficiencies, major organ damage, and skeletal damage, as well as hearing and vision impairments. Damage to the brain (central nervous system damage) results in developmental disabilities, including general learning difficulties, communication delays/disorders, behavioural, social and emotional difficulties, and sensory difficulties. The severity and type of foetal damage caused by maternal alcohol use depends on a variety of factors including:

- level and duration of drinking
- pattern of drinking
- timing of alcohol used (stage of foetal development)

- blood alcohol level
- genetic influences
- maternal age and health – physiological effects
- post-natal factors (such as caregiver/child interactions and home environment).

Chapter 12 discusses some of the issues relating to working with children with FAS and their families.

Consanguinity

The Department of Health UK Strategy for Rare Diseases (DoH 2013) estimates that rare diseases, including genetic conditions, affect the lives of over three million people in the UK. Of these people, a significant proportion are children and young people with genetic life-limiting and life-threatening conditions.

Consanguinity is when closely related people who share a similar gene pool produce a baby. The consequences of this can mean that a baby is born with congenital deformities, which may be life-limiting, and may result in the baby developing complex medical needs. The culture of first cousins marrying within Muslim communities is deeply rooted and continues today. It is not unusual for the majority of pupils in special schools in inner-city areas to be predominantly of Pakistani Muslim heritage. Erica Brown has written a case study drawn from her research to illuminate the reasons why this practice continues.

CASE STUDY 10.1

Faizan was born in the UK to parents who were second cousins.

The pregnancy was a difficult one and, following a 20-week scan, Alia was referred to a consultant because the baby did not appear to be developing as expected. Jointly, the couple decided they did not want to undergo any invasive pre-natal testing of their unborn baby, regarding the sanctity of their baby's life as very important. However, Alia and Aziz were understandably very distressed and they sought support and advice from the hospital, the midwife and the leader of their religious community. The imam advised the couple to delay screening until after the baby's birth. The couple's son was born by emergency caesarean section at 32 weeks and, as his parents had feared, the baby was diagnosed with a rare genetic life-limiting condition, although the syndrome was not given a name.

DAD'S STORY

 I am 28 years old and my wife Alia is 22 years old.

Soon after we were married we began to talk about having a baby and Alia became pregnant quickly. Sadly she miscarried early on but within a few

(Continued)

(Continued)

months she fell pregnant again and the hospital kept a close eye on her. Our first scan was very positive and we were both so excited to have photos of our baby boy in the womb. But Alia started to become poorly as the pregnancy continued and the 20 week scan revealed that our baby was very small. The paediatrician suggested that we undergo tests to try and determine the cause of our baby's lack of growth but it did not seem the right decision. After all, our son was a gift from Allah and we had both been brought up to believe that our religion would guide us in all things. At 30 weeks baby showed signs of distress and Alia was admitted to hospital. We were told that he might not survive after he was born and we were advised to have a caesarean section. At 32 weeks our son was born and he had to be resuscitated several times. We were asked whether this was the course of action we wanted to take because he was a very sick baby and we were told that if he survived that he would have disabilities. But how could we let him die? We had talked to him in the womb, held him, changed his nappy and chosen his name. The moment we first heard Faizan cry we knew that he was truly a gift from God and that we would be given grace to sustain us in caring for him.

REFLECTION

Faizan's story highlights the conflicts that can arise when a cultural practice such as consanguinity, and a religious belief that children are a gift from God, clash with medical knowledge and guidance:

- Consider this situation from Faizan's parents' point of view – how could you explain the reasons for their choices to colleagues?

- What knowledge and skills do you need in order to be non-judgmental of parents who hold views that are different to your own?

Trauma
At birth

Being born remains a high-risk activity despite the level of expertise that is available. On occasions, the birth process can still go wrong and babies may experience a period of time without oxygen, usually because the umbilical cord becomes wrapped around the baby's neck and restricts the oxygen supply to the brain. The interruption to blood flow causes brain damage and the impact on the child's body will depend on which part of the brain is affected. For example, if the speech centre is damaged, the child's speech will be affected.

After an injury

Damage to the body after a trauma, especially to the central nervous system – that is, the brain and/or the spinal cord – can leave a legacy of complex medical needs.

Before a child with complex medical needs arrives in your setting, it is likely that the child and family will have experienced a traumatic time and the parents are likely to have faced difficult decisions. Case study 10.2 explains the perspective of Margaret, a sister on a paediatric intensive care unit.

CASE STUDY 10.2   PAEDIATRIC INTENSIVE CARE UNIT SISTER'S PERSPECTIVE

Following the baby's birth, what should be a time of intense joy and celebration becomes a time of intense anxiety and uncertainty. The babies are transferred to our unit for life-saving treatment. We then start to assess the babies and we are faced with the situation where we try to predict the outcomes for the child as a consequence of their early birth or congenital problem. This is a very difficult task because what I have come to realise is that each child is truly unique. A set of circumstances that is devastating for one child and family can have less of an impact on another. All we can do is give the information, based on research, of what are the most likely outcomes. To help with this, we prepare an advanced care plan, which outlines the likely outcomes for the child and includes the details of what the parents' role will be in keeping the child alive.

Naturally, this information is given at a time of high emotion. Many parents feel incredibly guilty that their baby is in this situation and they blame themselves. Therefore, they want to do all they can to keep their child alive and do all they can to support their child, no matter what the consequences. Many parents feel a sense of loss for the baby they imagined they were going to have, and the vulnerability and smallness of their baby means that they are prepared, at that moment, to do anything for them. Sometimes, the baby that arrives with us is a longed-for first baby. Or, sometimes, the baby may be a twin, the other baby having died or being perfectly healthy. This can add to the complexity of the situation because some parents find it difficult to understand why their baby is in this position.

Trying to get the balance between being realistic and appearing harsh is also difficult. We try to get the message over that it's not just a disabled child we're sending home, but, to some extent, a disabled family. It's not easy.

The unique child

As Case study 10.2 explains, it is impossible to predict how a child's complex medical needs will impact on development. The many health conditions that can cause children to have complex medical needs can impact each child in unique ways. The impact of the disability can be as individual as each child is unique. Therefore, getting to know the child and family using a holistic approach is important. As always, observations are a valuable tool to learn about the uniqueness of each child. Gaining an understanding of the child's age and stage of development is possibly even more important for children with complex medical needs. Their cognitive development may be much lower than that expected of their chronological age and their methods of communication frequently non-verbal. Some may exhibit a range of emotional responses, in relation to managing their behaviour and in controlling their emotions. Cognitive ability may be impaired; therefore, partly depending on the educational environment they are in, they may experience feelings of low self-esteem. On the other hand, the need to face the impact of their health condition may have given them the opportunity to develop resilience. The aim of all who are involved in the care of children with complex medical needs is to promote as good a quality of life as possible, and educators working with such children are uniquely placed to work with the child, their family and other professionals to achieve this aim.

Working with other professionals

A child with complex medical needs will have a range of professionals who make a contribution to their care. The care they deliver may be as specialists at hospital appointments, which can be many miles away from the child's home. On the other hand, a child with complex health needs may come into daily contact with professionals in their setting, for example physiotherapists or school nurses. However the care is planned, careful communication and collaboration with other professionals will be important. As the educator and carer of a child with complex medical needs, you may be the professional who knows the child best and, therefore, you will have an important role in liaising and communicating with other professionals.

Working with parents

Working with the parents of all children is important and has been a cornerstone of good practice in early childhood for centuries. Working with parents is discussed in Chapter 5, but it is worth highlighting here that your role in developing ways of working with the parents of children with complex medical needs is even more critical to you being able to keep their child healthy and safe. Building relationships with parents of children who are at a special school can be challenging because parents may have minimal contact with the school due to their children being transported in minibuses organised by the local authority rather than by parents. This situation means that since on-going communication may be less easy, other methods of communication are very important. Some parents may have SEN themselves, so it is important to ensure that the method of communication is accessible to the family and carers who continue the care at home. Chapter 4 includes a section on how Rachel Wright, the mother of Sam, who has cerebral palsy, uses a communication passport to explain Sam's care.

Legislation and policy

The National Framework for Children and Young People Continuing Care Guidance (Department of Health 2016) is designed to assist Clinical Commissioning when assessing the needs of children whose complex needs cannot be met by universal or targeted services. The guidance promotes a multi-agency approach to making suitable arrangements for the health and education of such children. The guidance states that 'at the heart of the arrangements is an integrated Education, Health and Care (EHC) plan' (p. 7).

See Chapter 4 for more information on SENDA and Pupil Premium funding.

Implications for practice

Supporting the health of children with complex medical needs requires you to develop clinical skills to keep children as healthy as possible, and in some cases to keep them alive.

RESEARCH FOCUS: CLINICAL SKILLS

The skills listed in this section are those that have been developed and implemented by practitioners to support the health of children with complex medical needs in settings. All of the skills require training by professionals to ensure they are carried out safely and the risk of infection is minimised.

TUBE FEEDING – GASTROSTOMY FEEDS

Many children with complex medical needs cannot eat orally and need to have a gastrostomy tube inserted through their skin as a surgical procedure. The child is then fed via the tube where the nutrients are absorbed in the gut. Clearly, this is a skill that requires you to have training to be able to carry it out safely. The content of the feed is a commercially produced liquid, which is available on prescription. Increasing numbers of parents are introducing blended diets for their children (see Chapter 7 for more on this aspect of care).

LIFTING AND HANDLING

Children with complex medical needs often have impaired movement and will need to be moved by their carers. It is important that immobile children are moved regularly to avoid pressure sores from developing and to stretch muscles which can become contracted. In Case study 10.3, Rosie Dunn, a student practitioner, explains why it is important for you to be able to move and handle children safely.

CASE STUDY 10.3

Whilst on placement within this setting, I carried out a 'moving and handling' course to qualify with the assistance of moving children in and out of their wheelchairs. One of the children with complex medical needs is physically disabled and therefore cannot move around the classroom without the help of practitioners. As a result of what I learned on the course, I was able to help promote his inclusion in more activities. For example, when taking the class swimming I was able to hoist the child in and out of the pool, ensuring

(Continued)

(Continued)

he was provided with the same opportunities to participate as the rest of his peers. By attending the course, I was following the school policy. The aim of the school policy was to reduce the risks of manual handling by ensuring that risk assessments are carried out and equipment is used wherever appropriate. For this particular child, a two-person lift is required and when transporting the child in and out of the pool, a hoist and sling must be used. The child will often be measured and weighed accordingly to assess whether he is placed in the correct sling to cater for his weight. Under no circumstances are staff permitted to lift the child out of the chair by themselves, as this is a hazard both to the child and the staff member, which could lead to injury.

REFLECTION

- Consider how Rosie's ability to handle and move the child means that he is included in the physical activity of swimming. How do you think this child is likely to feel? What is the impact on his wellbeing and physical health?

- How does Rosie's understanding of the policy and willingness to attend training help with inclusion?

Managing pain and keeping children comfortable

Children with a complex medical need which results in reduced or no mobility are prone to experiencing frequent episodes of pain and discomfort. Some children may require muscle relaxants to prevent joint pain and spasms. Physiotherapy and regular movement can help to prevent and relieve discomfort. By observing the child, you will learn the positions that are more comfortable for them and also learn their preferred positioning and where they require support with cushions and bean bags.

Administering medication

Medication is a daily requirement for many children with complex medical needs, however swallowing can be difficult or dangerous and medication may need to be given in alternative forms. For example, rectal administration of diazepam may be required to control epileptic seizures. Liquid or powder forms of medication may need to be administered via a feeding tube.

Maintaining the airway: suction

Children with muscle incapacity may not be able to cough or swallow and this can compromise their airway. Rosie explains how she learned to care for a child with a compromised airway whilst on placement in a special school:

Ben requires suctioning to help clear secretions when he coughs; as he cannot swallow, immediate intervention is vital to prevent him from aspirating.

Great Ormond Street Hospital (2015, online) explains that 'suction is used to clear retained or excessive lower respiratory tract secretions in patients who are unable to do so effectively for themselves'; this is to enable the child to breathe more comfortably. To help keep the chest clear from secretions that can lead to infection, the child is given a nebulizer twice throughout the school day to help loosen the secretions so that they can be removed easily with suction.

Being trained appropriately to use the suction machine is crucial, as those who do not know how to handle the equipment properly can cause more damage to the child's health. When suctioning the child, he may also need a mouth sweep; this procedure cannot go any further than the back teeth as suction tubes can lead to complications such as choking the child. In order to support the child with their condition, the nurse often carries out chest physiotherapy if they become chesty and start to have difficulty breathing. Chest physio helps to reduce obstruction in the airways and helps increase the amount of air getting into the lungs. Physiotherapy can lead to a decrease in the number of chest infections the child develops.

Ventilation

If the child's breathing is very compromised, it may be necessary to support it using a ventilator. This approach requires on-going management. The Together for Short Lives website has a useful supporting ventilation toolkit available free of charge (see further reading section for the web address).

Caring for a tracheostomy

Some conditions can compromise the upper airway between the nose and the trachea. A surgically created hole or 'stoma' can be created and a tube can be inserted into the trachea. The tracheostomy requires careful management, which includes suction and changing dressings to protect the skin and anchor the trache. Cleaning and changing the trache are essential to maintain its safety and efficacy.

Bladder and bowel support

Complex medical needs may mean that children require support with intimate care. Some may be incontinent and require pads for all of their life. Some children may require *intermittent bladder catheterisation* to empty their bladder. Some children may have under-developed or malfunctioning bowels and may require the formation of a hole or stoma on their abdomen. The child will have an ileosotomy or colostomy, the name referring to where in the bowel the stoma is created. During a surgical procedure, the bowel is brought on to the abdomen and a bag can be attached to collect faeces. The child will require *stoma care*.

Vagal nerve stimulator (VNS)

VNS therapy involves a small electrical device which is implanted under the skin of the chest. The device sends electrical impulses to the brain through a nerve in the neck called the vagus nerve. The aim is to reduce the number of seizures and make them less severe (Epilepsy Society 2012).

Intravenous lines

Intravenous lines are tubes inserted into veins for administering medication or fluids straight into the bloodstream.

REFLECTION

- What are the benefits to the child of having the same practitioner carry out management of these skilled interventions?

- What are the challenges to you in relation to meeting these needs for children and their families?

Including children with complex medical needs

The EYFS or National Curriculum may be inappropriate for children with complex medical needs, who may need a different approach. Rosie, a student practitioner, describes how her setting uses a therapy-based curriculum.

Therapy-based curriculum

Children with special educational needs and disabilities (SEND) may require a more individualised approach due to the nature of their learning difficulties. By practitioners constructing lessons based on therapy and sensory play, they are adding to the children's sense of wellbeing. By shaping a curriculum to suit their needs, practitioners design therapy programmes to help those with low muscle tone and stiffened joints to relax and feel at ease in their learning.

Physical activity

Enabling a child with a complex medical need that inhibits their mobility can be a challenge. However, it is extremely important that children with reduced mobility have exercise for all the reasons we know are important for children with full mobility. Children with physical disability are even more prone to becoming obese with all of the attendant health problems. In addition, keeping the weight of a child with reduced mobility within a healthy range will have benefits for the carers who handle the child.

The muscle tone of children with reduced mobility can often be poor, however physical activity helps to strengthen all of the muscles of the body. Ensuring that the respiratory muscles are toned as much as possible is important to reduce chest infections. Children with complex medical needs and with reduced physical mobility are especially prone to developing chest infections, which are potentially life-threatening and are a common cause of death in such children. Ensuring that respiratory muscles are working as well as possible is important to help children clear mucous from their chests. If mucous stagnates, this is when infection can set in. Many children have physiotherapy sessions daily to exercise the muscles of limbs and chest. Some practitioners work closely with physiotherapists to learn how to carry out the physio treatments in order to ensure that children do not miss out in the absence of the physiotherapist in the setting.

Swimming can be therapeutic for children with complex medical needs, however there is a need for consideration if a child has a tracheostomy or another intervention designed to support bodily functions. Because of the uniqueness of each child, it is difficult to give definitive guidance about the suitability of swimming. Health professionals involved in their care will be able to advise on this, although the electronic newsletter *Complex Child* is a very useful source of guidance about how to manage children and ensure their safety.

Play

Play may have a different meaning for children with complex medical needs. Embracing play on their terms is even more important for them. Lack of ability to move or a negative reaction to sensory overload can make play hard work for them. In the same way that you should be observing any child to identify their preferences, observing children who are non-verbal and have reduced mobility is vital to ensure that you learn what interests them.

Play can be used as a way of keeping children healthy, for example children with reduced respiratory function may enjoy blowing bubbles. Doing so helps to exercise their respiratory muscles and reduces the risk of chest infection.

Absence from the setting

Children with complex medical needs often have higher levels of absence because they:

- are more at risk of becoming unwell due to often having a low level of immunity, which makes them vulnerable to infections
- often need intimate care and management of their bodily fluids by staff, and, as outlined in Chapter 8, this can pose a greater risk of the spread of infection
- may not have been able to receive childhood immunisations
- are more likely to require attendance at hospital, either for check-ups or admission for procedures.

Hospital visits

Children with complex medical needs are more likely to need hospitalisation because of the on-going treatment they require (see Chapter 5 for more information on preparation for children going into hospital).

Conclusion

This chapter has included the perspectives of a range of people who work with children with complex medical needs. The insights revealed have highlighted some of the difficult situations that parents and families face. The findings from the research that informs much of this book demonstrate the extent to which you can play an invaluable role and experience high levels of job satisfaction in supporting the health of children with complex medical needs.

Further reading

Birmingham Children's Hospital (no date) What it's Like Here? Available at: www.bch.nhs. uk/whats-it-like/topics/getting-ready (accessed 17 July 2016).

Epilepsy Society (2012) Vagus Nerve Stimulation. Available at: www.epilepsysociety.org.uk/ vagus-nerve-stimulation#.V2BQ51deI_V

Wright, R. (2016) *The Skies I'm Under.* http://theskiesimunder.co.uk/#the_book

Useful websites

Complex Child (an electronic newsletter) – http://complexchild.org

Together for Short Lives (a charity that supports children, families and professionals involved with children who have life-threatening and life-limited conditions) – www.togetherforshortlives. org.uk/professionals/childrens_palliative_care_essentials/definitions

11

COPING WITH THE DEATH OF A CHILD

CHAPTER AIMS AND OBJECTIVES

- To explain the causes and circumstances of child deaths
- To be able to share the experiences of practitioners who have been in the situation of having to cope with the death of a child in their setting

As you read the chapter, you are encouraged to consider:

- how equipped you are, and the colleagues you work with, to respond to the death of a child
- the knowledge and skills useful in helping you to cope
- if you have experienced the death of a child in your setting, how similar or different was your experience, and what have you learned from the experience to take forward in your professional and personal life?

Introduction

Government statistics (DfE 2015) reveal that there has been a reduction in the number of child deaths, however it is inevitable that despite medical advances and our awareness of health and safety, which have led to a reduction in child mortality, there will always be children who die.

The death of a child is always a tragic event, whether the death has been expected or is sudden and unexpected. Whatever the circumstances surrounding a child's death, there are implications for practitioners, families and the children in the setting. The death of a child is an event that is unthinkable to many of us, and you may wonder how you would cope. This chapter encourages you to consider how you can draw on your own inner resources and work with colleagues to make the event as bearable as possible for those involved and affected by the death.

Causes and numbers of death

The Department for Education collates the results of the reviews of child deaths annually. In March 2015, there were 3,515 deaths of children in England. The causes of children's deaths vary depending on their age; the first year of life is the most vulnerable. There are socio-economic, geographical and ethnic influences on child mortality.

Peri-natal period

A third of the child death reviews in 2015 were carried out on babies who died at birth, or 27 days after birth, usually as a consequence of being born with a condition that is life-limiting, such as a genetically inherited condition.

Children with complex medical needs

The March 2015 statistics revealed that 2,870 of the total deaths were as a consequence of a child's known health condition, with 149 deaths occurring in a hospice. In some cases the death of a child has been anticipated, for example children who survive the immediate post-natal period, when previously they would have died during or after birth, and are left with complex medical conditions that cause a degeneration of major body organs and are life-limiting. Children with complex medical needs are prone to life-threatening illnesses as a consequence of their condition. Some children have an impaired swallowing reflex and every time they eat or drink, they run the risk of aspirating into their lungs. This can cause pneumonia, which in some cases is fatal. Again, because of the deficiencies in the functioning of their bodies, infectious diseases can be very serious, and it is not uncommon for children with complex medical needs to die of dehydration following a virus.

Death as a consequence of accidental injury

After infancy, a common cause of death in children is road traffic accidents. There is a marked difference in the number of deaths of children between different socio-economic groups. A child is 13 times more likely to die from accidental injury, and 37 times more likely to die from the effects of house fire, if their parent(s) are unemployed, or have never worked, compared to the number of children in working families (Blair et al. 2010).

Death as a consequence of non-accidental injury and neglect

The exact figure of child deaths caused by non-accidental injury (NAI) or neglect is calculated to be three a week (NSPCC 2014). The incidence of children dying from NAI is higher in lower socio-economic groups.

Unexplained causes of death

Death as a consequence of an undiagnosed medical condition accounts for 10% of child death reviews.

Responses to the death of a child

As stated earlier, the death of a child is fortunately rare, however the enormity of such an event has implications for everyone who was involved in the child's life. The terms bereavement and grief are words often associated with death. In order to understand the responses to death, it is helpful to understand the terms associated with the emotional response that most people experience.

Bereavement is defined as the loss of a loved one, usually as a consequence of death.

Grief is defined as the deep mental anguish and emotional response to bereavement.

Anticipatory grief is the experience of imagining the loss of someone whose death is predicted. This is an emotion often experienced by parents who have a child with a life-limiting or life-threatening health condition. Rachel Wright is the mother of Sam who has cerebral palsy and complex medical needs. She writes in her book, *The Skies I'm Under* (2016, p. 194), about the anticipation of Sam's death:

> When I no longer have Sam, I won't grieve for what he could have been or what he failed to realise. I have been grieving those things since the day he was born. When I no longer have Sam, I will grieve that I no longer have Sam. I will miss him and miss our relationship. In the deepest way I will ache at no longer living with his spirit and character in my life and my home. I will miss the atmosphere and presence he creates by simply being him.

Bereavement has often been described as a 'process' or as having 'stages'. For example, the work of Elizabeth Kubler-Ross (1969) names five stages of the bereavement process, which are denial, anger, bargaining, depression and acceptance. Kubler-Ross's work has been widely accepted, but, as she pointed out herself in later work, this 'model' of bereavement is not typical and not everybody experiences the same responses. Whilst it is useful to have theories or research that inform our understanding of why things are the way they are, believing that becoming bereft of a loved one is a life event that one can go through a process of, via stages, implies that, at some point, the process will come to an end and that this part of life can be put down to experience and tidily put away. Going through 'stages' suggests that there is only time for grieving at that time. However, for many people, the 'process' of grief never ends and may stay with them for the rest of their lives. This can especially be the case for the family of a much-loved child.

The emotions that accompany the grief associated with bereavement can include anger and sorrow, which are emotions that most people will have experienced in their lives at some point. What is different about these emotions following a bereavement are the extremes of emotion, one moment laughing hysterically at a happy memory and the next moment, sobbing as the waves of loss threaten to overcome you. Understanding the emotions and the speed at which they can change following bereavement is helpful to know that this is a normal reaction.

Personal view

My daughter, Nicky, died unexpectedly and suddenly, aged 18 in 2006. We saw her at lunchtime on the day she died; she appeared as normal, perhaps a little tired and paler than usual. Her dad and I thought it was because she had been burning the candle at both ends; she was working in a pub to boost her student income and she was loving life. Seven hours after we last saw her, she died from an undiagnosed heart condition. In the initial hours and days following Nicky's death, I experienced extremes of emotions and in order to try and understand what was happening, I wrote down my thoughts:

> At the moment I feel numb, why am I not crying and full of anguish? How can I even think about doing something like writing down what is happening? I feel as if I have had an anaesthetic and it all seems bearable. The numbness is paralysing me, almost literally, I couldn't walk properly this morning, I didn't realise that grief could affect someone in such a physical way. This must be the 'shock' stage that I glibly used to describe to student nurses in my teaching. I feel so debilitated, how on earth am I supposed to do the ordinary, everyday things like cooking? How can I think about eating when I will never have my first-born daughter sitting at our table and eating with us ever again?

In the event of a child's death

An initial reaction to hearing about an unexpected death of a previously healthy child is often one of disbelief: 'Oh no', we often say, 'are you serious?' This can be followed by a sense of shock, which can make thinking straight difficult. As an ethical practitioner, your first thought may be: how can I keep this confidential? But, of course, it is impossible to keep a death confidential, though it is usually entirely appropriate to keep the events surrounding the death confidential. In the immediate aftermath of hearing the news of a child's death, there can be a sense of unreality and a feeling that it is very difficult to carry on as normal; in fact, it can feel disrespectful to the dead child to carry on as normal. At this time, it can feel as if nothing will ever be normal again. There are different perspectives to consider when a child in your setting dies. The following points are drawn from Jacky Avins' reflections on her experience as a manager following the unexpected death of a child in her setting:

- *The other children* will pick up on your distress and/or sadness and it will be important to respond to their questions.
- *Colleagues* may not have experienced death before, let alone the death of a child. The child's key person may have a special bond with the child and be especially upset, although such feelings are not confined to the key person and many staff may feel similarly.
- *Student practitioners on placement* may feel adrift and require support.
- *Other professionals* may have been in contact with the child in the setting.
- *The child's parents* – depending on the relationship you have with the child and family and the circumstances, it is likely that you will be in contact with the parents.

- *Other parents* will be upset and will require information about the circumstances of the death. It is particularly important to give factual information, especially if the death is sudden and unexpected, in order to allay fears, for example parents may worry about an infectious disease.
- *Police and Ofsted inspectors* will be involved if the death is sudden and unexpected in order to investigate any suspicious circumstances that may surround the death.
- *Journalists* may approach the setting if the death is thought to be newsworthy.

Legal requirements

In the first instance, a doctor needs to confirm a death. The coroner will be informed and, in some circumstances, a post-mortem may be carried out to determine the cause of death. In some cases, an inquest will be held.

Registration of the death and the issue of a death certificate are necessary before funeral arrangements can be made. The child death overview panel will examine the reasons and circumstances surrounding the death.

The need for leadership

It is important that someone takes the lead in managing the events following the death of a child, especially if it is an unexpected death. Because the impact of such an event is so great, it is worthwhile considering how you would respond to the unthinkable happening. Obviously, this is not an event that anyone would want to have to deal with, but thinking ahead and considering how you and your setting would manage it, is similar to the disaster and emergency planning that the NHS and the emergency services do.

Very rarely, a child dies in a setting, for example following a fall or from choking. This is an extremely difficult experience for a setting to endure. It is hard to accept that even when you've taken preventative steps, such as having policies in place that are designed to maintain the health and safety of children, a child can die. The death of a child in your care can understandably create feelings of intense guilt and deep regret. The process of coming to terms with a death occurring in such circumstances will be more difficult because of police and Ofsted investigations and possibly bad publicity. There will be a need for staff in such circumstances to engage with expert support in order to be able to manage their feelings.

Informing people

It is important that all involved are informed of the death. This needs to be done with sensitivity, and it is best to use plain language and to avoid platitudes and clichés. Colleagues need to know first of all, and this can be challenging. How to inform young children can be an area of conflict with other parents, who may be concerned about their child being burdened by such knowledge. Clearly, this requires careful handling and is an example of why it is a good idea to consider how you would work with other parents in the event of the death of a child. It is helpful to consider how you would give explanations and talk to children about death. Using phrases like 'fallen asleep' are not helpful to young children. Drawing on other experiences, such as the death of a family member or a pet, can help to frame the experience for a child.

Supporting the parents and family

The level of involvement you have with parents following the death of a child will vary depending on several factors. For example, if the child has siblings in your setting, it will be necessary for the parents to continue to attend the setting. The circumstances of the death may also influence the level of involvement you have with the parents. For example, if the child died as a consequence of a car crash, the parents and other family members may also have died or received injuries. If the family was abroad, reaching out to them may be more difficult. If a death happens over the summer holiday period and your setting is a school, news of the death may not reach you until several weeks afterwards. If there is suspicion surrounding the death, you may not be allowed to contact the parents. If the death of a child was anticipated, and the child was absent from the setting prior to the death, your relationship may appear to have diminished.

The support you offer the parents will partly depend on the relationship that you and your colleagues have with them. If the relationship is a warm and reciprocal one, it may be easier to reach out and offer support; after all, besides the parents, you and your colleagues may be the people who know the child best, so it will be natural that you share their grief.

The level of support that you offer will also depend on the family structure and the extent to which various family members are involved with the setting. If the siblings attend your setting, you may be an important source of on-going support for them. Especially poignant are the needs of a surviving twin, especially if the pair were identical twins. It is not difficult to imagine the acute sense of loss that is experienced by a surviving twin. The grief of grandparents can sometimes be overlooked; many grandparents play an active part in their grandchildren's care and if they are involved in your setting they may turn to you for support. They may feel a deep sense of injustice that their grandchild has died.

Single parents may have less support in their grief. Parents who have one of their children die, frequently turn to their other children for solace and purpose. However, parents who lose their only child are likely to have an extra dimension to their grief because of the complete loss of their offspring.

Children who have kinship carers, that is, carers who are related to the child but who are not their biological parents, have often experienced difficult situations that have resulted in them not being able to live with their parents. For example, a child born to a mother who was involved in substance abuse during her pregnancy, may have complex medical needs as a consequence of the impact of drugs and/or alcohol on their development in utero. Such circumstances around the child's death may add additional emotions into the mix for kinship carers.

Culture and religion

Culture and religion are different concepts that are frequently used interchangeably. There are many cultural and religious traditions that influence people's responses to a child's death and the arrangements for the funeral. The diversity of the UK means that there are a great number of cultures and religions within the population. In the event of a child's death, it is good ethical practice to be aware of the traditions of the family so that you can identify what your role may be in supporting that family. However, it is important that you do not make assumptions about the family's preferences or decisions based on what you think you know about their culture or religion. For example, a family who is not religious may choose to have a funeral in church.

Cultural and religious influences on death

Gaining an understanding of the influence of religion on how a parent responds to the death of their child will be helpful to you in identifying ways to support the parents.

Parents who hold strong religious faith may find comfort in their beliefs following the death of their child. A belief that their child is in heaven can be a comfort. Rachel Wright describes how, at the funeral of a child, Aidan, who died as a consequence of complex medical needs, 'we were encouraged by the priest to celebrate Aidan's life and have confidence that he was in heaven, doing cartwheels' (2016, p. 195). For the parents of a child who was severely disabled, it is easy to understand how such an image may be a comfort to them. On the other hand, parents may feel let down by their God and angry about the death of their child; and at a time when they have great need of their religion, they may turn away from it and reject the solace that they need. This may especially be the case if their child was killed in a needless or senseless way.

It is important to bear in mind that some people hold strong beliefs about abortion and will not consider terminating a pregnancy because of an abnormality. Consequently, there is a high risk of such babies dying early because of a condition that is likely to result in complex medical needs.

Erica Brown has shared Faizan's story to illustrate this point. Faizan was born in the UK to parents who were second cousins. His father Aziz describes his approach to Faizan's death:

> Faizan was allowed home from hospital but we were told that he had a very complex genetic abnormal medical condition and that he was life-threatened. Alia and I were advised to use contraception and to delay our decision that we would fulfil our role as parents by having another child as a brother or a sister to Faizan. Tragically Faizan died at 13 days old.
>
> When we consider our duty as parents we understand what the doctors have said to us but we also believe that tragedy can happen to anyone whether they are Muslim cousins or not. Faizan was an angel and we miss him even though his life was so short. But we do not feel alone. We were chosen by Allah to be Faizan's parents and we believe that as Muslims we do not own our children, we hold them in trust for Allah who gives them to us. It was Allah's will that he took our baby Faizan back to his home.

N.B. Names have been changed to protect the anonymity of the parents and their child.

Cultural and religious influences on funerals

In some cultures, a funeral is a private affair and attended by family and close friends. However, when the funeral is for a child, there may be less inhibition.

A child's death creates a strong reaction to the unfairness of life; there is a sense of unfinished business for a life cut short. Often, the parents are keen to share their child's life with all involved. Funerals are an opportunity to show the family your support and to demonstrate your regard both for them and the child. It is a mark of respect to share in saying farewell to the child.

In recent times, some people have moved away from having a solemn event where the mourners wear black towards holding a celebration of the child's life. Again, the decision made by the parents about their child's funeral may depend on the circumstances of the death. It is not unusual for a child who was old enough to understand that they were dying, to have a say in organising their own funeral. It may be surprising to discover that the funeral of a much-loved child can be an uplifting and joyful occasion. Conversely, for a child who is not at the centre of a family and, for instance, has been in care and was not surrounded by loved ones, the funeral may be a more solemn and joyless event. Funerals can be as unique as the child who has died. Many people are anxious about attending a child's funeral and can worry about their own response to the unknown and what is going to be a sad event. However, it is important to bear in mind that attending the funeral may be the last act of respect that you can pay to a child who has attended your setting. One of the concerns you may have about attending is what the parents' wishes are about you being there, therefore it is important to approach the parents and let them know that you would like to attend. Naturally, this needs to be done with sensitivity, so check with the parents that they are happy for you, and possibly colleagues, to represent this part of the child's life.

Obviously, there are religious practices that influence the kind of funeral that is arranged for the child. Erica Brown, in Brown and Warr (2007), describes how in Chinese culture the death of a child is regarded as a 'bad' death and parents and grandparents are not expected to go to the funeral. In England, the body following death is either buried or cremated. In some religions, one method of disposal is more acceptable than the other. It is important to be aware that there can be a clash of cultural expectations, and to be understanding and accepting. Whatever the cultural or religious influences, or the circumstances of a child's death, there are practical issues relating to the funeral service and there are ways that you and your colleagues can make a contribution to the memory of the child.

Jacky writes about her decision to attend the child's funeral:

> The next step was the funeral. I felt it was right, having shared everything as a team that we went to the funeral together, especially as some staff had never been to a funeral before, never mind a child's funeral. I talked to them all about what to expect, especially the size of the coffin. I gave notice to all the other nursery parents and we closed for the day, they were completely supportive of this decision.

Jacky asked her staff if, on reflection, they thought that attending the funeral was the right thing to do. They responded with the following:

> Yes, we all cared for her and knew her family very well. We bonded together and I'm sure that helped everyone emotionally. We were her nursery family.

Remembering the child

It is likely that your setting was a very important part of the child's life and you will instinctively want to preserve the memory of the child and celebrate the life of the child. There are various ways you can capture the essence of the child.

Following the death of my daughter, I received a memory book which had been initiated by her tutor. In the book, students and other tutors had written messages and drawn illustrations. This was hugely comforting and remains a treasured keepsake. In a similar way, you may want to ask children and their families and staff to write messages and draw pictures for a memory book for the family. Depending on the age and stage of development of the child at the time of death, you can include work, a learning journey or any memorabilia that will capture and celebrate the child's life in your setting.

Supporting others

Supporting other children

The age and stage of the children in the setting will influence their understanding of the death of a child. It is generally around the age of 7 that children understand that death is permanent. However, young children will be affected by the death of a friend. Brown and Warr (2007) explains that young children develop strategies to help them cope with events in their world. Such strategies can include play involving getting rid of bad and scary monsters. Young children will often ask the same questions repeatedly as they try to make sense of what has happened. It is important that they are answered using consistent and honest responses.

Even if the other children did not know the child or are very young, they will pick up on the atmosphere in the setting and this may impact on their behaviour. Following the usual routines of the setting will be very reassuring for children and for staff.

Besides play, children may gain understanding and make sense of the death of a friend by having books read to them. Michael Rosen's (2004) *Sad Book* is a delightful resource, which conveys the emotions that accompany grief as well as offering some achievable strategies for children, such as doing one thing every day that means they have a good time.

For older, primary school children with greater understanding of the permanence of death, Erica Brown has written a handbook to help support them (see further reading section).

Supporting staff

Jacky and her staff were able to support each other during the time they were bereaved of the child in their setting. How successfully staff in other settings manage to support each other in a similar way will depend on the relationships within the setting, between the staff and with parents. As pointed out previously, the circumstances of the death may also impact greatly on your response to the bereavement. Counsellors who specialise in bereavement are available and can be very useful to help you to understand the emotional response. But do remember that as long as you are well informed, your own resources and emotional intelligence will be helpful to respond appropriately. Do not be tempted to rely on bereavement counsellors as the main source of support; to do so may diminish confidence in your ability to manage and lead using your own instincts and knowledge about all involved. It is also useful to bear in mind that the concept of bereavement counselling is a relatively new one; in previous times, support was gained from the community. In many countries of the world, the concept of having a professional who is unknown to the individuals as a support in this time of need would be an alien one. This is because communities are able to support each other in their grief.

After the death of a child in her setting, Jacky asked her staff what helped them to cope with this event. They said the following:

- talking to others including the child's parents because I felt I was helping them; tell your family (if you can) and talk to other staff
- highlighting the positives in that child's life and remembering all the good times
- being given the OK to talk about it at work
- crying (not too much at work)
- time – take time, we all coped in different ways
- keeping busy at work and at home
- the website was useful but a bit impersonal.

Her staff found the following difficult:

- seeing and speaking with the parents and the sister for the first time
- seeing the child without her sister
- explaining to the other children why the child was not coming back to nursery
- explaining to the others why I was sad
- gathering up the child's things
- finishing her learning journey for her parents
- some days, just being in nursery and remembering her.

It would seem that the most helpful support mechanism for Jacky's setting was the opportunity to talk. Opportunities to talk may be informal, bearing in mind the proximity of others, especially children; or, in the early days, it may be a good idea to have a gathering of staff to check how everyone's day has gone. Some staff may find this helpful, though others may not.

The future

For anyone who has experienced the death of someone they love, whether in a personal or professional sense, in the early days one can wonder how life can ever be the same again. The truth is that life may never be the same again; it will be different and gradually people adjust to what becomes 'the new normal'. The 'new normal' is how Alice Terry (2012, p. 359) described the change in her life following her daughter's death. The passage of time usually helps to make reaching the 'new normal' more bearable, but how much time is an individual experience.

Caring for yourself

If you have been the member of staff who had to show leadership in managing the consequences of the death of a child in your workplace, it is important to be aware that doing so will draw on your emotional resources. It is likely to be one of the most challenging experiences of your professional life. You will be thinking deeply about your responses and may be anxious that you are doing 'the right thing'. Your levels of adrenaline will be high during the initial period; as events start to calm down and the 'new normal' emerges, you may find yourself exhausted and your emotions depressed. This is the time to ensure that you are looking after yourself and are taking time to do things that improve your wellbeing.

Conclusion

To a large extent, coping with the death of a child in your setting is a life event that cannot be taught. As with many events, living through them is what enhances your knowledge and skills. The purpose of this chapter is to help you consider how you can support all involved, especially the other children affected by the death. If you have had such an experience, perhaps you can reflect on how the event has helped you develop as a person and professionally. As one of Jacky's staff said:

I feel if it ever happened again I would still react in the same way but I would be more confident about how to deal with things like talking to the other children about death, and being less worried about talking to the child's parents.

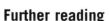

Further reading

Erica Brown has written resources to draw on to gain greater understanding of how to support bereaved children:

Brown, E. (2009) Supporting Bereaved Children: A handbook for primary schools. London: Help the Hospices. www.helpthehospices.org.uk

Brown, E. and Warr, B. (2007) *Supporting the Child and the Family in Paediatric Palliative Care*. London: Jessica Kingsley Publishing. This book includes information about religious influences on death and funerals.

Rosen, M. (2004) *Sad Book*. London: Walker Books.

Useful websites

Child Bereavement UK (comprehensive guidance and resources for families and professionals) – www.childbereavementuk.org/files/9314/0868/7136/Publications_Leaflet.pdf

NICE guidelines – www.nice.org.uk/guidance/GID-CGWAVE0730/documents/short-version-of-draft-guideline

12

APPLYING THEORY TO PRACTICE

Allergy

Allergy is an increasingly common contemporary health issue that affects children in developed countries. Moving from a simple lifestyle to a more complex one, where the use of antibacterials and antibiotics is commonplace, is one theory to explain why there is an increase in the number of children developing a range of allergies. Other contributory factors are changes to living conditions because of a move from draughty houses to homes that are sealed units. Most houses are insulated with double glazing and have sealed chimneys and this has led to a proliferation of the house dustmite which is linked with allergy. A common combination of allergy-related conditions is asthma, eczema and allergic rhinitis (allergy affecting the nasal passages and resulting in a runny nose).

Exposure to an allergenic substance at first contact can be uneventful, however the body's immune system works to produce an immune response. Consequently, the next time the allergen is ingested or inhaled, there is an overwhelming allergic response. Allergies can have a profound negative impact on children's quality of life.

Anaphylaxis

Anaphylaxis is a severe allergic reaction to a range of everyday substances. Common allergens that can trigger an anaphylactic reaction include fruit, nuts, kiwi and lactose. This means that the provision of food in settings requires a great deal of thought. Marilyn Duggins, who was assistant head at a large primary school, with a large number of children with allergies and anaphylaxis, shares the main points of her setting's policy for managing school meals for children with allergies and anaphylaxis:

Management of allergies policy

- On registration for a nursery place, parents are asked if their child has any needs.
- Prior to entry all parents have a 20–30-minute meeting with their child's key practitioner, phase leader and year leader responsible for nursery.
- All staff attend annual training on allergies and asthma.
- Some staff hold a current certificate for paediatric first aid. At least one member of staff is always in nursery and a first aider accompanies children on trips.
- All children with allergies have an individual care plan, which is displayed in the nursery and a copy is kept in the child's group register.
- Epipens/antihistamines are kept on a high shelf in the staff area. Each child has their own zip wallet containing their medication, a copy of their care plan and emergency telephone numbers.
- All phones have a yellow sheet on the wall next to the phone, including the school procedure for dialling an ambulance. The school postcode and telephone number are clearly displayed.
- All staff are aware of which children have allergies.
- There is a list on the kitchen wall to remind staff of foods that children with allergies must avoid prior to cooking/snack preparation.
- With parental permission, children wear an individually made badge.
- Frequent letters are sent to all parents to remind them not to allow children to bring any food into nursery.
- Nursery is a nut-free environment at all times.
- Parents are asked to sign a consent form giving permission to staff to administer medication. The form includes a statement informing parents that it is their responsibility to ensure the medication is in date.
- School keeps a database of all medication and expiry dates so we do our best to ensure medication is in date but it is ultimately the parents' responsibility.
- We work closely with health professionals at the allergy clinic and the children's hospital, as well as with health visitors and school nurses working in the community.
- School employs its own nurse paid for from the school budget.
- When children with an allergy leave nursery, the practitioner is supplied with a bum bag to put medication and the child's care plan in. Such children never leave nursery without medication, even to another part of the school.

- Practitioners teaching outside wear a whistle to summon emergency help.
- In school, in order to be able to summon emergency help, all classrooms and teaching areas have a 'red hand' which includes the location of where help is needed. This is given to a child to take to the main office to summon emergency help.

Reception dinners

- All dinner staff are made aware of children with allergies.
- Names and photos are displayed in the serving area.
- All reception classes have their own dinner supervisor who comes to know the children well.
- When children first start in reception, on entering the dinner hall they wear a high-visibility jacket. This is because the serving hatch is high up and catering staff can't see the child's badge.
- At first, a member of staff takes children with allergies into dinner before other children.
- Children are encouraged to know about their allergy and to develop the confidence to tell people about it.
- Children are encouraged not to share food.

REFLECTION

- How does the above detailed policy help to support children with anaphylaxis to food?

- How could this policy be adapted for your setting?

- What are the factors that will make this policy work successfully?

- What are the implications for working with all parents to make this policy work?

Asthma

Asthma is a chronic condition that can have a profound impact on children's wellbeing. Asthma is potentially life-threatening. In 2011, 18 children aged 14 and under died from an asthma attack (Asthma UK 2014). Karen, a manager at a large day-care setting, describes how she enables the environment and reduces the triggers for children with asthma:

We have had to adapt a few activities for children with asthma. For example, we used bark and straw in the role play area at Christmas time. This triggered some children's asthma symptoms, so it had to be removed from the room.

For some of the physical activities that take place both inside and outdoors, staff have to remember that some physical activities can affect the child's breathing.

This means they have to bear in mind the length of time they plan for some activities so that the children don't become over-exerted because this can trigger their asthma symptoms. In case children start to get asthma symptoms, inhalers are located in the child's room and they are taken outside when children are completing any physical activity. We have a medications policy for when we give inhalers to the children. The parents sign medical consent forms and careful records are kept of when we need to give inhalers. Practitioners are required to complete records prior to and after administering any medication, including inhalers.

All children with health needs such as asthma have a healthcare plan. They are really useful to help us understand children's asthma. The information is used to plan safe play opportunities to meet individual children's needs. It also informs us of how to respond appropriately if a child has an asthma attack. We rely on parents and carers to keep us updated and notify us of any changes to their child's health needs.

REFLECTION

What steps can you take to enable the environment for children with asthma?

Breastfeeding support

A reason that is given for mothers giving up breastfeeding is because they are returning to work. Student practitioner, Abi, describes how she supported a mum who wanted to continue breastfeeding:

Charlotte is 2 months old and her mum wants to continue breastfeeding after she returns to work. She is committed to the idea of breastfeeding and determined to breastfeed her baby because she believes that 'breast is best'. She has approached the setting to find out how they can help to support her to continue breastfeeding when she returns to work. She intends to return to work when her baby is 3 months old, although she has said that she may go into the office for short periods of time for meetings soon after the baby is born.

Abi describes how she approached this new initiative for her setting:

Charlotte's mum was really motivated and knowledgeable; she explained that part of the motivation was because there was a strong family history of eczema and asthma and she knew that breastfeeding could reduce the chances of Charlotte developing these conditions. In order to be able to supply us with enough breast milk, mum bought a pump and would express milk and store it in a sterile bottle. We decided that Charlotte's transition to nursery would include periods of time where mum could breastfeed her in the setting. She would then introduce Charlotte to expressed breast milk via a bottle. Then, as Charlotte's key person, I would give Charlotte bottles of expressed breast milk. This approach worked really well: Charlotte was really adaptable and very quickly she moved between breast and expressed breast milk bottle feeds with ease. Mum knew that she could come in any time and breastfeed Charlotte and she did do this in the first few weeks when she wasn't at work full time. However, I think it was more for mum's benefit than for Charlotte's!

Careful labelling and storage of the expressed breast milk is required so that the milk is not given to another baby. However, this is the same as for any bottle feeds that are brought in by parents.

REFLECTION

What are the benefits to Charlotte, her mum and the setting as a consequence of supporting mum's wish to continue breastfeeding?

Coeliac disease

Student practitioner, Jessica Houlston, explains how her knowledge of Lucy's family and knowledge of coeliac disease helped her to plan for Lucy' needs:

Lucy is a 6-year-old girl who has been diagnosed with coeliac disease. Coeliac disease is an autoimmune condition where the immune system mistakenly attacks the healthy tissue. Lucy's body mistakes the protein, called gliadin, in gluten as a threat to the body and attacks it. This causes damage to the lining of the small intestine. A gluten-free diet is required to prevent this damage (NICE 2016a). Lucy lives with her mum and dad and her younger sister. Both parents work, with mum working part time to allow for more time with the children. Lucy is a confident little girl who regularly discusses her condition with her friends; and she and is aware of what she can and cannot eat.

The NICE guidance for coeliac disease (2015) is very useful when it comes to dealing with Lucy's condition and provides valuable information for practitioners and parents. The guidelines enable them to understand more about the condition and how it can be managed. The guidance covers the recognition, assessment and management of the condition, as well as information relating to diagnosis.

It is important to plan activities to ensure that Lucy does not come into contact with gluten whilst ensuring that she fully engages with her environment. This means that sensory activities can be problematic, especially activities including play dough or spaghetti. In my setting, we used gluten-free flour in the playdough; this was a safe option for Lucy and was an inclusive approach because it could be used for all children within the setting and it ensured that Lucy's participation was maximised.

Lucy's condition means that her family faces added pressure. The condition can limit the choice of restaurants and also holiday destinations because careful research is required to ensure that they provide gluten-free options, making spur-of-the-moment plans very difficult. The condition can also provide additional financial pressure because gluten-free brands are more expensive. If Lucy becomes ill, her parents may also have to identify the cause and trace the source. This can be as simple as having gluten-free bread cooked in the same toaster as normal bread. The parents have been able to build up a wealth of knowledge on the condition and become experts on the child's health and the effect on the family (Brown 2009). This can be linked to the socio-economic status of the parents and Bourdieu's (1986) theory of cultural capital (in Bourdieu and Passeron 2000). It emphasises the importance of developing positive relationships and forms of communication between the setting and parents with regard to any changes in Lucy's health. Whilst this may not always be an easy process, it is crucial to develop these relationships in the best interests of the child (MacNaugton and Hughes 2009).

REFLECTION

- Consider how you can include a child with coeliac disease in your setting.

- What are the possible consequences for children with coeliac disease if parents do not support their child in the way that Lucy's parents do?

Dental caries

Student practitioner, Anna Cook describes the impact of Eli's dental caries on his development and education:

Eli had a very severe case of dental caries. Children's milk teeth start to fall out by the age of 5, to make way for adult teeth (NHS 2015b). Eli had a mixture of both milk and adult teeth, which were black and rotten. He was very conscious of his poor dental health and rarely opened his mouth to smile or talk. As a result, he had speech and language impairments and had daily one-to-one lessons with a speech and language therapist (SLT), the aim being to encourage him to open his mouth wider when he spoke and to learn to pronounce his words correctly. He often became frustrated and angry when failing to enunciate words correctly, which sometimes resulted in violent and aggressive behaviour and the whole year 2 class having to vacate the room.

As a result of poor speech and language development, along with little help and support at home, Eli's academic attainment suffered to the point of requiring daily interventions. This was made possible by the school, since the boy was entitled to claim the Pupil Premium grant, a sum of money, £1320 in 2015, claimed for each disadvantaged pupil, to be spent on addressing the child's individual issues to improve their attainment (Ofsted 2012).

REFLECTION

- What do you think your role is in supporting Eli? What are your thoughts about Heads et al.'s (2013) view that dental caries should be regarded as a sign of maltreatment?
- How could you work with Eli's parents?

Such is the scale of the problem of dental caries to children's health that many settings are taking on the responsibility for promoting dental hygiene in their settings. Read in the following how Paramjit developed this aspect of supporting children's dental health.

Paramjit has recently taken on the role of team leader for the pre-school children in the nursery where she works. The nursery is in an area of socio-economic deprivation and the majority of the children are entitled to free childcare. Paramjit is shocked at the condition of many of the 3-year-olds' teeth because many have advanced tooth decay. When she looks at the notes made by the health visitor during the 2-year-old health and development checks, she sees that the condition of the children's teeth has been noted. She contacts the health visitor, Miriam, to find out more about the children's teeth. Miriam explains that many parents are unaware of the importance of looking after children's first or 'deciduous' teeth because 'they are going to fall out anyway'. Paramjit is told about a 5-year-old who had to have an operation requiring a general anaesthetic in order to remove the child's teeth. Miriam pointed out that this meant that the child had an operation for an avoidable condition and even though general anaesthetic is mostly safe, there is still the possibility of an adverse reaction to it.

REFLECTION

- How can you promote good dental hygiene in your setting?
- How do you think good dental hygiene links to good wellbeing?

Eczema

Eczema is a common chronic health condition and there are compelling reasons for greater understanding of how eczema can affect children aged 3 and under so that adults can adapt children's environments in order to make them inclusive. First, it is now realised that eczema can be present in children in subtle forms, and the effect on children of a small patch of eczema can be just as profound as a larger area (Van Onselen 2009). Second, the physiological differences in the structure of white and black skin mean that eczema symptoms can appear milder in people with skin of colour, however the impact can be greater and more painful than it would be for white skin (Kelly and Taylor 2009). Both of these are examples of facts that may not be widely known, but this lack of awareness may mean that adults in children's environments may underestimate the effect of eczema on children and, as a result, practitioners may miss an opportunity to adapt the environment for children with seemingly 'mild' eczema, and, as a consequence, children may have reduced educational opportunities. Corrie describes how she worked with Ben to maximise his inclusion during a visit to the farm:

> In my placement, I work with Ben in a childminding setting; the childminder often takes the children to the local farm where they can participate in feeding the cows and sheep. This involves handling straw and hay, which can cause Ben's eczema to become very itchy and sore. Ben thoroughly enjoys visiting the farm and getting involved with feeding so the childminder worked with his mother to find a way that would allow Ben to fully enjoy the activity without risking him discomfort or pain. Ben's mother provided him with an extra long-sleeved top to wear to the farm and remove again once he returned. The majority of Ben's eczema was on the inside of his elbows and forearms so wearing a long-sleeved top that could be washed enabled him to feed the animals. The childminder applied Ben's medication, which is an ointment prescribed by the doctor, before and after feeding the animals. This helped to reduce the impact of the straw and hay on Ben's skin.

REFLECTION

What are the consequences for Ben if his childminder did not work with Ben's mum to maximise his participation in this activity?

Epilepsy

Epilepsy is caused by abnormal electrical impulses in the brain, set off by triggers either internally or in the environment. A student practitioner, Rosie Dunn, describes how she has learned to respond to Toby's epileptic seizures:

> Toby can often have a seizure due to different triggers, such as being in pain and discomfort, constipation or even being too hot. When dealing with children with epilepsy within a setting it is important to ensure children are out of direct lighting and it is the duty of practitioners to maintain a low level of lighting, keeping children away from bright flashing lights. To keep the room temperature cool, fans are kept on throughout the school day to make sure children don't become hot and flushed. These steps must be taken to prevent seizures from occurring. We must ensure work areas are free from obstructions and staff can get around to the child quickly if a seizure does occur.
>
> Toby has a vagal nerve stimulator magnet for when he has a seizure and this prevents the need for him to have emergency medication for epileptic seizures.

As a developing practitioner within the setting I became aware of the signs children portrayed when having a seizure. Once I had identified the child having the seizure it was then crucial I timed the length and and noted the type of seizure the child was having. This information then had to be passed on to parents and practitioners to record the amount of seizures displayed during the school day.

,

REFLECTION

- Learn more about epilepsy and vagal nerve stimulators from the Epilepsy Society (2012).

- What are the benefits to children of not having to take emergency medication for epileptic seizures?

Febrile convulsions

Febrile convulsions are alarming for all concerned, however, as Ferrier (2015) points out, understanding the reasons why febrile convulsion occurs is helpful because it can reduce the anxieties that this event can provoke. Having an understanding of the required response is helpful to you in fulfilling your role in supporting children's health.

Practice

Lucy, aged 24 months, looked sleepy when she arrived at nursery. As the morning wore on, her key person, Mollie, noted that she looked pale and had 'heavy eyes'. Lucy refused a snack, neither would she drink her juice, and she wanted her teddy. When Mollie changed Lucy's nappy, which was dry, she noticed that her skin looked pale and mottled. Mollie recalled her first aid training where she learned that a child with a high temperature may have such skin changes. She decided to use the nursery's electronic thermometer to record Lucy's temperature and the reading was 39.4. Mollie realised that Lucy needed medication such as ibuprofen or paracetamol to reduce her temperature. However, the nursery policy stated that parents must be contacted before the administration of medicines which was unplanned.

Mollie explained the situation to the manager who offered to speak to Lucy's mum. Mollie turned her attention to Lucy who had become still and sleepy, while her breathing had become shallow and fast. Mollie realised that the room was very warm, so she opened a window. In a very short space of time, Lucy became stiff and rigid, she started to jerk intensely and saliva accumulated in her mouth. Again, Mollie recalled her first aid training and realised that the priority was to ensure Lucy was safe from injury so she put her on her side on the floor away from furniture. She calmly asked the room leader to go and call for an ambulance and told her that Lucy was having a febrile convulsion. She asked another practitioner to take the other children to another room to avoid them becoming distressed by seeing Lucy and to preserve Lucy's dignity.

Mollie noted the time of the start of the convulsion so she could tell the paramedic staff. The crew arrived quickly and took over from Mollie in caring for Lucy. This meant that Mollie was able to turn her attention to Lucy's mum, who arrived just as the convulsion was easing off.

The paramedics confirmed that Lucy had experienced a febrile convulsion and they reassured Mollie and Lucy's mum that Mollie had responded to the situation in exactly the right way. Because this was the first time Lucy had experienced a convulsion, the paramedics took Lucy to the local hospital to have some investigations to find out the cause of the convulsion.

Management of a febrile convulsion

Febrile convulsions are a response to a higher than normal temperature and are caused by the immaturity of children's temperature control in their nervous system. They can happen as a consequence of a urinary tract or another infection, but can occur without an obvious cause.

A natural response to the child's production of saliva is to be concerned about aspiration and choking, however there are no reports of children aspirating during a febrile convulsion.

Administering ibuprofen or paracetamol does not prevent febrile convulsions, but it is effective in reducing temperature (NICE 2013a). Tepid sponging is no longer recommended, but cooling the room and removing clothing are recommended.

REFLECTION

- Are you confident that you would be equipped to manage a febrile convulsion?

- Do your policies reflect the actions necessary to respond swiftly and legally?

Female genital mutilation

Female genital mutilation (FGM) is defined as 'all procedures involving partial or total removal of the external genitalia or other injury to the female genital organs for non-medical reasons' (RCM et al. 2013, p. 8). FGM has become a contemporary health issue affecting women and girls' health and wellbeing. FGM is a cultural practice that is widely carried out in some African and Middle Eastern countries, sometimes on girls from birth. FGM is a cultural practice that conflicts with UK law because FGM is illegal in the UK and it is regarded as child abuse. The practice is medically unnecessary and causes a range of health problems for women. Professionals are required to report cases under the Working Together to Safeguard Children (HM Government 2015) guidance. Further guidance has been published by the Department of Health (2015b) on FGM for professionals, which states:

Since October 2015 registered professionals in health, social care and teaching also have a statutory duty (known as the Mandatory Reporting duty) to report cases of FGM to the police non-emergency number 101 in cases where a girl under 18 either discloses that she has had FGM or the professional observes physical signs of FGM. (p. 1)

The legal responsibilities have consequences for practitioners working in areas where there are communities who practice FGM. Read Jan's account of safeguarding and FGM:

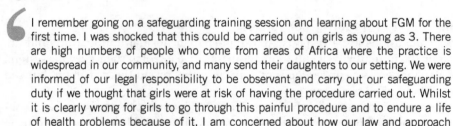

I remember going on a safeguarding training session and learning about FGM for the first time. I was shocked that this could be carried out on girls as young as 3. There are high numbers of people who come from areas of Africa where the practice is widespread in our community, and many send their daughters to our setting. We were informed of our legal responsibility to be observant and carry out our safeguarding duty if we thought that girls were at risk of having the procedure carried out. Whilst it is clearly wrong for girls to go through this painful procedure and to endure a life of health problems because of it, I am concerned about how our law and approach can be a barrier to working with parents. It may even mean that girls are not able to access their early education and care because of parents' fears. It is really difficult.

Jan's example from practice highlights the cultural and legal tension that surrounds FGM. Clearly, heavy-handed approaches should be avoided, however it is essential to convey the correct health messages. The Wave Trust/DfE report (APPG 2013) states that prevention and screening efforts for female genital mutilation are 'best framed in relation to benefits for women's health, rather than opposing traditional practices or beliefs about women's rights' (p. 14).

REFLECTION

- How can an understanding of FGM help you to develop cultural competence in working with families who support the practice?

- Considering the perspective of girls who do not have FGM, what are the consequences to their status in their society? Is this an ethical dilemma?

Foetal Alcohol Syndrome

Foetal Alcohol Syndrome (FAS) is an increasing problem and can be under-diagnosed. Carolyn Blackburn has researched the effect of alcohol on pregnancy, and here is an extract from her research (Blackburn, Carpenter and Egerton 2012):

Rachel (not her real name) drank heavily and used marijuana throughout pregnancy. When her son David (not his real name) was born she was motivated to change her drug and alcohol habits. However, she found it difficult:

> When I was pregnant I couldn't get up in the morning without throwing up and having a drink and I knew that I shouldn't, but I couldn't function without a drink. I am impatient and I am fiery and he's also learned a lot of that, I did find it hard to be a single mum and when I did put the drink down when he was about 6 months, and the marijuana when he was about a year, then I had a wake-up call, and then I had to decide just which one am I going to choose? My son, or the drugs (visibly upset). Mentally I was unfit, I had suicidal thoughts, I had thoughts about harming my son, was seeing things, I was a mess, so having a baby and trying to deal with my head was difficult.

During his infancy period, therefore, David's experience of care-giving interactions and early relationships is best described as unpredictable and insensitive. In addition, he was sexually abused at the age of 3 by a young adolescent. Consequently, he now experiences difficulties in forming relationships with peers, engaging in learning, expressing his emotions and physical contact with others:

> When he started going to Nursery, I knew he needed a lot of support, but I thought it might be my parenting skills. Social Services were involved then and I had to see a Counsellor. I asked for CAHMS to be involved when he was sexually abused, but that support only started this year. A nursery place was also provided for him. Speech and Language therapy was involved when he was quite young.

David now attends a special school for children with social, emotional and behavioural difficulties, where he has the additional socio-emotional support necessary to promote engagement in learning and self-regulation. However, family life continues to be dominated by his often aggressive outbursts as a result of damage to his central nervous system and difficult relationships. As stated by Rachel:

> Help to deal with the guilt, we are newly married, David has known my husband since he was about 2 or 3, but now I think we're all going to need help getting used to living together. My husband can't sometimes tolerate my son's behaviour and then I'm stuck in the middle, and I find that difficult. We (David and I) are staying at my mum's at the moment while she's away, because my husband was totally ignoring my son. He (my husband) knows that his behaviour is not good; I think we just need support gelling as a family.

The impact of FAS on children's development changes over time as children mature. If FAS is not recognised in early childhood, difficulties for children increase as they progress through the education system, resulting in so-called secondary disabilities such as poor mental health, disrupted school and ultimately criminal activity.

REFLECTION

How can recognising and understanding FAS help you to meet children's needs and work with parents?

Obesity

The obesity epidemic is minimising children's participation in their early education. Read Ellen's account of the impact of obesity on Lily's inclusion:

Every day in nursery, I found myself being concerned about Lily and how she was going to manage to join in with the activities that were planned. Lily was 3 but she wore clothes made for an 8 year old. Because she was average height, her jogger bottoms and the sleeves of her sweatshirt were rolled up. When it came to playing outside, she could not keep up with the other children because she easily became out of breath. Consequently, she avoided joining in with the games that the other children played. She would follow the adults around and became more and more apart from the other children. With gentle encouragement we would try to help her to join in with the outdoor play but it became difficult and added to Lily's unhappiness. Her lunch box usually contained food such as chocolate bars and crisps, or even white bread jam sandwiches. Lily's parents were lovely, but both of them were very overweight and appeared very poor. The best part of Lily's day was when both parents arrived to pick her up from nursery and the first thing they gave her was a bag of sweets. The thing that I found most upsetting was when Lily had to sit on a chair when we joined the school for assembly; she was so overweight that she could not sit on the floor and cross her legs in the same way that the other children did; she was too overweight. It broke my heart to see how she was excluded from this everyday activity because of her obesity.

REFLECTION

Such a scenario may be one that you have encountered in your practice and there are many challenges to consider:

- What are the ethical issues relating to working with Lily's parents?

- How can you plan to include Rosie in activities?

- How helpful do you think the National Child Measurement Programme is going to be in raising Lily's parents' awareness of obesity?

Observations and inclusion

Observations are critical to maximising inclusion for children in activities. The following observations were carried out as part of my research. They are included to illustrate how at 20 months, DJ, who is allergic to many foods, noticed difference.

30 March 2012, 14:50 The 'orange incident' snack time – children are called to the table. A brightly coloured bowl containing orange quarters still in their skins is put in the middle of the table. The room smells of oranges and the spring sun is shining on the oranges and they are glistening. DJ is gazing at the oranges, as the children are invited to help themselves. DJ looks with interest at the children sucking on the

oranges. DJ and another boy are given a breadstick by a practitioner: 'Oranges aren't for you, DJ and Josh'. DJ gazes at the breadstick and then turns his gaze to a child eating a piece of orange; he repeats this action but looks at a different child each time.

15:05 The children are still sitting at the table. DJ is given another breadstick. DJ points at the bowl, then his hand slowly goes towards the bowl, he puts his fingers on the edge of the bowl and a practitioner says, 'No, DJ'. He removes his hand but then repeats the action and sits for about 30 seconds with his hand on the bowl, his gaze alternating between looking at the breadstick and the orange segments. He takes small nibbles at the breadstick. He then slowly tries to move the bowl closer to him ... a child is having his hands wiped and is told he can leave the table. DJ looks at the child who is toddling to the outdoor area. DJ makes a small sound, puts his half-eaten breadstick on the table, then leaves the table and runs to the door and returns to the outdoor play area.

A year later, when DJ is 32 months old, the following observation suggests that he is still noticing difference in relation to food:

21 March 2013, lunchtime: DJ watches the practitioner handing out bowls of food to the other children. The other children have meatballs and pasta in a red-coloured tomato sauce. DJ is given meatballs and pasta in a brown-coloured gravy sauce.

DJ looks at the other children's food. *The other children do not look at each other's food!* He starts to feed himself, but it is hot and he stops. A student practitioner who is sitting beside DJ tries to feed him. She asks the practitioners if DJ's food is different; they respond briefly: 'Yes, he cannot eat tomatoes, so he has to have a different sauce'. The student continues to make comments such as 'Gravy with pasta is weird'; she asks DJ, 'is that nice?' DJ nods and starts to eat his food independently.

The children are offered a serving of dessert. DJ continues to glance and occasionally gaze at their food. DJ is served a portion from the communal bowl. *Other children do not look at each other's food.* DJ nibbles at his pudding, but does not complete eating the portion.

REFLECTION

How could you plan mealtimes for DJ so that his participation is maximised and differences in food are less obvious?

Refugee children

Children who have been forced to leave their home country because of war and civil conflict may present with many health challenges. Most countries that people are migrating from have poor or no health services available. The effect of civil strife and destruction from bombing over the course of many years has damaged the infrastructure of such countries. A lack of sanitation and a limited availability of food can result in infections, infestations and malnourishment. In addition, many children will have witnessed deeply disturbing sights before leaving their country. The work of organisations such as Freedom from Torture reports that some children have been forced to watch their parents being tortured, or even forced to torture their parents. The long journey from their home country to the UK will have been perilous and the outcome uncertain. Hunger, thirst and boredom will have contributed to their discomfort. Their arrival in their host country can be a traumatic experience; they are disenfranchised people, possibly at further disadvantage because of a lack of English.

CASE STUDY 12.1

Emma is a practitioner in an inner-city Children's Centre which has a hostel for refugees from Syria. Read her account of Rosa:

Rosa is 6 and has recently arrived in England from Sudan. The country has experienced a civil war for decades and in 2011 the country was divided into South Sudan and Sudan; this makes South Sudan the newest country to be created in the world. During the civil war, many people were persecuted because of their religious and political beliefs. Rosa's grandparents were burnt to death by rebel soldiers and Rosa, who was 3 years old at the time, watched this event as it happened. Shortly after this, Rosa's parents fled the country and arrived as refugees seeking asylum in England. They arrived in England following a long and dangerous journey with no possessions and no money. Rosa's parents are finding the adjustment to living in the UK difficult, but are trying to be positive about the future. They are especially keen that Rosa benefits from education in the local primary school. Rosa has become selectively mute and is experiencing separation anxiety. She sits inactive for long periods of time and cries inconsolably. Her parents are desperate for Rosa 'to get better'.

REFLECTION

- How could you work with other professionals to support Rosa and her parents?
- What are her immediate health needs?
- What are the positive aspects of Rosa's situation?

School readiness

The 'school readiness' agenda that is part of the Early Years Foundation Stage (DfE 2014a) has several health-related items that need consideration. Public Health England (2014) aims to increase the number of children who are ready for school at age 5. The transition from pre-school to school increases the expectations on children in many ways and your role in preparing them for some of the health-related issues so that they are well prepared for school may help to alleviate stress on children at a time of change for them. In addition, the health promotion activities that you adopt for pre-school children can mean that they stay healthier and miss less school, thus helping them to make a good transition.

The following health-related areas contain suggestions for you to consider when preparing children for transition.

Toileting

For a number of reasons, it is important that children are as independent as possible in managing their own toilet needs before they start school. It is especially important for their own dignity, which, in turn, helps to promote a sense of independence and greater self-esteem. In addition, it is more pleasant for everyone if children are not incontinent or relying on others to support them in their toileting. The small adult-to-children ratio in school means that it may be more difficult to give sensitive and individual care to children who find toileting difficult. Strategies put in place in pre-school to support toileting include ensuring that:

- staff work with parents to ensure that children are showing positive signs of being prepared for toilet training, usually around the age of 2
- toileting routines are regular throughout the day and positive reinforcement is given when children manage their toileting needs well, or sensitive support and guidance if they do not do so
- toilets are inviting and kept clean and well stocked with equipment
- children are kept well hydrated.

Children can be engrossed in activities and ignore the signs that they need to empty their bladder. Regular visits in the routine should help with this, but if children start to cross their legs and wriggle it may be a sign that they need a reminder to pay a visit.

Unexpected wetting accompanied by strong-smelling urine may indicate an infection and this requires a medical opinion. It should be noted that urine problems may indicate a safeguarding issue, or the presence of an infestation with a parasite, such as worms. Some children may avoid visiting the toilets because of anxiety. (For a useful video about bladder control and an explanation of how to manage such problems in practice, see North Devon Healthcare Trust 2015.)

An important part of the toileting routine includes washing hands after visiting the toilet (see further explanation of how to encourage this important preventative health measure in Chapter 8).

Dietary needs

How capable are children of managing their own dietary restrictions? Have you taught the other children about a child's dietary restrictions?

Speech and language

'Language proficiency is a key predictor of school success' (Public Health England 2016c). Therefore, ensuring that any barriers, such as dental caries, to the development of children's speech and language skills are looked at, is an important part of your role in preparing children for school and promoting their chances of being successful.

Children with chronic or complex medical needs

For children with chronic or complex medical needs, a primary focus of their readiness for school will be the school's readiness to manage their health needs. Careful planning in collaborative and integrated ways is essential. Whether the school is a specific one for children who have complex and special educational needs, or a mainstream school that is planning how to meet the healthcare needs of children with complex needs, the role of the school nurse will be a vital one in creating the link between the child, professionals from education and health and the parents or carers. Central to effective integrated working and communication will be the preparation of education, health and care plans, written in collaboration with parents.

Conclusion

This chapter has developed some of the content of previous chapters in this book, giving examples that practitioners have encountered in practice. The examples highlight the need for deep reflection and critical thinking in relation to your role in supporting children's health.

Further reading

Department of Health (2015) Female Genital Mutilation Safeguarding and Risk: Guidance for professionals. Available at: www.gov.uk/government/uploads/system/uploads/attachment_data/file/525390/FGM_safeguarding_report_A.pdf (accessed 25 July 2016).

Public Health England (2015) Improving School Readiness Creating Better Start For London. Available at https://www.gov.uk/government/uploads/system/uploads/attachment_data/file/459828/School_readiness_10_Sep_15.pdf (accessed 16 January 2017).

BIBLIOGRAPHY

Action for Children (2010) Deprivation and Risk: The case for early intervention. Available at: www.actionforchildren.org.uk/media/52765/the_case_for_early_intervention.pdf (accessed 3 August 2012).

Alderson, P. (2011) Trends in research about health in early childhood: economics and equity, from micro-studies to big business. *Journal of Early Childhood Research*, 9(2): 125–36.

All Party Parliamentary Group (APPG) (2013) Conception to Age 2: The age of opportunity. Wave Trust/DfE. Available at: www.wavetrust.org/sites/default/files/reports/conception-to-age-2-full-report_0.pdf (accessed 12 July 2016).

All Party Parliamentary Group (2015) A Fit and Healthy Childhood: Play. Available at: www.activematters.org/uploads/pdfs/Play-Report-final.pdf (accessed 12 July 2016).

All Party Parliamentary Group (ND) A Fit and Healthy Childhood: The early years. Available at https://gallery.mailchimp.com/b6ac32ebdf72e70921b025526/files/APPG_Report_Early_YearsFINAL.pdf (accessed 28 October 2016)

Allen, G. (2011) *Early Intervention: The Next Steps*. An independent report for HM Government. London: Cabinet Office.

Allen, G. and Duncan Smith, I. (2008) *Early Intervention: Good Parents, Great Kids, Better Citizens*. London: Centre for Social Justice and The Adam Smith Institute.

Appleby, K. (2010) Reflective Thinking; Reflective Practice. In Reed. M. and Canning. N. (eds.) *Reflective Practice in the Early Years*. London: Sage.

Asthma UK (2014) – www.asthma.org.uk

Ayliffe, G.A.J., Babb, J.R. and Quoraishi, A.H. (1978) Six Stage Hand Washing Technique (poster). Available at: www.ahpo.net/assets/handwashing-poster-.pdf (accessed 26 July 2016).

Baldock, P., Fitzgerald, D. and Kay, J. (2009) *Understanding Early Years Policy* (2nd edn). London: Sage.

Bentley, J. (2013) Vitamin D deficiency: identifying gaps in the evidence base. *Nursing Standard*, 27(46).

Blackburn, C., Carpenter, B. and Egerton, J. (2012) *Educating Children and Young People with Fetal Alcohol Spectrum Disorders, Construing Personalised Pathways to Learning*. London: Routledge.

Blair, M. and Barlow, J. (2012) Chapter 6: Life Stage – Early Years in the Chief Medical Officer's Annual Report: Our children deserve better. Available at: www.gov.uk/government/uploads/system/uploads/attachment_data/file/252656/33571_2901304_CMO_Chapter_6.pdf (accessed 23 July 2016).

Blair, M., Stewart-Brown, S., Waterston, T. and Crowther, R. (2010) *Child Public Health* (2nd edn). Oxford: Oxford University Press.

Bourdieu, P. and Passeron, J. C. (2000). *Reproduction in Education, Society and Culture* (2nd ed). London: Sage Publications.

Bowes, J., Lowes, L., Warner, J. and Gregory, J.W. (2008) Chronic sorrow in parents of children with Type 1 diabetes. *Journal of Advanced Nursing*, 65(5): 992–1000.

British Medical Journal (2005) Management of severe malaria in children: proposed guidelines for the United Kingdom. BMJ, 331, doi: http://dx.doi.org/10.1136/bmj.331.7512.337 (published online 4 August 2005).

Bronfenbrenner, U. (1979) *The Ecology of Human Development: Experiments by Nature and Design*. Cambridge: Harvard University Press.

Bronfenbrenner, U. (1994) Ecological models of human development. *International Encyclopaedia of Education* (2nd edn), Vol. 3, pp. 1643–7.

Brown, D.G., Krieg, K. and Belluck, F. (1995). A Model for Group Intervention with the Chronically Ill: Cystic Fibrosis and the Family. *Social Work in Pediatrics*, 21 (1): 81-94.

Brown, E. (2009) Supporting Bereaved Children: A handbook for primary schools. London: Help the Hospices. www.helpthehospices.org.uk

Brown, E. and Warr, B. (2007) *Supporting the Child and the Family in Paediatric Palliative Care*. London: Jessica Kingsley Publishing.

Burton, M., Pavord, E. and Williams, B. (2014) *An Introduction to Child and Adolescent Mental Health*. London: Sage.

Centre for Social Justice (2011) Making Sense of Early Intervention. Available at: www.centreforsocialjustice.org.uk/UserStorage/pdf/Pdf%20reports/20110707_early_years_report_web_v3.pdf (accessed 1 July 2016).

Children's Food Trust (2016) available at http://www.childrensfoodtrust.org.uk (accessed 28 October 2016).

Children's Society (2015) The Good Childhood Report. Available at: www.childrenssociety.org.uk/sites/default/files/TheGoodChildhoodReport2015.pdf (accessed 9 November 2015).

Children's Workforce Development Council (CWDC) (2008) Integrated Working Explained. Available at: www.gov.uk/government/uploads/system/uploads/attachment_data/file/182200/integrated_working_explained.pdf (accessed 13 July 2016).

Chugani, H., Behan, M., Muzik, O., Juhasz, C., Nagy, F. and Chugani, D. (2001) Local brain functional activity following early deprivation: a study of post-institutionalised Romanian orphans. *Neuroimage*, 14: 1290–301.

Clark, C.D. (2003) *In Sickness and in Play: Children Coping with Chronic Illness*. New Brunswick, NJ: Rutgers University Press.

Closs, A. (2000) *The Education of Children with Medical Conditions*. London: David Fulton Publishers.

Coleman, A. (2006) *A Dictionary of Psychology* (2nd edn). Oxford: Oxford University Press.

Corsini, A.C. and Viazzo, P.P. (1993) The Decline of Infant Mortality in Europe 1800–1950: Four national case studies. Available at: www.unicef-irc.org/publications/pdf/hisper_decline_infantmortality.pdf (accessed 12 January 2016).

Coventry Local Safeguarding Children Board (LSCB) (2013) Daniel Pelka Serious Case Review: Overview report. Available at: www.coventry.gov.uk/downloads/file/17081/daniel_pelka_-_serious_case_review_overview_report (accessed 22 January 2016).

Cowley, S., Whittaker, K., Grigulis, A., Malone, M., Donetto, S., Wood, H., et al. (2013) *Why Health Visiting? A review of the literature about key health visitor interventions, processes and outcomes for children and families* (Department of Health Policy Research Programme, ref. 016 0058). London: National Nursing Research Unit, Kings College London.

Cuthbert, C., Rayns, G. and Stanley, K. (2011) All Babies Count: Prevention and protection for vulnerable babies. Available at: www.nspcc.org.uk/services-and-resources/research-and-resources/pre-2013/all-babies-count/ (accessed 26 July 2016).

Department for Children, Schools and Families (DCSF) and Department of Health (DoH) (2008) The Child Health Promotion Programme: Pregnancy and the first five years of life. Available at: http://webarchive.nationalarchives.gov.uk/20130401151715/http://www.education.gov.uk/publications/eOrderingDownload/DH-286448.pdf (accessed 23 September 2016).

Department for Education and Skills (2003) *Every Child Matters.* London: The Stationery Office.

Department for Education (DfE) (2014a) Statutory Framework for the Early Years Foundation Stage: Setting the standards for learning, development and care for children from birth to five. Available at: www.gov.uk/government/uploads/system/uploads/attachment_data/file/335504/EYFS_framework_from_1_September_2014__with_clarification_note.pdf (accessed 5 August 2016).

Department for Education (2014b) Free School Meals. Available at: www.gov.uk/guidance/universal-infant-free-school-meals-guide-for-schools-and-local-authorities (accessed 12 July 2016).

Department for Education (2014c) Supporting Pupils at School with Medical Conditions: Statutory guidance for governing bodies of maintained schools and proprietors of academies in England. Available at: www.gov.uk/government/publications/supporting-pupils-at-school-with-medical-conditions—3 (accessed 6 July 2016).

Department for Education and Department of Health (2011) *Supporting Families in the Foundation Years.* London: DfE and DoH. Available at: www.gov.uk/government/uploads/system/uploads/attachment_data/file/444788/SFR23-2015.pdf

Department for Education and Department of Health (2014) Special Educational Needs and Disability (SEND) Code of Practice: Children aged 0– 25 years. Available at: www.gov.uk/government/uploads/system/uploads/attachment_data/file/398815/SEND_Code_of_Practice_January_2015.pdf (accessed 12 July 2014).

Department for Education (2015) *Child Death Reviews: year ending 31 March 2015.* Available at https://www.gov.uk/government/statistics/child-death-reviews-year-ending-31-march-2015 (accessed 28 October 2016).

Department for Work and Pensions (DWP) (2013) Reporting of Injuries, Diseases and Dangerous Occurrences (RIDDOR) Regulations. Available at: www.legislation.gov.uk/uksi/2013/1471/pdfs/uksi_20131471_en.pdf (accessed 3 January 2016).

Department of Health (DoH) (2004) National Service Framework for Children, Young People and Maternity Services: Core standards. Available at: www.gov.uk/government/uploads/system/uploads/attachment_data/file/199952/National_Service_Framework_for_Children_Young_People_and_Maternity_Services_-_Core_Standards.pdf (accessed 4 August 2016).

Department of Health (2009) The Healthy Child Programme. Available at: www.gov.uk/government/uploads/system/uploads/attachment_data/file/167998/Health_Child_Programme.pdf (accessed 4 August 2016).

Department of Health (2013) The UK Strategy for Rare Diseases. Available at: www.gov.uk/government/uploads/system/uploads/attachment_data/file/260562/UK_Strategy_for_Rare_Diseases.pdf (accessed 27 September 2016).

Department of Health (2013) *Our Children Deserve Better: Prevention Pays – Annual Report of the Chief Medical Officer 2012.* London: Department of Health.

Department of Health (2014) Overview of the Six Early Years High Impact Areas. Available at: www.gov.uk/government/uploads/system/uploads/attachment_data/file/413127/2903110_Early_Years_Impact_GENERAL_V0_2W.pdf (accessed 12 January 2016).

Department of Health (2015a) Guidance on the Use of Emergency Salbutamol Inhalers in Schools. Available at: www.gov.uk/government/uploads/system/uploads/attachment_data/file/416468/emergency_inhalers_in_schools.pdf

Department of Health (2015b) Female Genital Mutilation Safeguarding and Risk: Guidance for professionals. Available at: www.gov.uk/government/uploads/system/uploads/attachment_data/file/525390/FGM_safeguarding_report_A.pdf (accessed 25 July 2016).

Department of Health (2016) National Framework for Children and Young People: Continuing Care Guidance. Available at: www.nhs.uk/CarersDirect/guide/practical-support/Documents/National-framework-for-continuing-care-england.pdf (accessed 7 June 2016).

Department of Health/NHS England (2015) Future in Mind. Children and Young Peoples' Mental Heath. Available at https://www.england.nhs.uk/2015/03/martin-mcshane-14/ accessed 25 October 2016

Doherty, J. and Hughes, M. (2009) *Child Development: Theory and Practice 0–11*. Harlow: Pearson.

Douglass, F (To Follow)

Driessnack M. (2006) 'Draw-and-Tell Conversations' with children about fear. *Qualitative Health Research*, 16(10): 1414–35. doi: 10.1177/1049732306294127.

Early Intervention Foundation (2014) Getting it Right for Families: A review of integrated systems and promising practice in the early years. Available at: www.eif.org.uk/wp-content/uploads/2014/11/GETTING-IT-RIGHT-FULL-REPORT.pdf (accessed 1 July 2016).

Edwards, M. and Davis, H. (1997) *Counselling Children with Chronic Medical Conditions*. Leicester: the British Psychological Society.

Eiser, C. (1985). Changes in Understanding of Illness as the Child Grows. *Archives of Disease in Childhood*, 60, 489-92.

Envy, R. and Walters, R. (2013) *Becoming a Practitioner in the Early Years*. London: Sage.

Epilepsy Society (2012) Vagus Nerve Stimulation. Available at: www.epilepsysociety.org.uk/vagus-nerve-stimulation#.V2BQ51deI_V

Evans, J. (2016) *Little Meerkat's Big Panic*. London: Jessica Kingsley.

Ferrier, R. (2015) Understanding the pathophysiology behind febrile convulsions. *Nursing Children and Young People*, 27(2): 20–3.

Field, F. (2010) *The Foundation Years: Preventing Poor Children Becoming Poor Adults*. The Report of the Independent Review on Poverty and Life Chances. London: Cabinet Office.

Fink, E., Patalay, P., Sharpe, H. Holley, S., Deighton, J. and Wolpert, M. (2015) Mental Health Difficulties in Early Adolescence: A comparison to two cross-sectional studies in England from 2009-2014, *Journal of Adolescent Health*, 56(5) : 502–7.

Fitzgerald, D. and Kay, J. (2016) *Understanding Early Years Policy*, 4th edn. London : Sage.

Fuller B to follow

Fuller, S. (2014) Gaining evidence on the value of health visiting. *Nursing Times*, 26 November, 110(48): 20.

Gerhardt, S. (2004) *Why Love Matters: How Affection Shapes a Baby's Brain*. London: Brunner-Routledge.

Gibran, K. (1923) *The Prophet*. London: Penguin.

Gillespie, C., Woodgate, R. L., Chalmers, K. I. and Watson, W. T.(2007) Living with risk: mothering a child with food-induced anaphylaxis. *Journal of Paediatric Nursing* , 22 (1): 30–42.

Goleman, D. (1995) *Emotional Intelligence*. New York: Bantam Books.

Great Ormond Street Hospital (GOSH) (2015) [online] Available at : http://www.gosh.nhs.uk/health-professionals/clinical-guidelines/suction (accessed 26 April 2016).

Hall, D. and Elliman, D. (2006) *Health for All Children* (4th edn). Oxford: Oxford University Press.

Heads, D., Ahn, J., Petrosyan, V., Petersen, H., Ireland, A. and Sandy, J. (2013) Dental caries in children: a sign of maltreatment or abuse? *Nursing Children and Young People*, 25(6): 22–4.

HM Government (2003) Every Child Matters. Available at: http://webarchive.nationalarchives. gov.uk/20130401151715/www.education.gov.uk/publications/eOrderingDownload/ CM5860.pdf (accessed 10 November 2015).

HM Government (2015) Working Together to Safeguard Children. Available at: www.gov. uk/government/uploads/system/uploads/attachment_data/file/419595/Working_ Together_to_Safeguard_Children.pdf (accessed 5 August 2016).

Horn, P. (1974) *The Victorian Country Child*. Stroud: Sutton Publishing.

Howard, J. (2010) The developmental and therapeutic potential of play: re-establishing teachers as play professionals. In J. Moyles (ed.) *The Excellence of Play* (3rd edn). Maidenhead: McGraw-Hill/Open University Press.

Howell, R. and Brimble, M. (2013) Dental health management for children with special healthcare needs. *Nursing Children and Young People*, 25(5): 19–22.

Kelly, S. and Taylor, S.C. (2009) *Dermatology of Skin of Colour*. New York: McGraw-Hill.

Kelmanson, I.A. (2015) Recurrent respiratory infections and psychological problems in junior school children. *Early Development and Care*, 185(9): 1437–51.

Kolak, A.M., Frey, T.J., Brown, C.A. and Vernon-Feagans, L. (2013) Minor illnesses, temperament, and toddler social functioning. *Early Education and Development*, 24(8): 1232–44.

Kubler-Ross, E. (1969) *On Death and Dying*. New York: Scribner.

Laevers, F. and Heylen, L. (eds) (2003) Involvement of children and teacher style: insights from an international study on experiential learning. *Studia Paedagogica* 35. Leuven: Leuven University Press.

Laming, H. (2003) *The Victoria Climbié Inquiry*. London: HMSO.

Legislation.gov.uk (2014) The Children and Families Act. Available at: www.legislation.gov. uk/ukpga/2014/6/contents/enacted (accessed 5 August 2016).

Lumsden, E. (2012) The Early Years Professional: A new professional or a missed opportunity? PhD thesis, University of Northampton. Available at: http://nectar.northampton. ac.uk/4494/1/Lumsden20124494.pdf

Lumsden, E. (2014) Changing landscapes in safeguarding babies and young children in England. *Early Childhood Development and Care*, 184(9–10): 1347–63.

MacNaughton, G. (2005) *Doing Foucault in Early Childhood Studies: Applying Poststructural Ideas*. Abingdon: Routledge.

McDowall Clark, R. (2013) *Childhood in Society for the Early Years* (2nd edn). London: Sage.

McMillan, M. (2012) *The Nursery School*. London: Forgotten Books.

Marmot, M. (2010) *Fair Society, Healthy Lives: Strategic Review of Health Inequalities in England Post 2010*. London: DoH.

Maslow, A.H. (1954) *Motivation and Personality*. New York: Harper & Row.

Messenger, W. (2013) Professional cultures and professional knowledge: owning, loaning and sharing. *European Early Childhood Education Research Journal*, 21(1): 138–49.

Moss, P. (2014) Early childhood policy in England 1997–2013: anatomy of a missed opportunity. *International Journal of Early Years Education*, 22(4): 346–58.

Moss, S. (2015) Managing risks in a fearful world: why children need a sense of adventure. Keynote address, European Early Childhood Research Conference. Universitat Autònoma de Barcelona. September 2015.

Moyles, J. (ed.) (2010) *The Excellence of Play* (3rd edn). Maidenhead: McGraw-Hill/Open University Press.

Musgrave, J. (2014) How do Practitioners Create Inclusive Environments for Children with Chronic Health Conditions? An exploratory case study. Thesis for Doctor of Education, University of Sheffield. Available at: http://etheses.whiterose.ac.uk/6174/1/Jackie%20 Musgrave%20-%20Final%20Thesis%20incl%20Access%20Form%20for%20submission%2019-5-14.pdf (accessed 24 July 2016).

National Institute for Health and Care Excellence (2008) Social and emotional wellbeing in primary education. Available at : https://www.nice.org.uk/guidance/ph12/resources/social-and-
emotional-wellbeing-in-primary-education-1996173182149 [accessed 19 December 2016).
National Children's Bureau (NCB) (2015) The Integrated Review: Bringing together health
and early education reviews at age two and two and a half. Available at: www.ncb.org.uk/
media/1201160/ncb_integrated_review_supporting_materials_for_practitioners_
march_2015.pdf (accessed 4 August 2016).
National Health Service (NHS) (2015a) NHS Family Nurse Partnership. Available at:
http://fnp.nhs.uk/about-us (accessed 5 August 2016).
NHS (2015b) NHS Choices: Health A–Z – Conditions and treatments. Available at: www.
nhs.uk/Conditions/Pages/hub.aspx (accessed 27 September 2016).
NHS England (2015) Maternity and Breastfeeding. Available at: www.england.nhs.uk/statistics/
statistical-work-areas/maternity-and-breastfeeding/ (accessed 29 January 2016).
National Institute for Health and Care Excellence (NICE) (2007) Atopic Eczema in Under
12s: Diagnosis and management. Available at: www.nice.org.uk/guidance/cg57 (accessed
24 July 2016).
NICE (2008) Social and Emotional wellbeing in primary education. Available at www.nice.org.
uk/guidance/ph12/resources/social-and-emotional-wellbeing-in-primary-education-
1996173182149 (accessed 19 December 2016).
NICE (2010) https://www.nice.org.uk/guidance/ph28/resources/lookedafter-children-and-
young-people-1996243726021
NICE (2011) Food Allergy in Children and Young People. Available at: https://pathways.nice.
org.uk/pathways/food-allergy-in-children-and-young-people (accessed 14 October 2011).
NICE (2012) Social and Emotional Wellbeing: Early years. Available at: www.nice.org.uk/
guidance/ph40/resources/social-and-emotional-wellbeing-early-years-1996351221445
(accessed 23 March 2016).
NICE (2013a) Feverish Illness in Children: Assessment and initial management in children
younger than 5 years. Available at: www.nice.org.uk/guidance/cg160/evidence (accessed
15 March 2016).
NICE (2013b) Quality Standard for Asthma. Available at: www.nice.org.uk/Search.
do?x=-994&y=- 200&searchText=asthma+young+children&newsearch=true (accessed
6 June 2013).
NICE (2015) Coeliac Disease: Recognition, assessment and management. Available at:
www.nice.org.uk/guidance/ng20 (accessed 27 September 2016).
NICE (2016a) Social and Emotional Wellbeing of Vulnerable Children Guidance. Available at:
http://pathways.nice.org.uk/pathways/social-and-emotional-wellbeing-for-children-and-
young-people#path=view%3A/pathways/social-and-emotional-wellbeing-for-children-and-
young-people/social-and-emotional-wellbeing-for-children-and-young-people-overview.
xml&content=view-index (accessed 11 July 2016).
NICE (2016b) Sepsis: Recognition, diagnosis and early management. Available at: www.nice.
org.uk/guidance/ng51/resources/sepsis-recognition-diagnosis-and-early-management-
1837508256709 (accessed 14 July 2016).
North Devon Healthcare Trust (2015) Bladder Control and Potential Problems.
Available at: www.youtube.com/watch?v=OzD6nBe-mYI&feature=youtu.be (accessed
29 June 2016).
NSPCC (2014) Child Killings in England and Wales: Explaining the statistics. Available at:
www.nspcc.org.uk/globalassets/documents/information-service/factsheet-child-
killings-england-wales-homicide-statistics.pdf
NSPCC (2016) Looking after Infant Mental Health. Available at: www.nspcc.co.uk/preventing-
abuse/child-protection-system/children-in-care/infant-mental-health/ (accessed 11 July
2016).
Nutbrown, C. (2012) *Foundations for Quality. The Independent Review of Early Education
and Childcare Qualifications. Final Report*. Runcorn: Crown Copyright. Available at:

Nhttps://www.gov.uk/government/uploads/system/uploads/attachment_data/file/175463/Nutbrown-Review.pdf (accessed 16 April 2014).

Nutbrown, C. and Page, J. (2008) *Working with Babies and Children from Birth to Three*. London: Sage.

Nutbrown, C., Clough, P. and Atherton, F. (2013) *Inclusion in the Early Years* (2nd edn). London: Sage.

Office for National Statistics (ONS) (2016) Measuring National Wellbeing: Life in the UK. Available at: www.ons.gov.uk/peoplepopulationandcommunity/wellbeing/articles/measuringnationalwellbeing/2016#childrens-well-being (accessed 11 July 2016).

Office for National Statistics (2016) Childhood cancer survival in England: Children diagnosed from 1990 to 2009 and followed up to 2014 (experimental statistics) http://www.ons.gov.uk/peoplepopulationandcommunity/healthandsocialcare/conditionsanddiseases/bulletins/childhoodcancersurvivalinengland/childrendiagnosedfrom1990to2009andfollowedupto2014experimentalstatistics

Office for National Statistics (2016) Measuring national wellbeing: life in the UK. Available from https://www.ons.gov.uk/peoplepopulationandcommunity/wellbeing/articles/measuringnationalwellbeing/2016#childrens-well-being (accessed 11 July 2016).

Ofsted (2015) *The Report of Her Majesty's Chief Inspector of Education, Children's Services and Skills, 2015: Early Years*. Manchester: Ofsted.

OUP (2010) *Concise Medical Dictionary* (Oxford Quick Reference). Oxford: Oxford University Press.

OUP (1986) *Oxford English Dictionary* (OED). Oxford: Oxford University Press.

Padmore, J. (2016) *The Mental Health Issues of Children and Young People*. Maidenhead: Open University Press.

Penn, S. (2015) Overcoming the barriers to using kangaroo care in neonatal settings. *Nursing Children and Young People*, 27(5): 22–7.

Piaget, J. (1951) *Play, Dreams and Imitation in Childhood*. Abingdon: Routledge.

Pike, E.R. (1966) *Human Documents of the Industrial Revolution in Britain*. London and Woking: Unwin Brother Ltd.

Piko, B.F. and Bak, J. (2006) Children's perceptions of health and illness: images and lay concepts in pre-adolescence. *Health Education Research*, 21(5): 643–53.

Pitchforth, E., Weaver, S., Willars, J., Wawrzkowicz, E., Luyt, D. and Dixon-Woods, M. (2011) A qualitative study of families of a child with nut allergy. *Chronic Illness*, 7(4): 1–12.

Public Health England (2010) Guidance on Infection Control in Schools and other Childcare Settings. Available at: www.gov.uk/government/uploads/system/uploads/attachment_data/file/522337/Guidance_on_infection_control_in_schools.pdf (accessed 1 April 2016); poster available at: www.publichealth.hscni.net/sites/default/files/A2%20Schools%20poster_1.pdf

Public Health England (2013) Green Book: Immunisation against infectious diseases – poliomyelitis. Available at: www.gov.uk/government/uploads/system/uploads/attachment_data/file/148141/Green-Book-Chapter-26-Polio-updated-18-January-2013.pdf (accessed 11 January 2016).

Public Health England (2014) Guidance on Infection Control in Schools. Available at: www.gov.uk/government/uploads/system/uploads/attachment_data/file/522337/Guidance_on_infection_control_in_schools.pdf (accessed 5 August 2016).

Public Health England (2015) Rapid Review to Update Evidence for the Healthy Child Programme 0–5. Available at: www.gov.uk/government/uploads/system/uploads/attachment_data/file/429740/150520RapidReviewHealthyChildProg_UPDATE_poisons_final.pdf (accessed 17 July 2016).

Public Health England (2016a) Health Matters: Giving every child the best start in life. Available at: www.gov.uk/government/publications/health-matters-giving-every-child-the-best-start-in-life/health-matters-giving-every-child-the-best-start-in-life (accessed 28 May 2016).

Public Health England (2016b) National Child Measurement Programme 2016: Information for schools. Available at: www.gov.uk/government/uploads/system/uploads/attachment_data/file/531904/NCMP-information-for-schools.pdf (accessed 23 July 2016).

Public Health England (2016c) Improving School Readiness: Creating a better start in London. Available at: www.gov.uk/government/publications/improving-school-readiness-creating-a-better-start-for-london (accessed 6 July 2016).

Public Health England (2016d) Routine Immunisation Schedule. Available at: www.gov.uk/government/uploads/system/uploads/attachment_data/file/532787/PHE_Complete_Immunisation_Schedule_SUMMER2016.pdf (accessed 27 September 2016).

Public Health Nurses (Devon) (2015) The Importance of Fluid Intake. Available at: www.youtube.com/watch?v=WyLBntO9FQQ&feature=youtu.be (accessed 29 June 2016).

Quigley, M., Hockley, C., Carson, C., Kelly, C., Renfrew, M. and Sacker, C. (2012) Breastfeeding is associated with improved child cognitive development: a population-based cohort study. *Journal of Pediatrics*, 160: 25–32.

Rapley, G. (2015) Baby-led weaning: the theory and evidence behind the approach. *Journal of Health Visiting*, 3(3): 144–51.

Renton, Z., Hamblin, E. and Clements, K. (2016) Delivering the Healthy Child Programme for Young Refugee and Migrant Children. Report for the National Children's Bureau. Available at: www.ncb.org.uk/media/1284015/delivering_hcp_for_young_refugee_and_migrant_children.pdf (accessed 6 June 2016).

Reunamo, J., Kalliomaa, M., Repo, L., Salminen, E., Less, H. and Wang, L. (2014) Children's strategies in addressing bullying situations in day care and preschool. *Early Development and Care*, 185(6): 952–67.

Rosen, M. (2004) *Sad Book*. London: Walker Books.

Royal College of Midwives (RCM), Royal College of Nurses (RCN), Royal College of *Obstetricians and Gynaecologists* (RCOG), Equality Now and Unite (2013) *Tackling FGM in the UK: Inter-collegiate Recommendations for Identifying, Recording and Reporting*. London: RCM.

Sloan, S., Sneddon, H., Stewart, M. and Iwaniec, D. (2007) Breast is best? Reasons why mothers decide to breastfeed or bottlefeed their babies and factors influencing the duration of breastfeeding. *Child Care in Practice*, 12(3): 283–97.

Statham, J. and Chase, E. (2010) *Childhood Well-being: A Brief Overview*. Childhood Well-being Research Centre Briefing Paper 1, August 2010. Available at: www.cwrc.ac.uk/documents/CWRC_Briefing_paper.pdf (accessed 5 August 2016).

Tassoni, P. (2016) Home learning: a parent's guide to self-regulation. *Nursery World*, 27 June.

Tedam, P. (2014) Witchcraft branding and the abuse of African children in the UK: causes, effects and professional interventions. *Early Child Development and Care*. Published online 14 April. Available at: http://dx.doi.org/10.1080/03004430.2014.901015

Terry, A.W. (2012) My journey in grief: a mother's experience following the death of her daughter. *Qualitative Inquiry*, 18(4): 355–67.

The Thrive Approach (no date) available at : https://www.thriveapproach.com (accessed 19 December 2016).

Thomas, S. (2016) Blended diets: a challenge at the coalface. Poster presentation at the Royal College of Nursing Children and Young People and Royal College of Paediatric and Child Health Conference. Liverpool, May.

Trueland, J. (2014) Rising to the sickle cell challenge. *Nursing Standard*, 23(38, 47) : 22-3.

Underdown, A. (2007) *Young Children's Health and Well-being*. Maidenhead: Open University Press.

Unicef (2013) Innocenti Report Card 11: Child well-being in rich countries – a comparative overview. Available at: www.unicef.org.uk/Images/Campaigns/FINAL_RC11-ENG-LORES-fnl2.pdf (accessed 9 November 2015).

Unicef (2016) The State of the World's Children 2016 Report: A fair chance for every child. Available at: www.unicef.org/publications/files/UNICEF_SOWC_2016.pdf (accessed 11 July 2016).

United Nations (UN) (1989) *United Nations Convention on the Rights of the Child*. Geneva: United Nations.

United Nations Development Programme (UNDP) (2015) Sustainable Development Goals: Goal 3 – Ensure healthy lives and promote wellbeing for all at all ages. Available at: www.un.org/sustainabledevelopment/health/ (accessed 10 July 2016).

Van Onselen, J. (2009) Unlocking the misery of childhood atopic eczema. *British Journal of Nursing*, 18(10): 590-99.

Whitington, V., McInnes, E. and Diamond, A. (2015) The wellbeing classroom. Presentation at EECERA conference. Barcelona, September.

Wilkin, A., Derrington, C. and Foster, B. (2009) *Improving the Outcomes for Gypsy, Roma and Traveller Pupils: A Literature Review*. Department for Children Schools and Families https://www.gov.uk/government/uploads/system/uploads/attachment_data/file/181669/DFE-RR043.pdf

World Health Organization (WHO) (1986) Glossary of Humanitarian Terms. Available at: www.who.int/hac/about/definitions/en (accessed 1 September 2012).

WHO (1992) The ICD-10 Classification of mental and behavioural disorders: Diagnostic criteria for research. Available at :http://www.who.int/classifications/icd/en/GRNBOOK.pdf

WHO (2015a) Health Impact Assessment: The determinants of health. Available at: www.who.int/hia/evidence/doh/en/

WHO (2015b) Children: Reducing Mortality. Factsheet No. 178. Available at: www.who.int/mediacentre/factsheets/fs178/en/

WHO (2015c) Millenium Development Goals. Factsheet No. 290. Available at: www.who.int/mediacentre/factsheets/fs290/en/

WHO (2015d) Interim Report of the Commission on Ending Childhood Obesity. Available at: www.who.int/mediacentre/news/releases/2014/world-health-assembly67/en/ (accessed 17 January 2016).

Wright, R. (2016) *The Skies I'm Under*. http://theskiesimunder.co.uk/#the_book

INDEX

Added to a page number 'f' denotes a figure and 't' denotes a table.